Nathanael West:

the cheaters and the cheated

Nathanael West:
The Cheaters and the Cheated
A Collection of Critical Essays

edited by **David Madden**

EVERETT/EDWARDS, inc.

POST OFFICE BOX 1060
DELAND, FLORIDA 32720

Library of Congress Catalog Card Number: 72-90913
Standard Book Number: 0-912112-01-8
Everett/Edwards, inc., DeLand, Florida 32720
© 1973 by David Madden

For
Robie Macauley

CONTENTS

THE DAY OF THE LOCUST

ILLUSTRATIONS

(Following Page 178)

PREFACE

The essays gathered here were entered in a competition
for the best essay on Nathanael West, sponsored jointly in
1969 by Everett/Edwards, inc. and the *Southern Review*.
With the exception of the winning essay, T. R. Steiner's
"West's Lemuel and the American Dream" (published by the
Southern Review) these essays appear in print for the first
time. Given honorable mention in the competition were:
Warwick Wadlington for "Nathanael West and the Confidence
Game" and John M. Brand for "A Word Is A Word Is A
Word."

The editor and the contributors (except three) are in
their thirties; several are in their twenties. Thus, this
collection represents an appraisal of West by men and women
who grew up in the forties and fifties and for whom his work
has a special significance.

Although I would have felt comfortable enough writing a
conventional introduction to this collection, I decided that
another way, just as appropriate, to express my own insights
and feelings about West was to select carefully and juxtapose
deliberately groups of quotations: from West's fiction, from
his letters, and other sources; from his friends; from works
that have perhaps influenced West or that reveal evocative
parallels; from writers who were perhaps influenced by West's
work; from critics (usually from pieces that do not deal
primarily with West); and from the contributors' essays—as a

sort of preview. I have also included direct comments of my own now and then. For ease in reading, references to the sources of the quotations are omitted.

Grouping these voices, I had in mind Sergei Eisenstein's definition of montage: "from the collision of two given factors arises a concept." The reader will discover, within this confluence of voices, motifs that recur and areas in which the voices seem to speak to each other as in a symposium; and the essays themselves often echo insights expressed by the voices. Following a general, introductory section, the voices recur throughout the volume at major breaks in organization.

The theme of the American Dream and Nightmare has tied all my critical works together since the first, *Wright Morris*, appeared in 1964: *Proletarian Writers of the Thirties; Tough Guy Writers of the Thirties; American Dreams, American Nightmares; James M. Cain;* and *Nathanael West: The Cheaters and the Cheated.*

★ ★ ★ ★

I want to thank Lewis Simpson, Donald Stanford, and Rima Drell Reck, editors of the *Southern Review*, for permission to reprint T. R. Steiner's "West's Lemuel and the American Dream" (Summer, 1971). I want to thank George M. Pisk, Calvin W. Evans, Mark McCloskey, Mary Graham Lund, Jonathan Holden, Joseph Angell, Carmen Weinstein, and Steven J. Lautermilch for entering essays in the competition. I'm grateful to Irving Malin, James Light, Marcus Klein, Alvin Greenberg, Frederick I. Carpenter, Sanford Pinsker, and Jay Martin for their interest in this volume. My wife, Robbie, provided me, as usual, with her keen editorial sense and patience.

D. M.

INTRODUCTION: A CONFLUENCE OF VOICES
Arranged by David Madden

Leslie Fiedler: Nathanael West appears to us from our present vantage point the chief neglected talent of the age.

F. Scott Fitzgerald: . . . the growing cowardice of the reviewers. Underpaid and overworked, they seem not to care for books, and it has been saddening recently to see young talents in fiction expire from sheer lack of a stage to act on: West, [Vincent] McHugh and many others.

Harvey Swados: . . . West wrote in humble gratitude for the praise Fitzgerald had bestowed upon him. . . .

Raymond Chandler: . . . somehow [Marquand's] successful, oh-so-successful souffles always make me think of little lost books like *Gatsby* and *Miss Lonelyhearts*—books which are not perfect, evasive of the problem often, side-stepping scenes which should have been written. . . but somehow passing along, crystallized, complete, and as such things go nowadays eternal, a little pure art. . . .

Swados: Kazin's *On Native Grounds* is surely still the outstanding literary study of the period. . . . one searches the book in vain for even an index listing, much less an appraisal, of such writers as Nathanael West or Daniel Fuchs or Henry Roth.

Malcolm Cowley: By 1946 . . . the percentage of transatlantic imports was beginning to decline. In France it was still growing. Not only were the French translating or planning to translate dozens of the more prominent American novelists. . . . they were also discovering and publishing, in the midst of a paper shortage, American books that had been largely neglected at home; for example, the fantastic *Miss Lonelyhearts*, by Nathanael West, which . . . had promptly gone out of print.

Wallace Fowlie: The young Frenchmen have been struck not only by the tragic stories of the American novels, but also by the example of the many writers who have died young and who before dying left brilliant testimonials of their experiences. Nathanael West, author of *Miss Lonelyhearts*, killed at thirty-six, at the wheel of his auto.

Jean-Paul Sartre: When I was passing through New York in 1945, I asked a literary agent to get the rights of translation of *Miss Lonelyhearts*. . . . He did not know the book and came to a gentleman's agreement with the author of a certain *Lonelyheart*, an old maiden lady who was very surprised that someone was thinking of translating her into French. He learned his mistake and, continuing his search, he finally found West's publisher who admitted that he did not know what had become of the author. I urged them to investigate and finally they learned that West had died several years earlier in an automobile accident. It seems that he still had a bank-account in New York and the publisher was still sending him checks from time to time. . . .

Fiedler: West's long neglect by official writers on the period is now being over-balanced by his enthusiastic rediscoverers. . . . West does not seem to me finally a really achieved writer; his greatness lies like a promise just beyond his last novel and is frustrated by his early death.

Helen Taylor: The cult of Westiana has grown steadily since the late '50's to its present height, and, with the plethora of new material which is constantly appearing, has become a bibliographer's proverbial nightmare.

★ ★ ★ ★

Liber Brunensis (1924): [Nathanael Wallenstein Weinstein] seems a bit eccentric at times, a characteristic of all geniuses. To predict his future would indeed be a hard task, so we'll leave the answer to the crystal and the astrologer.

Lillian Hellman: When we were very broke, those first years in New York, Hammett got a modest advance from Knopf and began to write *The Thin Man*. He moved to what was jokingly called the Diplomat's Suite in a hotel run by our friend Nathanael West. It was a new hotel, but Pep West and the depression had managed to run it down immediately. . . . part of my idle time could be spent with Pep snooping around the lives of the other rather strange guests.

David Madden: Although he revived *Contact* with West and published three issues, William Carlos Williams couldn't remember his face at the time he wrote his autobiography.

William Carlos Williams: I confuse him with someone else, a lawyer, but he was a thin, slightly stooped individual with the same half-embarrassed black eyes.

Gerald Lochlin: West was in his personal relationships a lovable if eccentric man of many faces. Those qualities which repell so many readers of his books did not seriously threaten his friendships. But he was also a victim of profound mental suffering, tormented by his rejection of Jewishness and the subsequent lack of security, by the lack of popular and, in some cases, critical enthusiasm for his work, and by his uncomfortable relations with his mother. And his suffering ran in even deeper currents, possibly augmented by sexual unfulfillment, or at least, a profound aloneness.

★ ★ ★ ★

West: [The theater is] a bonanza, an El Dorado, a Golden Hind.

Madden: West's first play, written with Perelman was never produced.

Martin: Even Stephen satirizes publishing and publicity practices. . . . sensational novels of exposure and sex, college professors and their wives, newspapermen, romantic young poets, and mad scientists.

Madden: Gentlemen, the War was the former title of *Good Hunting*, West's second, produced play.

Martin: The final curtain rang down to puzzlement. Were these the kind of warriors who would defeat Hitler? This audience, at least, refused to think so and was not amused. . . . *Good Hunting* closed after two performances. . . . . [West] never again spoke of writing for the theater.

Madden: Many plays of the past two decades provide parallels and possible comparison with the novels of West: Harold Pinter's *The Caretaker*, Samuel Beckett's *Endgame*, Jean Genet's *The Balcony*, Eugene Ionesco's *Rhinoceros*, and Edward Albee's *The American Dream*.

Albee-Young Man: I have no talents at all, except what you see. . . . my person; my body, my face. In every other way I am incomplete, and I must therefore . . . compensate.

Albee-Grandma: You're the American Dream, that's what you are.

★ ★ ★ ★

James T. Farrell: Come along with me, Pep, and get arrested.

Marcus Klein: West picketed, and he was one of the many involved in the first American Writers' Congress, in 1935, and he worked for Loyalist Spain, among other things. He also wrote a political novel, *A Cool Million*—he did not have a talent for political expression.

Daniel Aaron: Out in California . . . 250 writers from East of the Rockies gathered in San Francisco on November 13 [1933: Upton Sinclair, Mike Gold, William Saroyan, John Steinbeck, Irwin Shaw, Budd Schulberg] . . . and the most talented writer of them all, Nathanael West, who spoke on "Makers of Mass Neuroses."

Harvey Swados: Perelman himself was writing for the *New Masses* even while he did scripts for the Marx Brothers movies.

Fiedler: . . . every revolution, failing inevitably at all of its ends but terror, produces a laureate of terror: the original Divine Marquis in 1789, Nathanael West in 1935. . . . West is a virtuoso of the macabre.

★ ★ ★ ★

Madden: Like the best of the tough guy writers—all of whom wrote for the movies (James M. Cain, Horace McCoy, Dashiell Hammett, Raymond Chandler)—West was a master of pace, that element which vitalizes all others in a novel—especially a short novel. Except for his favorite writer, Dostoyevski, West admired mostly poets and novelists known for their aesthetic qualities. Far too little has been written about West's style—his deliberate use of clichés, for instance—and his techniques and devices, among which the flow and drive of his narratives is especially remarkable.

Nathanael West: Lyric novels can be written according to Poe's definition of a lyric poem. The short novel is a distinct form especially suited for use in this country.

Madden: West's works are among the great American short novels: Poe's *The Narrative of Arthur Gordon Pym*; Twain's *The Mysterious Stranger*; Melville's *Billy Budd*; Crane's *Maggie: Girl of the Streets*; James's *Washington*

Square; Porter's *Pale Horse, Pale Rider*; William Carlos Williams' *The Great American Novel*; Edith Wharton's *False Dawn*; Faulkner's *The Bear*; Gertrude Stein's *Melanctha*; Glenway Wescott's *Pilgrim Hawk*; Fitzgerald's *The Great Gatsby*; Wright Morris' *Man and Boy*; Saul Bellow's *Seize the Day*.

West: Forget the epic. . . . In America, fortunes do not accumulate, the soil does not grow, families have no history. Leave slow growth to the book reviewers, you have only time to explode.

Chandler-Philip Marlowe: A screen star's boudoir, a place of charm and seduction, artificial as a wooden leg.

West: [Faye] left the couch for a red chair that was swollen with padding and tense with live springs.

Chandler-Marlowe: It was raining again the next morning, a slanting gray rain like a swung curtain of crystal beads.

West: The gray sky looked as if it had been rubbed with a soiled eraser.

Chandler-Marlowe: You can have a hangover from other things than alcohol. I had one from women. Women made me sick.

West: A blood-shot eye appeared, glowing like a ruby in an antique iron ring.

Chandler-Marlowe: Neither of the two people in the room paid any attention to the way I came in, although only one of them was dead.

West: The old man began to scream. Somebody hit Miss Lonelyhearts from behind with a chair.

Jay Martin: [West] cultivated an art free from personal emotion. He regarded art as identical with form and as resulting in escape from emotion, though his own emotional responses were always deeply involved in the groundwork of his art.

★ ★ ★ ★

Madden: As I searched for a title for this collection of essays, these occurred to me: *The Dismantling of the Dream and Nathanael West; Nathanael West and the American Dream and Nightmare; Dream Dump of the West.*

William Carlos Williams: I asked him, "How did you get that name?" "Horace Greeley said, 'Go west, young man.' So I did."

Fiedler: [West] is an American everyman. . . .

Madden: West's assumed name is ironic. He did indeed go West, and his life was a play on the many variations of what the West has meant to Americans. In *Fiction of the Forties*, Chester Eisinger discusses the idea of the West as expressed in Southern and Western novelists; the great myth of the American Dream that the West fostered was a nightmare from the start: Carolyn Gordon, *Green Centuries*; Eudora Welty, *The Robber Bridegroom*; Wallace Stegner, *Big Rock Candy Mountain*; Robert Penn Warren, *All the King's Men*; Andrew Lytle, *A Name for Evil*; all the novels of Wright Morris and of Walter Van Tilburg Clark. But a Northeastern Jew, Nathanael West, wrote the most visionary novels of East and West, polar deadends for both Dream and Nightmare: *Miss Lonelyhearts* and *The Day of the Locust*. Leo Marx has written of the Machine in the Garden. West wrote of the newspaper and then of the movie camera in the Garden.

Robert Penn Warren-Jack Burden: So I fled from the fact, and in the West, at the end of History, the Last Man on that Last Coast, on my hotel bed, I had discovered the dream. That dream was the dream that all life is but the dark heave of blood and the twitch of the nerve.

Frank Norris: The West is different, and the Pacific Coast is a community by itself.

Madden: Whitman sang of all Americans through himself. When West came along, there seemed no American self left to sing—only a whimpering echo to resound.

T. R. Steiner: The [Horatio] Alger material becomes very sophisticated and the skeleton for, as well as merging with, a whole series of American motifs, fictions and myths. . . . *Cool Million* is the encyclopedia of mythic "America." And West realizes that the Dreams mask horrors and coexist with nightmares. . . .

Madden: For West, Hart Crane's mythic Brooklyn Bridge, "harp and altar," lay on the back lot at Universal, moldering.

T. S. Eliot: Their only monument the asphalt road / And a thousand lost golf balls.

Ezra Pound: The enormous tragedy of the dream in the peasant's bent shoulders.

James H. Bowden: Lonelyhearts follows the same tack used by the Preacher in Ecclesiastes: here are all the baals, he says, now do you not realize they are no more than gold-painted bulls?

Robert I. Edenbaum: The Day of the Locust represents . . . not only the prophecies of Jeremiah, but also his lamentations; it comes after the fact. The machine is here and it is mechanizing. . . . West's conception of the conditioned response acting as defense against a mechanized world is a brilliant irony: it turns Pavlov into Christ.

Walter Allen: [West] can now be seen as the first of a whole generation of American novelists whose work has been motivated by what has been called "the vision of the ludicrous catastrophe". . . . characterized by black comedy often farcical and outrageously funny even when, and in a sense because, it is being pessimistically nihilistic. . . . [These novels are linked to the later works of] Herman Melville and even more, perhaps, to the fiction of Franz Kafka.

Alvin Greenberg: Only in . . . *The Day of the Locust* does the dream of the demonic apocalypse . . . approach the possibility of reality. The final scene of mob violence parallels the destruction of Harlem in *Invisible Man*. . . . the apocalyptic redemption in the process of destroying the redeemers. . . .

Henry Miller: We inhabit a mental world, a labyrinth in whose dark recesses a monster waits to devour us. Thus far we have been moving in mythological dream sequence, finding no solutions because we are posing the wrong questions. . . . I had the misfortune to be nourished by the dreams and visions of great Americans—the poets and seers.

THE MAN BEHIND THE NOVELS
By Gerald Locklin

Nathanael West, surely the most underrated and unjustly neglected American writer since Herman Melville, was born Nathan Weinstein on October 17, 1903, in New York City.[1] At Manhattan's DeWitt Clinton High School, he took no active interest in either the school literary magazine or the school newspaper. He distinguished himself only by his unflinching mediocrity in subjects, and in June, 1920 he left school without graduating. With the aid of an incorrect transcript, which the school has no record of having sent, he gained admittance to Tufts University in September, 1921. He did not immediately reverse the trend of his previous academic endeavors, and in November of that year he was advised to withdraw from Tufts for academic reasons. Nevertheless, the young man soon applied to Brown University, using a slightly different first name than he had at Tufts. According to James Light, the University received a different Nathan Weinstein's transcript, an excellent one, good for approximately two years of college credits, including many of the sciences which would no doubt have proved most uncongenial to this restless mind. The first day of Spring Semester, 1922, found West a bonafide Ivy Leaguer. He remained at Brown two and a half years and, after an inauspicious first semester, settled down to acquiring the degree, which was awarded in June, 1924 (Light, 4-6).

After spending a few months at home with his parents

and two sisters, West succumbed to that highly contagious virus of the twenties, the lust for Paris. His family was consulted and approved the trip. Thus, late in 1924, West sailed for the city of dadaist ashes and surrealist flames. A friend, Jack Sanford, remembers that by 1924 he had been subjected to most of the comic inspirations which West eventually wove into his first novel, *The Dream Life of Balso Snell* (Light, 30). It is more than likely that the novel was written largely during West's stay in Paris.

He returned to New York early in 1926 and worked for a time for his father, a reasonably successful building contractor. In 1927 he switched to assistant manager of the Kenmore Hall Hotel on East 23rd Street, a position that afforded him increased time for reading. Later he moved to the same position at the Sutton on East 56 Street, a more exclusive establishment.

By the summer of 1931, which he spent in the Adirondacks with Sanford, also an aspiring writer, West was already hard at work on his second novel, *Miss Lonelyhearts*. This same year saw the publication of *Balso Snell*, which went almost unnoticed by reviewers and public alike. The bizarre fable did, however, sow the seeds of a word-of-mouth reputation among other young literary people. In 1932 he edited three issues of *Contact* with William Carlos Williams. In the early fall of that year, Josephine Herbst and her husband, John Hermann, followed Williams' suggestion to "look up young West."[2] They lured him from the Sutton to a weekend idyll in Bucks County, Pennsylvania, where West confided that he had been at work on his new novel for three years. They convinced him to take a leave-of-absence from the Sutton, where he had not been able to work steadily on his novel, and soon after that he moved to nearby Frenchtown, New Jersey, and finished *Miss Lonelyhearts*.

This book was published in 1933 with an excellent advance critical reception. But a stroke of ill fortune of the type which all young writers fear crippled the sales of the book. Liveright, the publisher, went bankrupt after the printer had delivered only a few hundred copies to bookstores. By the time a second edition could be arranged under the aegis of Harcourt, Brace, the public had forgotten about the book. Nevertheless, Twentieth Century Fox bought the novel and brought West to Hollywood. He was given little to do on the film (which became a Lee Tracy thriller), and he was released in July, 1933. This same year his one published story, "Business Deal," appeared in *Americana*, and a Marxist poem appeared in *Contempo*. In August, 1933, he became Associate Editor of *Americana*.

West had returned from Hollywood to Bucks County, and it was here that he wrote *A Cool Million, or The Dismantling of Lemuel Pitkin*, published in June, 1934. The reviewers were kind but sensed a falling off from *Miss Lonelyhearts*. West was discouraged. During the summer of 1934 he wrote a number of short stories, all of which he considered unsatisfactory, and none of which his agent was able to sell.

Early in 1935 the author who had failed to make any sort of living as a creative writer accepted a hack job with Republic Studios. Although he remained in Hollywood until his death in 1940, none of the pictures on which he worked was of permanent value, and most were to a greater or lesser degree cases of the usual Hollywood multiple authorship. He collaborated in 1936 on *Ticket to Paradise, Follow Your Heart,* and *The President's Mystery*, and adapted *Rhythm in the Clouds* in 1937. In 1938 he wrote an original screenplay, *Born to Be Wild.* Moving to RKO and Universal, he worked on *Five Came Back, I Stole a Million, Men Against the Sky,* and *The Spirit of Culver* in 1939 and 1940. During this same period he wrote an unproduced play, *Even Stephen*, in collaboration with S. J. Perelman, and with Joseph Shrank produced *Good Hunting*, which enjoyed a two-day run on Broadway.

His last novel, *The Day of the Locust*, set in Hollywood, published by Random House in 1939, was greeted by mixed reviews, and sold poorly. In April, 1940, West married Eileen McKenney, the original of *My Sister Eileen*, and his life seems to have been taking a happier turn. But on December 22, 1940, returning with his wife from a trip to Mexico, West missed a stop sign and skidded into another car on wet pavement. He and his wife were both killed in the crash.

Each of West's four novels is unique. There are, however, two qualities shared by all four. All are short on words and long on pessimism. What sort of man was this who wrote "as carefully as if he were chiseling each word in stone with space around it . . . as if he were so composing cablegrams to a distant country, with the words so expensive that not one of them could be wasted, yet never forgetting that the message, at any cost, must be complete and clear"?[3] What sort of man was this who exercised such precise and imaginative art in the service of a nihilism so unrelenting that it denied the validity of art itself?

He was, it seems, an amiable person. William Carlos Williams, in his *Autobiography*, remembers that he was "a firm admirer" of West (and of *Miss Lonelyhearts*), and calls West "a great guy."[4] Quentin Reynolds, a classmate of West's at Brown, worked with him one summer on a construction job. His account is gratifying:

> Most of the laborers on the construction job were Italian or Irish. It used to amaze me to see how Pep endeared himself to these ignorant and rather rough characters. They never knew he was the Boss's son; they just liked him. Most college kids in the 1920's were strictly nonlisteners. Pep was one of the few who would listen, and when he talked, he talked their language—the language of the Bronx where he too had grown up.[5]

At Brown, West aspired to be an exemplary collegian, introducing new dances and playing the banjo (Light, 15). In spite of fraternity prejudice against Jews, he was reportedly "welcome at any house on campus" (Light, 16). The Brown yearbook typed him as "an easy-going fellow. . . . He passes his time in drawing exotic pictures, quoting strange and fanciful poetry, and endeavoring to uplift *Casements* (the student literary magazine). He seems a bit eccentric at times, a characteristic of all geniuses" (Light, 31).

West's natural generosity was remarked by his classmates at Brown and by his friends in later life. Erskine Caldwell did not forget that West allowed him to stay at the Sutton for a

token fee during the difficult days of the early depression
and that the gesture was made with delicate *savoir-donner.*[6]
West rendered this same service to a number of writers. He
extended hospitality to James T. Farrell and his wife "when
we had no money and no place to go; he did it simply and
unobtrusively as though it were a matter of course. When I
next saw him in '34-'35, he did not even mention it. He did
us this favor without expecting any return or any particular
thanks."[7]   It was at the Sutton that a penniless Dashiell
Hammett finished *The Maltese Falcon* (Light, 64-65).

William Faulkner joined West on occasional hunting trips
when they were both in Hollywood. The men did not discuss
writing, but Faulkner later recalled that West "was an
excellent marksman and did his share, and more, in the
chores of the hunt" (Light, 146).

These complimentary descriptions of West contrast
strongly with the image of the author that arises from his
novels. They indicate, among other things, that West's
criticism of life cannot be dismissed as the histrionics of a
cantankerous misanthrope. West was by no means personally
anti-social; his dark vision had its roots far beneath the
surface aspects of personality.

Unfortunately, West's admirable fellowship does not
represent the sum total of his personality. His friends did not
mistake his geniality for happiness. Robert Coates struck the
essence of West's personality and his art: "I think the key to
his character was his immense, sorrowful, sympathetic but all
pervasive pessimism. He was about the most thoroughly
pessimistic person I have ever known" (Light, 128). Between
the poles of geniality and pessimism, West lived a life of
paradoxes which kept his friends perpetually off guard:

> No one could satisfactorily explain the many clashing
> elements in his nature and interests. He despised military men,
> yet was an authority on armies and strategies from the time of
> Caesar on ("When he took out a girl, he sometimes spent the
> evening telling her about some battle of Napoleon's," one
> friend remembers); he regarded organized religion as a hoax,
> but was on intimate terms with the structure, organization,
> and financial condition of the Catholic Church. He was tall,
> awkward and disarming in appearance, but he dressed with

excessive propriety in Brooks Brothers clothes and travelled
with an incredible collection of trick luggage. He had an acute
feeling for words, but couldn't spell; he hated business and
workaday occupations, but was successful as a hotel clerk for
several years. Born and raised a city boy, he spent most of his
childhood on the Upper West Side in New York (he was a poor
athlete, and once disgraced himself in a baseball game by
dropping an easy catch that would have meant a win for his
side), but when he finally became an outdoor man he was a
comic personification of Nimrod. Next to writing, hunting was
his main interest, so much so that it continually impinged upon
his work interest, as evinced by his liberal use of references
and metaphors in *The Day of the Locust*. . . . Josephine
Herbst . . . has suggested that hunting assumed such importance in his life because it was a way of finding an
uncomplicated kinship with rural people—he got on very well
with his neighbors in the country—who were not afflicted with
the frustrated desires and guilts indigenous to the sophisticated
world in which he customarily travelled.[8]

At their first meeting Miss Herbst became aware of the
unreconciled extremes in the author's psyche:

> This tall slim young man with the warm handclasp and
> infectious smile was the author of *Balso Snell*, and it was no
> surprise. His composure, his quick repartee, his sudden
> silences, resounding like a pebble dropped into a well,
> suggested the complexities, the contraries to be found in his
> work. He could hand you a drink with the grace of someone
> offering you a rose; could stand at ease, listening, with the
> aristocratic air of detached attachment. He could flash and
> blaze; then, suddenly, you were looking at the opaque figure
> of a man gone dumpy, thick, who might be brooding behind a
> cash register in a small shop on a dull day (Herbst, 621).

There begins to emerge the image of a whirlpool mind,
bottomless and violently Protean. Perhaps it was the impossibility of articulating the permanent and dominating traits of
West that led his good friend and brother-in-law, S. J.
Perelman, to prefer burlesque when called upon to describe
the young writer:

> To begin with, the author of *Miss Lonelyhearts* is only
> eighteen inches high. He is very sensitive about his stature and
> only goes out after dark, and then armed with a tiny umbrella
> with which he beats off cats who try to attack him. Being
> unable to climb into his bed, which is at least two feet taller

than himself, he has been forced to sleep in the lower drawer of a bureau since childhood, and is somewhat savage in consequence. He is meticulously dressed, however, and never goes abroad without his green cloth gloves and neat nankeen breeches. His age is a matter of speculation. He claims to remember the Battle of the Boyne and on a fine night his piping voice may be heard in the glen lifted in the strains of "For She's My Molly-O." Of one thing we can be sure; he was seen by unimpeachable witnesses at Austerlitz, Iena, and Wagram, where he made personal appearances through the courtesy of Milton Fink of Fink & Biesemyer, his agents. What I like about him most is his mouth, a jagged scarlet wound etched against the unforgettable blankness of his face. I love his sudden impish smile, the twinkle of those alert green eyes, and the print of his cloven foot in the shrubbery. I love the curly brown locks cascading down his receding forehead; I love the wind in the willows, the boy in the bush, and the seven against Thebes. I love coffee, I love tea, I love the girls and the girls love me.[9]

This is nonsense (the description strangely suggests Alexander Pope), but some truth is dimly reflected. West *was* a dandy dresser and an expert on Austerlitz, among other battles. His satire may very well have been partly motivated by an inferiority complex of the stereotype which Perelman depicts. But it is more likely that Perelman was simply trying to be as inaccurate and ridiculous as possible. Nevertheless, it is significant that Perelman did not try to state directly what West really was like.

One possible source of self-conflict, a psychological factor which James F. Light repeatedly cites as forming a basis for the disillusionment of West's novels, is his rejection of Jewishness. At Brown, West avoided the "insistently 'Jewish' Jew and had nothing to do with organized Jewish activities on campus."[10] His change of name may or may not have ethnic implications. (His own explanation to William Carlos Williams was that Horace Greeley had said, "Go West, young man," so he did [Williams, 301]). It is certain that his fiction does not reflect the rich possibilities of the Jewish situation in America, which have been so profitably exploited by Salinger, Roth, Bellow, Malamud, and others. Apparently West wanted very badly to belong to one of the Brown fraternities and resented the roadblock posed by his being Jewish.[11] At any rate, one of the closest of his friends, Jack Sanford, saw West's Jewishness as a constant albatross about his neck:

> More than anyone I ever knew, Pep writhed under the accidental curse of his religion. I'm Jewish myself, and I've had many a painful moment . . . but Pep stands at the head of the list when it comes to suffering under the load. So far as I know, he never denied that he was a Jew, and so far as I know, he never changed his faith (it's a joke to call it that, because he had as much faith as an ear of corn). But he changed his name, he changed his clothes, he changed his manners (we all did), in short he did everything possible to create the impression in his own mind—remember that, in his own mind—that he was just like Al Vanderbilt. It never quite came off (Light, 132).

Another source of personal dissatisfaction was the young writer's inability to achieve either financial security or a wide reputation as an artist. Sanford attests that "more than anyone I ever knew, Pep was dedicated to his writing" (Light, 132). His former roommate, Philip Lukin, confirms (in a paraphrase by James Light) that "West took his writing very seriously. He was consumed by the desire to write well and filled with 'self-torture' . . . by the compulsion to get his visions on paper" (Light, 29). After West's first book had settled into oblivion, Erskine Caldwell recalls that the neophyte "had not been embittered by the notices of the reviewers, but he was puzzled by their unsympathetic attitude and by the lack of understanding of his purpose" (Caldwell, 110). After the publication of *The Day of the Locust*, a book such as any author might reasonably expect to be handsomely received by critics and public alike, West wrote to F. Scott Fitzgerald: "So far the box score stands: Good reviews—fifteen per cent, bad reviews—twenty-five per cent, brutal personal attacks—sixty per cent."[12] In a letter from Hollywood to Edmund Wilson, West explained:

> I once tried to work seriously at my craft but was absolutely unable to make even the beginning of a living. At the end of three years and two books I had made the total of $780 gross. So it wasn't a matter of making a sacrifice, which I was willing to make and still will be willing, but just a clear cut

impossibility . . . I haven't given up, however, by a long shot, and although it may sound strange, am not even discouraged (Gehman, xviii).

This undaunted confidence is not bluff, since West at that time was blocking out *The Day of the Locust*. Nevertheless, it is clear that West did suffer from his inability to prove himself, so to speak, as a writer.

No doubt West's Jewishness and his unrewarded writing contributed to his pessimism. There is also evidence that he was bothered by sexual frustrations of some sort or, at least, by an uncomfortable attitude towards sex.

There was no doubt in the mind of Mrs. Richard Pratt that he was

> a deeply disturbed person, aware of the repressed violence in himself and others, fascinated by the macabre and offbeat. He was monopolized by a possessive mother and quite unable, at the time, to free himself from this thralldom. Certainly he was a lonely man and quite often full of despair. What saved him was that he was immensely alive, full of curiosity about everything. His strong sense of the droll and the ironical colored all his thinking.[13]

West's relationship with his family was an all too typical one. His mother was a strong-willed materialist, who had no sympathy whatsoever for his literary ambitions. Even his first three published books failed to sway her, mainly because they did not represent any income to speak of. She visited West for long periods of time and he respected her almost to the point of fear. West's father was meek and gentle, and West liked him very much. Light has suggested a link between West's rejection of Jewishness and his attempts through art to reject his mother. He bases this analysis on Jungian psychology (Light, 52-53). For our present purposes it is enough to note that West was apparently the victim of the classic possessive, domineering mother and that no psychologist has recommended this familial situation as conducive to vigorous mental health.

West was not close to one of his sisters who resembled his mother. But he idolized his sister Laura to such a degree that all other women paled in comparison. At Brown he swore by

Odo of Cluny's description of woman as a *saccus stercoris,* and was wont to defend the double standard (Light, 24). He seems to have exalted his sister at the expense of womankind. In the light of his fiction, this misogyny cannot be dismissed as a collegiate pose.

West did not marry until the last year of his life. Josephine Herbst points out that "though he wasn't a man without women, none of his friends mentions any romantic love affair in Light's account of him." She reaffirms that "he had closer ties to his family than any of the other young writers of the period whom I knew" (Herbst, 628). At one time West carried in his pocket for three years a marriage license with which he hoped to bind himself to Alice Shepard, the "A. S." to whom *Balso Snell* is inscribed. One cannot help wondering how the girl interpreted the dedication of this singularly anti-romantic book. At any rate, religious and financial difficulties eventually killed the engagement.

In summary: West was in his personal relationships a lovable if eccentric man of many faces. Those qualities which repel so many readers of his books did not seriously threaten his friendships. But he was also a victim of profound mental suffering, tormented by his rejection of Jewishness and the subsequent lack of security, by the lack of popular and, in some cases, critical enthusiasm for his work, and by his uncomfortable relations with his mother. And his suffering ran in even deeper currents, possibly augmented by sexual unfulfillment or, at least, a profound aloneness. After his ideal marriage in the last year of his life, "West noted that he was no longer interested in pessimistic writing; in the future—and not just because such art sold—he planned to write simple, warm, and kindly books, one of which he had already planned."[14]

This sketch of West would not be adequate without some mention of his reading. He was an insatiable reader and the lines and colors of his own imagination take on a more distinct cast when viewed in the context of his participation in literary history.

Information concerning West's reading commences at the age of ten, at which time he was burrowing or buried, as the case may be, in the pages of Tolstoy. By the age of thirteen, he had also discovered French literature, *Madame Bovary* in particular (Light, 8). The French and Russians remained favorites of West's, and Flaubert and Dostoevsky, whom West never ceased to re-read, influenced his novels noticeably. By the time he reached Brown, however, his taste had shifted to *Salammbo* and *The Possessed*. Dr. Wilhelm Stekel has remarked on the extremely sadistic tone of these two books.[15] West's own novels are certainly rife with scenes of sadistic cruelty; for example, the sacrifice of the lamb and the interrogation of the clean old man, both from *Miss Lonelyhearts*.

James Joyce was soon added to the trinity of masters. West read *transition* avidly and had a special reverence for the Irish writer's narrative experimentation.[16] In the desultory manner of an Ivy League Coleridge, West wandered through the diabolism of Huysmans and Eliphas Levi; Celtic Mysticism and such contemporary Celts as Padraic Colum, AE, and James Stephens; Baudelaire, Verlaine, Rimbaud, Arthur Symons, and other symbolists; Church history and hagiography; the dry ice of Mencken, Nathan, and the *Smart Set;* the novels of one of the professors at Brown, Percy Marks; and miscellaneous stragglers, such as Machen, Saltus, Beerbohm, and France. He published an essay on Euripides, heavily indebted to the Dionysian cultism of Huneker, in the school literary magazine, *Casements* (Light, 24-29).

He arrived in Paris in 1924. The fires of dadaism had gone out after the debacle of Breton's projected *"Congress International pour la Determination des Directives et la Defense de l'Esprit Moderne"* in 1922. But the spirit of nihilistic laughter still endured and all the notions of the movement were accessible to the young American. Moreover, in 1924 Breton published the *Surrealist Manifesto.* West met Hemingway in Paris. One might expect that West would find much in common with his fellow writer and outdoorsman, but instead Hemingway "impressed him as something of a poseur who talked at length, like a character from *The Sun Also Rises,* about Spain and the fishing and the bulls" (Light, 62).

West returned to the States and set about at once initiating his friends into the new literature. Jack Sanford recalls some of the names that he first heard from West: "T. S. Eliot, Ezra Pound . . . Walter Pater, a young guy named Hemingway, Max Beerbohm, Aubrey Beardsley, Picasso, Modigliani, Sherwood Anderson, Joyce, Kafka, William Carlos Williams."[17] From his vast reading West eventually distilled certain original ideas on the novel: "Lyric novels can be written according to Poe's definition of a lyric poem. The short novel is a distinct form especially suited for use in this country. France, Spain, Italy have a literature as well as the Scandinavian countries. For a hasty people we are too patient with the Bucks, Dreisers, and Lewises. Thank God we are not all Scandinavians.[18] He had also been reading widely in psychology and suggested that Freud could not teach human nature to the modern writer, but that the collection of case histories could be used as a modern Bullfinch (West, p. 1). Among the more important authors in his mature reading were Spengler and Valery.[19]

West was a writer among writers and he must have assimilated a good deal from the numerous writers with whom he rubbed elbows. Among his literary friends and acquaintances were Frank O. Hough, Quentin Reynolds, Robert Coates, Wells Root, S. J. Perelman, Dashiell Hammett, I. J. Kapstein, Josephine Herbst, John Hermann, Alexander King, William Carlos Williams, James T. Farrell, Erskine Caldwell, Matthew Josephson, Malcolm Cowley, Edmund Wilson, William Faulkner, F. Scott Fitzgerald, and, briefly, Hemingway. And if he knew these people, he must have known many more through them.

The material and spiritual conditions of the twenties and the thirties provided ample food for West's pessimistic nature. The moral scruples mentioned earlier could not help being troubled by the laxness of the Jazz Age. In the thirties West associated with various protest groups and moved always further to the left. He was a contributor to and later an associate editor of the nihilistic *Americana*, edited by Alexander King, George Grosz, and Gilbert Seldes. The first issue produced this manifesto:

> *We Are Not REPUBLICANS Because . . .*
> the present office holders have dismally failed in leadership and intelligence and because the moneyed oligarchy that runs and ruins this country is animated by stupid and shameless greed best exemplified by the Republican party. As for Mr. Hoover personally, we rest content by presenting the record of his flabbiness and incompetence.
>
> *We Are Not DEMOCRATS Because . . .*
> the Democratic party is no less corrupt than the party in power and is simply striving to glut its vicious and insatiable appetite at the public money trough. As for Mr. Roosevelt personally, we consider him a weak and vacillating politician who will be an apt tool in the hands of his powerful backers.
>
> *We Are Not SOCIALISTS Because . . .*
> the erstwhile sentimental liberalism of the Socialists has degenerated to the bourgeois mouthing of their spokesman, Norman Thomas.
>
> *We Are Not COMMUNISTS Because . . .*
> the American Communist party delegates its emissaries to bite the rear ends of policemen's horses and finds its chief glory in spitting at the doormen of foreign legations. We are also opposed to Comrade Stalin and his feudal bureaucracy at Moscow.
>
> We are Americans who believe that our civilization exudes a miasmic stench and that we had better prepare to give it a decent but rapid burial.
>
> We are the laughing morticians of the present.[20]

In February, 1933, West published "Christmass [sic] Poem" in *Contempo:*

> The spread hand is a star with points
> The first a torch
> Workers of the World
> Ignite
> Burn Jerusalem
> Make of the City of Birth a star
> Shaped like a daisy in color a rose
> And bring
> Not three but one king

> The Hammer King to the Babe King
> Where nailed to his six-branched tree
> Upon the sideboard of a Jew
> Marx
> Performs the miracle of Loaves and fishes
>
> The spread hand is a star with points
> The fist a torch
> Workers of the World
> Unite
> Burn Jerusalem.[21]

Although the poem strikes one as forced and cold, the diction is precise. Moreover, it is obvious that West at least wanted to sympathize emotionally with the Movement. This sympathy landed him in jail overnight in 1935 as a result of picketing a department store. The experience was nearly traumatic.[22] On November 13, 1936, West, "the most talented writer of them all," spoke on "Makers of Mass Neuroses" at the Western Writers' Congress, an activity of the League of American Writers (Aaron, 307).

One last, but very important, influence must be mentioned. West had a lifelong interest in painting. This was, of course, a *sine qua non* among the surrealists with their cult of the image. He had spent a good deal of time drawing while in college and among his most prized possessions was a collection of Max Ernst prints (Light, 95). The pictorial technique is prominent in all of West's novels, and in *The Day of the Locust* it is raised to the level of a mystique. West's tour of duty as a screen writer added the dimensions of time and the moving perspective to his already acute eye for still life.[23]

FOOTNOTES

1. James F. Light, *Nathanael West: An Interpretative Study* (Evanston, Ill., 1961), p. 1. Most of the information in this chronology is gleaned from Light's book, the most important study of West to be published to date.

2. Josephine Herbst, "Nathanael West," *Kenyon Review*, XXIII (1961), 621.

3. Malcolm Cowley, "Introduction" to *Miss Lonelyhearts* (New York, 1959), p. 96.

4. New York, 1951, p. 302.

5. Quoted in Light, p. 10.

6. Erskine Caldwell, *Call It Experience: The Years of Learning How To Write* (New York, 1951), pp. 110-12.

7. Quoted in Light, p. 65.

8. Richard B. Gehman, "Introduction" to *The Day of the Locust* (New York, 1950), p. xii.

9. S. J. Perelman, "Nathanael West: A Portrait," *Contempo*, III (July 25, 1933), 4.

10. Quoted in Light, p. 17.

11. Quoted in Light, pp. 16-17.

12. Quoted in Gehman, p. xi.

13. Quoted in Light, p. 109.

14. Quoted in Light, p. 182.

15. Wilhelm Stekel, *Sadism and Masochism: The Psychology of Hatred and Cruelty*, II, trans. by Louise Brink (New York, 1939), 369.

16. Quoted in Light, p. 28.

17. Jack Sanford, quoted in Light, p. 63.

18. Nathanael West, "Some Notes on Miss Lonelyhearts," *Contempo*, III (May 15, 1933), 1.

19. Quoted in Light, p. 127.

20. Quoted in Daniel Aaron, *Writers on the Left: Episodes in American Literary Communism* (New York, 1961), p. 175.

21. *Contempo*, III (February 21, 1933), 4.

22. Quoted in Light, p. 114.

23. For a fuller and more recent account of the life of Nathanael West, see Jay Martin's *Nathanael West: The Art of His Life* (New York: Farrar, Straus and Giroux, 1970).

A CONFLUENCE OF VOICES:
THE DREAM LIFE OF BALSO SNELL

Madden: When *The Dream Life of Balso Snell* appeared in 1931, *The Good Earth* by Pearl S. Buck was at the top of the bestseller list. Vicki Baum's *Grand Hotel* and Fannie Hurst's *Back Street* were also on the list, along with novels by Bess Streeter Aldrich, Warwick Deeping, Mazo de la Roche, Erich Maria Remarque, John Galsworthy, and Willa Cather.

Martin: [Balso] is a direct descendant of Mark Twain's Innocents, and of the other indigenous comic characters discussed by Constance Rourke in her *American Humor*, published the same year as *Balso*.

West-Gilson: People say that it is terrible to hear a man cry. I think it is even worse to hear a man laugh.

Norman Podhoretz: Utterly open, limitlessly impressionable, possessed of something like total recall and a great gift for intellectual mimicry, I also succeeded, and without conscious intent, in writing papers for each of my professors in a different style—one which invariably resembled his own. . . . I was a *Partisan Review*-type intellectual and I was also the man the *New Yorker* was choosing to review such classy authors as Simone de Beauvoir, Camus, Nathanael West, and Faulkner.

Madden: Have you read *The Dream Life of Balso Snell* yet?

Helen Taylor: Half. I couldn't finish it. It was too true of my own experiences as a graduate student just now. I had to go to bed. To finish it now would be disastrous.

Oscar Wilde: Dorian Gray had been poisoned by a book.

West-Gilson: The books smelt like the breaths of their authors; the books smelt like a closet full of old shoes through which a steam pipe passes.

Rabelais: . . . the fart that [Pantagruel] let made the earth tremble for nine leagues around, and the foul air he emitted begot more than fifty-three-thousand little men, dwarfs, and misshapen fellows; while with a poop that followed, he begat the same number of little crouching females. . . . he called them Pygmies. . . . these little runts . . . are naturally of a choleric disposition. The physiological reason is that their heart lies so near their crap.

Jonathan Swift-Lemuel Gulliver: . . . [The Yahoo] roared so loud, that a herd of at least forty came flocking about me from the next field, howling and making odious faces. . . . Several of this cursed brood getting hold of the branches behind leaped up into the tree, from whence they began to discharge their excrements on my head.

West: In case the audience should misunderstand and align itself on the side of the artist, the ceiling of the theatre will be made to open and cover the occupants with tons of loose excrement.

Pope: Lo! thy dread Empire, CHAOS! is restor'd; / Light dies before the uncreating word: / Thy hand, great Anarch! lets the curtain fall; / And Universal Darkness buries All.

Franz Kafka: As Gregor Samsa awoke one morning from a troubled dream, he found himself changed in his bed to some monstrous kind of vermin.

Fiedler: Though lonely in his own time, West was not really alone in his attempt to redeem French horror for the American soul, as Poe had once redeemed that of Germany; Djuana Barnes (whom he probably did not even know) had made a similar, even less popular essay in *Nightwood* [1937].

Marcus Klein: Balso Snell ... is ... clearly an initial effort within a new moment of history. ... Balso's adventures ... make an equivalence between modish literary chatter and sexual perversions. ... The characters invented by Balso are all perverse because they are all derivatives, without flesh and blood of their own. They are frustrated, self-conscious poseurs. ... And the necessity faced by West, behind Balso, is to get free of this posturing, into something new.

Antonin Artaud: One of the reasons for the asphyxiating atmosphere in which we live without possible escape or remedy—and in which we all share, even the most revolutionary among us—is our respect for what has been written, formulated, or painted, what has been given form, as if all expression were not at last exhausted, were not a point where things must break apart if they are to start anew and begin fresh.

West-Gilson: ... like Rimbaud, I practiced having hallucinations.

Matthew Josephson: We pretended to be interested chiefly in the abnormal, the morbid, and the neurotic, posing as frightful cynics and even as decadents.

West-Janey Davenport-Beagle Darwin: I said that death is like putting on a wet bathing suit.

Anais Nin: [Surrealism] was not even recognized as such when it appeared in Nathanael West's work or in Henry Miller's novels. ... There is no purely surrealistic writer, but there are writers who use surrealism to convey a flight from naturalism: Nathanael West, John Hawkes, Henry Miller.

Theodore Solotaroff: . . . . a mode of satiric vision . . . is strongly marked in the work of the other American surrealist of note, Nathanael West. However, it is [Henry] Miller's example rather than West's that seems most characteristically American. . . .

West-C. M. Doughty: The Semites are like a man sitting in a cloaca to the eyes, and whose brows touch heaven.

Fiedler: S. J. Perelman [West's brother-in-law] has been conducting a strange experiment, whose end is the transformation of Surrealist gallows humor into commercial entertainment. . . . The avant-garde images of twenty-five years ago and the grotesquerie which distinguished the short-lived *Contact* have become now the common property of gifte shoppes and greeting card racks, fall as stereotypes from the lips of hip twelve-year-olds. . . . the "sick" joke popularizes the nauseated giggle before violence, which not so long ago belonged only to books like *Miss Lonelyhearts*.

West: Prodded by his conscience [Miss Lonelyhearts] began to generalize. Men have always fought their misery with dreams. Although dreams were once powerful, they have been made puerile by the movies, radio and newspapers. Among many betrayals, this one is the worst.

John Brand: In *Balso Snell* the spoken word is allowed to run its course and achieve nothing. As the biblical writers try to authenticate the Divine Word in its human counterpart, West is equally determined to establish its absence. . . . this work needs to be understood as the lament of a Jew whose time is Wordless.

West-Guide: Art is sublime excrement.

West-Gilson: Written while smelling the moistened forefinger of my left hand.

Isaac Rosenfeld: In West's use of [surrealistic and pop culture] imagery he straddles the two worlds of his own sensibility, the poetic and the popular. . . . The result is neither an apology nor a condemnation of the popular. It has independent status. . . . West was in touch with the popular culture over its whole range.

Gerald Locklin: Snell is an exercise in total nihilism cast in an ingenious nihilistic form. By means of his nihilistic dialectic, the author systematically disposes of the various contestants in the world's intellectual arena. . . . His attack is comprehensive and it is at one with the method in which it is carried out.

Terence Martin: Beyond the hoaxes, puzzles, and grotesque distortions which manifest Poe's imagination at play lies the central mood of destruction. If one is not willing to die, he can't really play. . . . He is our one author who makes an absolute commitment to the imagination—who releases the imagination into a realm of its own where, with nothing to play *with*, it must play *at* our destruction.

J. Martin: [West] began to work on the original screenplay he had come out to do. This he titled first *The American Family Anderson*, and later *Return to the Soil*. All the satisfactions and powers which West denied to rural life in *Miss Lonelyhearts* he would be able to attribute to it here in the free fantasy-world of a Hollywood movie. If his work at the hotel and his life in New York had given him insight into the collective wishes inspected coolly in his novels, picture writing allowed him to indulge his own deep personal attachment to fantasy.

Fiedler: [West] is the inventor of a peculiar kind of book, in which the most fruitful strain of American fiction is joined to the European fiction of avant-garde. . . . The Westian or neo-gothic novel has opened up . . . possibilities of capturing the quality of experience in a mass society—rather than retreating to the meaningless retailing of fact or the pointless elaboration of private responses to irrelevant sensations.

Thomas Pynchon: Benny Profane. . . . walked, he thought, sometimes, the aisles of a bright, gigantic supermarket, his only function to want. One morning Profane . . . decided on a whim to spend the day like a yo-yo. . . . "Why don't you hunt alligators, like my brother," Kook said [in the sewers under New York City].

Ishmael Reed: No one says a novel has to be one thing. It can be anything it wants to be, a vaudeville show, the six o'clock news, the mumblings of wild men saddled by demons. . . . Just then a white python fell from the chandelier and coiled itself around John Wesley Hardin, its ruby red tongue and eyes staring directly into the famous gunslinger's face.

THE DREAM LIFE OF BALSO SNELL:
JOURNEY INTO THE MICROCOSM
By Gerald Locklin

Even today, when Nathanael West's star seems well into its ascendancy (negative critics may claim that it has passed its apex), little attention is paid to *The Dream Life of Balso Snell*. Malcolm Cowley, an admirer of *Miss Lonelyhearts* and *The Day of the Locust*, dismisses *Balso Snell* and *A Cool Million* as "barely worth reprinting."[1] A. M. Tibbetts, who complains that all of West's novels are presently overrated, brands the two lesser works as "universally condemned."[2] He is not altogether accurate. The reviewer in *Contempo* perceived a promising talent in a work that certainly did not warrant "condemnation":

> This is a first novel. And, considering the usual unevenness of first novels, Mr. West has effected a splendid and craftsman-like book. Perhaps it would be rather impertinent to call this facile, buoyant book a novel, but whatever the author ordains to baptize his work it is, not too superlatively, a distinguished performance in sophisticated writing. True, there is nothing tremendously significant in it either of style or technique. Yet there is a suavity of phrase and execution in *The Dream Life of Balso Snell* that makes for excellent reading.[3]

A few others are willing to admit a fondness for the book. S. J. Perelman betrays his affection for *Balso* when he terms it "Goyesque,"[4] as does Alan Ross in his imaginative summation of it as "a sneer in the bathroom mirror at Art."[5] James F. Light is cautious in his evaluation, but he admits that

"Balso Snell is an intriguing book for anyone interested in Nathanael West, just as *This Side of Paradise* is important for anyone who wishes to understand Scott Fitzgerald."[6]

The novel does not deserve either neglect or disparagement. It is one of the most complex books this side of James Joyce, and its complexity is coherent, not chaotic. West was a widely read young man. In his first book, he reacted to his reading in three ways: he rejected the ultimate value of literature; he laid the foundation for his novel in allusions of an unusually destructive sort; and he put into practice a number of the lessons he had learned from his favorite authors, while succeeding in creating an unmistakably original work. I hope to show that the novel, when its originality is properly understood, is of considerable merit in its own right and is an indispensable aid in understanding West's later novels.

The novel is divided by spacing in the text into seven chapters. Each of these is apt to break down into two or more relatively discrete episodes. True to its title, the novel is a dream from start to finish. There is no frame of waking reality. The reader is initiated into the unconscious mind of Balso Snell, contemporary American bard and bawd. Balso's unconscious is externalized as the Trojan Horse, into which he journeys by way of the alimentary canal. Simultaneously, he and the reader explore the bowels of human nature. For Balso's dream, like Earwicker's, is a microcosm of humanity. The adventures of the journeyer Balso are of very little interest as they pertain to that caricature alone. But the entire contents of the dream, when spread out as a mural of condensed types, becomes an original generalization about man's total condition. Balso's unconscious is both personal and collective.

The inscription sounds the keynote of this novel and of West's life and work: "After all, my dear friend, life, Anaxagoras has said, is a journey."[7] This quotation not only places the novel in the historical context of the picaresque novel, but it articulates the philosophical basis from which the genre takes its validity and effectiveness. If life itself is a

journey, then what more realistic structure than the picaresque?

Although *Balso Snell* shares the linear structure and
profane episodes of such novels of the road as *Lazarillo de
Tormes, The Scavenger,* and *The Adventures of Augie March,*
its differences from them are at least as important as its
similarities. The most obvious difference is the fantastic,
uncharted course that Balso pursues. Wandering among the
ruins of Troy, he comes upon the famous horse, and decides to
inspect more closely this relic of the great epics. Unfortunately,
"the mouth was beyond his reach, the navel provided a cul-de-
sac" (3). He is obliged to travel third class, up the remaining
orifice. "O Anus Mirabilis!" comments the lyrical narrator (3).

This allusion to Dryden's poem is neither the last nor the
least of the book's puns. Balso comes at once upon wall
scribblings. Engraved in a Valentine heart is a monument to
self-love and literary pretentiousness, the Emperor Nero's
dying gasp, "Ah! Qualis . . . Artifex . . . Pereo!" (4). Balso
responds with "O Byss! O Abyss! O Anon! O Anan!" (4). He
re-inforces this word play with a parody of the invocation of
Stephen Daedalus: "O Beer! O Meyerbeer! O Bach! O
Offenbach! Stand me now as ever in good stead" (4). Balso
feels right at home among these echoes from the literary past
and he is further reassured by identification with such heroes
as "the one at the Bridge, the Two in the Bed, the Three in
the Boat, the Four on Horseback, the Seven Against Thebes"
(4).

West has wasted no time in proclaiming his book a
portrait of the artist turned inside-out. This technique of
announcing the multiple motifs of a novel on the first one or
two highly compressed pages is precisely that of James Joyce.
The first two pages of *A Portrait of the Artist as a Young
Man* foreshadow all the themes of the book. The epigraph to
Balso introduces, ironically, the ignoble journey of the
protagonist, the journey of the reader into the microcosm of
humanity's dream life, and the life-long search of West for
some escape hatch from his ironclad nihilism. The mention of
Anaxagoras prepares us for the problem of the One and the

Many, the metaphysical question which has occupied philoso-
phers in one form or another since the pre-Socratics and
which occurs in bizarre contexts in *Balso.*

The Trojan Horse is an apt symbol for the alleged dual
nature of man because it is an animal, but it is also an
ingenious creation of the mind. Mythical, it suggests Homer,
the flower of Greek culture.

Balso, as a poet, should be a paragon of man's spiritual
life. His name, however, suggests something different, either
"the balls of Snell," or "the smell of balls." West seems to
have intended the association of "Snell" and "smell" (Light,
p. 30). The novel argues that art is not a sublime excretion,
but simply excrement. The invocations to the Muse are
burlesqued. Nero, an artist by self-designation only, is one of
the first artists to leave his mark on Balso. From then on, all
the characters Balso meets are artists; the one exception is an
aesthetician.

West then has not simply parodied Joyce; he has imitated
him in a very thorough manner. The first section launches the
novel's attack on the apotheosis of the artist and the deluded
use of art as a hermetic world of its own, a refuge from the
material reality of life, a self-contained system of meanings
and values with no reference to the world from which the
raw materials of art are drawn. The "real" world, from which
people are always trying to escape, is painted in images of
vulgarity and abnormal sexuality, here the only too obvious
anal eroticism which Balso's dream betrays.

West's unusual gift for startling imagery and diction is
evident even in these first published pages of his work: "the
navel proved a cul-de-sac," "along the lips of the mystic
portal," "he entered the gloom of the foyer-like lower
intestine" (3-4). His "particular kind of joking" is also
indulged in. Sometimes, of course, West is funny in a way
that can be universally appreciated. At other times, however,
his humor seems purposely designed to offend the reader by
its silliness or vulgarity or obscenity or blasphemy. This is the
humor which West learned from the dadaists, whose "saint,"
Jacques Vache, defined humor as "a sense of the theatrical

and joyless futility of everything, when one knows."[8] West's humor often provokes an initial grin or grimace, rather than a smile or belly laugh, and its cumulative effect is one of purgation or inoculation, rather than ephemeral amusement. Neither West nor the dadaists felt any obligation to offer an audience comic relief. They condemned the theory that art is to be enjoyed, and preferred to wreak their art upon their audiences.

Balso is comfortable only in the web of literary associations; the minute that he is left alone with nothing to read and no one to reply to his invocations, he feels it necessary to compose a song (4-5). The desire for ideal Unity is expressed in the song in Balso's preoccupation with such circular objects as ani, buttons, wheels, brass rings, the potbelly of a satyr, the structural principle of Giotto's painting (medieval unity, as personified for Henry Adams in the Virgin), a goblet, a navel, a mouth, stigmata, and nails (Light, p. 43). Even as he longs for a unifying God or, at least, an Earth Mother, Balso reduces the deity to physical reality by the insistence of his imagery. West also creates an opportunity to sneer at both Christianity and Judaism.

Balso considers a number of titles for his ode, the most successful of which are "Anywhere Out of the World, or a Voyage Through the Hole in the Mundane Millstone," and "At Hoops with the Ani of Bronze Horses, or Toe Holes for a Flight of Fancy" (5). These could serve as subtitles for the whole novel. The first (half of which is the title of a Baudelaire prose-poem) indicates a real despair at the limitations of material existence, while the second is more in the mood of a dadaist joke. The combination of genuine ennui and sophisticated detachment contributes to the novel's unusual atmosphere.

Balso is not relieved by "the gaiety of his song" (5). His fears are aggravated by his recollection of the Phoenix Excrementi, who "eat themselves, digest themselves, and give birth to themselves by evacuating their bowels" (5). The fertile imagination of Balso invented these people while he lay in bed one Sunday afternoon. This is the first instance of

erotic daydreaming, a preoccupation of many West characters. The Excrementi may be considered, as Light asserts, as
emblem of the hopeless, circular sameness of a monistic
universe (Light, p. 43). Or they may represent the vicious
circle of the artistic process, in which the imagination feeds
upon its own creations and from these gives birth to further
fictions. Or it may simply be an image of the life process, in
which everything is prime matter under different forms.
Balso's infantile cloacal concept of birth is betrayed by his
confusion of evacuation and generation.

Balso bursts forth in another series of exclamations that
seem to parody the artist's hackneyed use of flowers, wells,
fountains, and so forth, as life-symbols. He attracts the
attention of a tour guide. Balso quotes one of his own
senseless aphorisms in order to prove that the *poete maudit* is
beyond the pale of social authority. The guide, in the name
of the Old World, welcomes Balso as an envoy from the New
World. The two fail to see eye to eye. The guide ineptly
praises America's premier contribution to world culture, the
automatic water-closet. Balso retaliates by pricking the
guide's illusion that a decayed pile, which they pass in the
canal, is a Doric sculpture. He proceeds to advance as
incontrovertible proof of America's cultural hegemony Grand
Central Station, the Yale Bowl, Holland Tunnel, and Madison
Square Garden. The guide falls back on platitudes about the
hallowed ground of the ancients and then turns abruptly
upon Balso with the twentieth-century formula heard on
both sides of the Atlantic, "If you don't like it here, why
don't you go back where you came from" (6). Just as
abruptly, he remembers the correct relationship of guide to
tourist and offers to tell Balso a colorful folk tale.

The truce between the two is broken when Balso
realistically calls a hernia a hernia. Seeing the guide's
discomposure, he tries to advance a theory of non-referential
word music: " 'Hernia,' he said, rolling the word on his
tongue. What a pity childish associations cling to beautiful
words such as hernia, making their use as names impossible.
Hernia! What a beautiful name for a girl! Hernia Hornstein!

Paresis Pearlberg! Paranoia Puntz! How much more pleasing to the ear . . . than Faith Rabinowitz or Hope Hilkowitz" (p. 7). Balso has not only reduced to absurdity the Symbolist aesthetic of poetry as music, but he has also piqued the guide's racial inferiority complex. " 'I am a Jew!' " he cries, " 'and whenever anything Jewish is mentioned, I find it necessary to say that I am a Jew. I'm a Jew! I'm a Jew!' " (8-9). Hoping to disperse the smokescreen of habitual formulae with a single breath of truth, Balso succeeds only in quoting the most gauche, offensive aphorism available: " 'The semites . . . are like to a man sitting in a cloaca to the eyes, and whose brows touch heaven' " (8). Balso's imagery, of course, runs to cloaca on all occasions.

Both the Jews and their critics have come off very poorly in that exchange. The conversation now switches to aesthetics. Fittingly enough, the intestinal tour guide swears by George Moore's dictum that "Art is a sublime excrement." Irrelevantly, Balso observes that Picasso believes there are no feet in nature. The guide takes flight on a theory of points that links the aesthetic problem of realism versus abstraction to the epistemological problem of universals versus nominalism to the metaphysical problem of monism versus pluralism (8-9). Balso, driven to the wall by the guide's logic, intrudes a statement from Cezanne, "Everything tends toward the globular," (just as Balso's song certainly did), and escapes the discussion.

West here ridicules the sterility of aesthetics and of philosophical reasoning in general, but he displays a thorough understanding of the principles involved. Ultimately, he declares all such questions inconsequential and not worth pursuing, but his satire gains authority from the evident keenness of his mind. He is not an intellectual adolescent, afraid of complex problems (as is Balso); his nihilism is that of one who understands thoroughly what he is rejecting, whether it be religion, philosophy, or art.

Two nihilistic methods predominate in this first chapter: facetious allusion and mock dialectic. The opposition of thesis and antithesis (Christianity versus Judaism, the Old

World versus the New, and so forth) does not, as in Hegel, issue in a synthesis, but rather in a reduction of both terms to absurdity. Thesis versus antithesis equals nothingness—that is the Western dialectic.

In the second chapter, Balso comes upon Maloney the Areopagite. Just as the guide hastened to stereotype himself as Jewish, Maloney identifies himself as "a catholic [sic] mystic" (10). Maloney is an idealist, but he seeks to liberate his spirituality not through art, but through the abnegation of the body. He is naked except for a derby of thorns, and he is attempting to crucify himself with thumbtacks. Just as Balso is secure in a literary tradition, Maloney foots the well-trod path of such Catholic mystics as Marie Alacoque, Suso, Labre, Lydwine of Schiedam, Rose of Lima, Notker Balbus, Ekknard le Vieux, Hucbald le Chauve. And in his own fashion, Maloney is also a devotional poet (10). Like any mystic worth his salt, Maloney spends the proper time concerned with the least of his brethren—the vermin. He is, in fact, the biographer of Saint Puce, a flea who was born, lived, and died in the armpit of Christ.

Maloney tries to document the continuity of the Classical and Christian traditions and in so doing he implicates Dionysus and Athene, Leda and Europa, in the satire. West has great fun at the expense of the Virgin Birth. Puce's life is, inevitably, one protracted communion with divinity. As a culmination of his travels about the body of Christ, he authors his magnum opus, *A Geography of Our Lord*. The day comes when Christ's arms are stretched on the cross and Puce's armpit cathedral is exposed to the ravages of sun and climate. Puce refuses to desert the ship, and his martyrdom follows close upon that of the Master.

Maloney is brought to tears by his own telling. Once again the realistic Balso staunchly opposes such neurotic behavior: " 'I think you're morbid. . . . Don't be morbid. Take your eyes off your navel. Take your head from under your armpit. Stop sniffing mortality. Play games. Don't read so many books. Take cold showers. Eat more meat' " (13). After dispensing this advice, so typical of a healthy American, Balso continues his pilgrimage.

The mortification of the body does not yield spirituality. It yields morbidity and is a type of masochism. Largely by allusion and comic parallel, West includes in his indictment not simply modern-day Maloneys, but all ascetics and their prototype, Christ. West does not reduce Christ to a good man or to a beautiful myth, as many unorthodox thinkers have done. He reduces Christ to absurdity. The effect of the Incarnation, theologically, is to raise humanity virtually to the level of the deity. West's interpretation of the doctrine lowers the concept of the deity to the level of man, and the force of the novel is to reduce man to the level of the animal.

Religion, then, is not, in West's opinion, the way to spirituality. But West also exposes Balso's way—a healthy mind in a healthy body—as too banal even to require detailed satire. Any boob, the author implies, can see that animal existence is not enough—it is what we are all trying to escape—but man's illusions of spirituality require a certain amount of effort to debunk.

The function of the imagery is to diminish the thing described in the very proportion that it purports to be enhancing it: "The hot sun of Calvary burnt the flesh beneath Christ's upturned arm, making the petal-like skin shrivel until it looked like the much-shaven armpit of an old actress' " (12).

Around the next bend of the intestine, Balso finds hidden in a hollow tree an English theme written by John Gilson for his eighth-grade teacher, Miss McGeeney. The precocious theme is a *Crime Journal*, written in obvious imitation of *Crime and Punishment* and *Notes from the Underground*. Gilson abhors the use of "masks, cardboard noses, diaries, memoirs, letters from a Sabine farm, the theatre" because these are forms of illusion and Gilson considers himself an honest man. West was probably similarly impatient with literary forms. Nevertheless, Gilson settles on the diary form, for he is a man divided against himself and must compromise to exist. After a picturesque lament for the inaccessibility of the Real, he concludes his first entry with the sobering detail, "Written while smelling the moistened forefinger of my left hand" (14). Gilson's awareness of his animal nature forces him to parody his intellectual dilettantism.

This alternation of the serious and the burlesque continues. Gilson makes a few apt observations on the art of the diary, in particular the tendency of amateur diaries to deteriorate quickly after the first entry: "The white paper acts as a laxative. A diarrhoea of words is the result. The richness of the flow is unnatural; it cannot be sustained" (14). He admits his own split-personality. At times he is "honest Iago" and at times Raskolnikov, but he is never simply John Gilson. He who abhors personae exists only in the shells of literary creations. His schizophrenia supports Alan Ross's statement that "*Balso Snell* analyzes only the disintegration of the Self, and its illusion of superiority at its most pathetic moment of neurotic isolation" (Ross, p. xi).

Signing himself "John Raskolnikov Gilson," the young psychotic composes a journal within a journal, entitled *The Making of a Fiend*. He is residing in an asylum where he notices that his mother, during her visits, is much more disordered than himself. He first asserts that "order is the test of sanity," and then that "order is vanity" (15). The reader soon infers that there is little to choose between the hysteria of the mother and the intellectual cancer of the incarcerated son. Suspecting that someone is reading his diary, Gilson leaves the note, "You who read these pages while I sleep, please sign here" (15). His schizophrenia is confirmed when he rises at night to sign the incriminating page himself.

From this point in the diary, West allows the narration to become steadily more serious, without the moments of self-mockery. The Crime Journal becomes Dostoevsky in miniature, sharing the Russian master's preoccupation with the divided man. West first debunks the myth of the possessed artist. Gilson confesses that there is nothing romantic or spiritual about madness.

As a book-sorter in the public library, Gilson got a taste of the fruit of the world's intellectual efforts: "The books smelt like the breaths of their authors. As I handled them they seemed to turn into flesh, or at least some substance that could be eaten." The books were never more than excretions of their authors and they are as dead as their authors are or soon will be. The people who consult them are cannibals, trying to feed their own illusions on dead illusions.

On the top floor of Gilson's rooming house lives an idiot dishwasher. The idiot comes to personify for Gilson man's animality. It is this animality which all the "fervors, deliriums, ambitions, and dreams" of art are designed to transcend (17). It is the awareness of this animality that has disordered Gilson's mind. Gilson describes this "noble savage" without sentimentality: "He was a fat, pink and grey pig of a man, and stank of stale tobacco, dry perspiration, clothing mold, and oatmeal soap. He did not have a skull on the top of his neck, only a face; his head was all face—a face without side, back or top, like a mask" (18). The most irritating thing about the idiot is that "a beast of laughter always seemed to be struggling to escape from between his teeth" (18). He is reminded of this laughter by an incident at a performance of Gounod's *Faust*. The basso was at first unable to summon up a stage laugh on cue. When the laughter finally caught fire, it consumed the man and he was unable to cease his hysterics. Gilson has had enough of this cosmic joke. He returns home determined to murder the idiot. After an interlude of Dostoevskian soul-searching, he commits the crime with a heavy knife. It is patterned on Raskolnikov's murder and on the *acte gratuit* of *Lafcadio's Adventures* in that it is not inspired by any of the motivations popularized by detective writers and criminologists. Gilson explains that he killed the man to restore his balance, just as, during his childhood, he always had to kill the flies in his room before he could go to sleep.

That this compulsion neurosis has the usual sexual causes is demonstrated by the manner of the crime. In spite of Gilson's intellectual pretensions, it becomes an inverted sex murder. He chooses a knife because "as a child I always took pleasure in cutting soft, firm things" (20). The murder has been magnified into a ritual castration of man's animal nature. But Gilson is defeated in his attempt to cut the mind free from the body because his mind is seduced by the sexual gratification of the murder: "Naked: I felt cold: and I noticed that my genitals were tight and hard, like a dog's, or an archaic Greek statue's—they were as though I had just come out of an ice-cold bath. I was aware of a great excitement; an excitement that seemed to be near, but not quite within me" (21). Thus Gilson commits the murder in the nude. He makes a mess of it and is possessed by fear until he can deposit the knife in the river. Then he undergoes a blissful transformation. Freed of his maleness, his anima is able to assert itself: "I caressed my breasts like a young girl who has suddenly become conscious of her body on a hot afternoon. I imitated the mannered walk of a girl showing off before a group of boys. In the dark I hugged myself" (22). He tries to attract some sailors, but they laugh at him. Finally, he sits down on a bench and is sick to his stomach with self-disgust. The murder has already become malignant within him. The murder, as James Light has explained, is a crisis in the struggle between Gilson's mind and body, a battle instigated by the mind, but turned to its own purposes by the body (Light, 46).

Gilson's sex life is arrested, juvenile. Nevertheless, it is in regard to his isolation, his introspection, his sadomasochism, that the first touch of pathos slips into the book. The reader sympathizes with the boy's lonely quest for freedom from himself. Nor does West rebuke Gilson with any *carpe diem* nonsense about enjoying the animal pleasures. The animal pleasures are embodied in the idiot.

West and Dostoevsky shared this concern for the intellectual divided against himself. The *doppelganger*, consequently, abounds in their works. West, however, differs from Dostoevsky in three important respects. First, he goes beyond his analysis of the divided man to satirize himself for becoming serious in a world that does not reward serious inquiries with usable answers. Secondly, he rejects Dostoevsky's mysticism outright. Thirdly, he employs an imagistic style that contrasts with the Russian's passionate abundance. Gilson finds striking images for his self-analysis:

> Inside my head the murder has become like a piece of sand
> inside the shell of an oyster. My mind has commenced to form
> a pearl around it. The idiot, the singer, his laugh, the knife, the
> river, my change of sex, all cover an irritating grain of sand. As
> the accumulations grow and become solidified, the original
> irritation disappears. If the murder continues to grow in size it
> may become too large for me to contain; then I am afraid it
> will kill me, just as the pearl eventually kills the oyster (22).

West has led himself and the reader into a trap. The
fourth chapter opens with Balso returning the manuscript to
the tree and sadly musing that "the world was getting to be a
difficult place for a lyric poet" (22-23). His lament is sharply
interrupted by Gilson himself, who demands, "Well, nosey,
how did you like my theme?' (23). Balso's reply is a subtle
blending of dilettantism and parental cleanmindedness: 'Interesting psychologically, but is it art? . . . I'd give you
B-minus and a good spanking' (23).

Gilson is a little realist who gladly prostitutes his art for
financial or sexual remuneration. When he discovers Balso is a
poet and without any market value whatsoever, the youngster's scorn knows no bounds. Balso, the bard of suburbia,
regurgitates stock prescriptions for mental health: " 'What
you ought to do, child, is to run about more. Read less and
play baseball' " (23). Gilson dismisses this YMCA advice,
although he does admit that he once wrote a poem to seduce
a fat girl who only sleeps with poets (23). In spite of his
triumph with this exclamatory, allusive, freely-formed masterpiece, Gilson's vocation is not a labor of love: "I'm fed up
with poetry and art. Yet what can I do; I need women and
because I can't buy or force them, I have to make poems for
them. God knows how tired I am of using the insanity of Van
Gogh and the adventures of Gauguin as canopeners for the
ambitious Count Six-Times. And how sick I am of the
literary bitches. But they're the only kind that'll have me"
(23-24). In order to rid himself of the gremlin, Balso buys a
copy of Gilson's latest autobiographical pamphlet.

Once again West has revealed the physiological basis for
cultural activity. The sex appeal of the poet has been
prominently advertised since Byron. But Byron, whether a

poseur or not, was at least serious about his art. Gilson is the last phase in a movement that has seen the image of the writer become decidedly phallic, almost to the exclusion of interest in his works.

We are dealing with two Gilsons, however. The Gilson of the *Crime Journal* is a tortured seeker of truth. The Gilson who created Raskolnikov is a cynic who has not contested the claims of the body, but capitulated totally. He is partially refreshing as an antidote to Raskolnikov's delirium and Balso Snell's bromidic banalities. But he is also depressing, because he is deluded in his cynicism and vulgarity. That "beast of walls," the "walled-in fat girl," is even less worth our while than arid philosophy.

Strangely, the Pamphlet, which Gilson has offered as "a brief outline of my position" is a complete departure from the brattish tone of its author. It is closer to that of the *Crime Journal*. The narrator, however, is not psychotic and, if he is neurotic, he is at least articulate in the probing of his neuroses. The roots of his troubles are the same as those of Raskolnikov Gilson—an acute metaphysical ennui and an abnormal sex life.

The pamphlet opens with the unnamed narrator receiving word of the death of his mistress Saniette. He uses this event as an excuse for not shaving. As usual he is self-critical: "I recognized the cardboard and tin of my position (a young man, while shaving, dismisses death with a wave of his hand)" (24). He views the situation from every angle in search of an emotion. None arrives. At last, he is forced to admit that he is irrevocably committed to "the side of intellect against the emotions . . . the side of the brain against the heart" (24). This clinical, intellectual coldness is, of course, the unforgivable sin of Ethan Brand, as well as of Ivan Karamozov, Stavrogin, and Raskolnikov.

Gilson's emotional block stems from the prefabricated responses from which he is compelled to choose in every situation. He has been trained by literature to react to various situations in various ways. He has been taught by literature that all responses are ultimately constructs. To death, for instance, his response may be "sentimental, satirical, formal" —his choice is one of convenience and appropriateness. He has no virgin sensibility with which to react un-selfconsciously to experience. His spontaneity has been eroded first by daily life (in which society demands conventional masks at funerals, weddings, and so forth), and secondly by literature (where the social responses are exposed as masks, but where characterization still depends on credible, consistent behavior). When he is finally driven to admit that his search for pure emotion is hopelessly stymied by his education in formal emotions, Gilson tries to elevate his emotional impotence to a heroic stance by practicing "a few sneers in the bathroom mirror" (25).

Saniette's deathbed struggles afford West a chance to ridicule another religion, Christian Science (25). Gilson implies that health and illness may be psychosomatic, but that it is probably the body causing mental illness, rather than the opposite. Nevertheless, as much as he despises his own cold plight, he loathes even more the unquestioning optimism of the world's Saniettes, who force experience into their own mental molds:

> The inevitability of death has always given me pleasure, not because I am eager to die, but because all the Saniettes must die. When the preacher explained the one thing all men could be certain of—all must die—the King of France became angry. When death prevailed over the optimism of Saniette, she was, I am certain, surprised. The thought of Saniette's surprise pleases me, just as the King's anger must have pleased the preacher (25).

He has a further reason for disliking Saniette. She represented the world's audiences, all those observing eyes that force one to play a role. Their actor-audience relationship came to epitomize for him the sexual charade: "I have forgotten the time when I could look back at an affair with a woman and remember anything but a sequence of theatrical poses—poses that I assumed, no matter how aware I was of their ridiculousness, because they were amusing. All my acting has but one purpose, the attraction of the female" (26). The narrator repeats, in a different tone, Gilson's defense of his intellectual prostitution. Lacking physical charms, he had to substitute "strange conceits, wise and witty sayings, peculiar conduct, Art, for the muscles, teeth, hair, of my rivals" (26).

The narrator, then, is driven to artificiality not only by the demands of society, not only by his literary self-consciousness, but also as a compensation for his lack of other gifts. This is the paradox of the Wound and the Bow, but it does not have the heroic implications that Edmund Wilson accords it. For, if the narrator could be a Hamlet or a tragic clown, he would be satisfied to make a stage of life. But he always finds it necessary to "burlesque the mystery of feeling at its source; I must laugh at myself, and if the laugh is 'bitter' I must laugh at the laugh" (27). This explains the curious ambivalence of the novel's humor. West is laughing at life, but he is also laughing at laughter. He leaves no honorable recourse to humans, neither sainthood nor cynicism. Nor can an author be serious or humorous with impunity.

Driven by the implacability of such knowledge as this, the narrator seeks relief in causing pain: he beats Saniette. A hotel clerk breaks in upon them. In another brilliant monologue the narrator tries to describe to them the torment of simply being flesh and blood:

> "This evening I am very nervous. I have a sty on my eye, a cold sore on my lip, a pimple where the edge of my collar touches my neck, another pimple in the corner of my mouth, and a drop of salt snot on the end of my nose. . . .
> . . . It seems to me as though all the materials of life—wood, glass, wool, skin—are rubbing against my sty, my cold sore and my pimples; rubbing in such a way as not to satisfy the itch or convert irritation into active pain, but so as to increase the size of the irritation, magnify it and make it seem to cover everything—hysteria, despair. . . .
> . . . If I could only turn irritation into pain; could push the whole thing into insanity and so escape. I am able to turn irritation into active pain for only a few seconds, but the pain soon subsides and the monotonous rhythm of irritation returns. O how fleeting is pain!—I cry (28).

The narrator's sadomasochism is not the result of some

childhood trauma, but the natural recourse of one who cannot obliterate the constant displeasure of his body in any other way. I think that West has here hit upon something more than an effective *tour de force* of characterization. He has isolated a bizarre human universal—the ever-present physical discomfort—which previous novelists have only touched upon in passing. Moreover, the force of the passage gives a much greater reality to his nihilism than the somewhat adolescent complaints of many of the characters.

Saniette and the clerk cannot cope with this original insight. They must take their "truth" in familiar doses. Saniette concludes that Gilson does not love her "because a gentleman would never strike a lady," and the clerk threatens to call the police (29). But Gilson drops the names of the Marquis de Sade and Huysman's Gilles de Rais. Saniette and the clerk are people of the world and thus familiar with the sadists of literature; all is accounted for because all is categorized—the clerk withdraws and Saniette goes back to bed.

The next day Gilson tries once more to pierce through to Saniette's understanding. He tells her of an animalistic chauffeur, named The Desire to Procreate, a creature reminiscent of Raskolnikov Gilson's idiot, who lives within him: "Can you imagine how it feels to have this cloth-covered devil within one? While naked, were you ever embraced by a fully-clothed man? Do you remember how his button-covered coat felt, how his heavy shoes felt against your skin? Imagine having this man inside of you, fumbling and fingering your heart and tongue with wool-covered hands, treading your tender organs with stumbling feet" (30). Saniette finds the image monstrously funny. She smiles superiorly.

Gilson's snowballing resentment of Saniette generates a magnificent fantasy of revenge. She now represents a specific kind of audience, one which relishes the performance of such eccentrics as Gilson. This audience is "the smart, sophisticated, sensitive yet hardboiled, art-loving frequenters of the little theatres" (30). He dreams of producing a play for "the

discriminating few: art-lovers and book-lovers, school teach-
ers who adore culture, lending librarians, publisher's assistants, homosexualists and homosexualists' assistants, hard-
drinking newspaper men, interior decorators, and the writers
of advertising copy" (30). The play will be properly
avant-garde. Gilson will compliment the audience "on their
good taste in preferring Art to animal acts" (30). Then the
cast will march to the footlights and declaim from Chekhov:
"It would be more profitable for the farmer to raise rats for
the granary than for the bourgeois to nourish the artist, who
must always be occupied with undermining institutions"
(30). As a *pièce de résistance*, "the ceiling of the theatre will
be made to open and cover the occupants with tons of loose
excrement. After the deluge, if they so desire, the patrons of
my art can gather in the customary charming groups and
discuss the play" (31). There is, in other words, nothing to
choose from between Art and animal acts, deluded optimism
and knowing pessimism, prostituted art and "serious" art,
lack of consciousness or the constant irritation of consciousness.

The novel is more than an attack on Art; it is an attack
on the complete artificiality of consciousness. Art, history,
religion, philosophy, psychology, bourgeois axioms—these are
all aspects of Artificiality, the Westian transcendental. And
this transcendental artificiality leaves no possibility of un-
adulterated spirit. Not only is the mind harassed by the body;
it is also divided against itself.

Once again Balso discards Gilson's work with a parental
sigh. Fortunately, the decline of the younger generation has
been more amply, more complacently documented than any
other recurrent phenomenon. Thus Balso, drawing upon the
artificiality of amateur sociology, blames, "the war, the
invention of printing, nineteenth-century science, communism, the wearing of soft hats, the use of contraceptives, the
large number of delicatessen stores, the movies, the tabloids,
the lack of adequate ventilation in large cities, the passing of
the saloon, the soft collar fad, the spread of foreign art, the
decline of the western world, commercialism, and finally, for

throwing the artist back on his own personality, the renaissance" (31).

Naturally, Balso is relieved after this analysis. He has cured the evil by classifying its causes. Turning once more to the *beau ideal,* he asks rhetorically, " 'What is beauty, saith my sufferings then?' " In answer, there appears a young girl, bathing naked in a public fountain, reminiscent of the apparition of the Muse to Stephen Dedalus as he walked along the strand. In that case, the young artist perceived his "call" to the artistic life. Here, the girl heralds, in a paean of baroque imagery, Balso's call to the erotic; and her imagery becomes progressively less ethereal. Balso interrupts her by sticking his tongue in her mouth. A metamorphosis occurs. The girl becomes Miss McGeeney, John Gilson's school-teacher, an authoress in her own right, described as "a middle aged woman dressed in a mannish suit and wearing horn-rimmed glasses" (32).

Miss McGeeney is writing a biography of Samuel Perkins. Perkins is the biographer of E. F. Fitzgerald, who is the biographer of D. B. Hobson, who is the biographer of Boswell. Miss McGeeney shrewdly predicts that someone will "take the hint" and write a life of Miss McGeeney. The chain biographers "will all go rattling down the halls of time, each one in his or her turn a tin can on the tail of Doctor Johnson" (33).

Miss McGeeney will not be satisfied with a pedestrian narration of dates and events in her book; she has attempted to isolate the quintessence of Samuel Perkins. Her book is entitled *Samuel Perkins: Smeller* for "at an age when most men's features are regular, before his personality had been able to elevate any one portion of his physiognomy over the rest, Perkins' face was dominated by his nose" (33). She accounts for his olfactory prowess by a theory of natural compensation: "He was deaf and almost blind; his fingers fumbled stupidly; his mouth was always dry and contained a dull, insensitive tongue. But his nose! ... Nature had strengthened this organ and had made it so sensitive that it was able to do duty for all the contact organs" (34). The reader discovers he has been led into a clever burlesque of synaesthesia, the poetic device of interpreting one type of sensation in terms of another which was raised to the level of a mystique by the Symbolists. According to Miss McGeeney, "Perkins was able to translate the sensations of sound, sight, taste, and touch, into that of smell. He could smell a chord in D minor, or distinguish between the tone-smell of a violin and that of a viola. He could smell the caress of velvet and the strength of iron. It has been said of him that he could smell an isosceles triangle; I mean that he could apprehend through the sense of smell the principles involved in isosceles triangles" (35). Subsequently, Miss McGeeney refers to Rimbaud's sonnet "Voyelles" and to Des Esseintes, the epicurean hero of *A Rebours*, as believers in synaesthesia.

There is more involved here than the burlesque of an overused literary device. Baudelaire's synaesthesia reflects a Swedenborgian monism, the belief in a transcendent reality of which all the phenomena of this world are symbols. This hidden immanence is the ground for the unity of the senses. West, likewise, extends his satire into metaphysical realms:

> "Rather than a tread-mill, I should call the senses a circle. A step forward along the circumference is a step nearer the starting place. Perkins went, along the circumference of the circle of his senses, from anticipation to realization, from hunger to satiation, from naivete to sophistication, from simplicity to perversion. He went ... from the smell of new-mown hay to that of musk and vervain (from the primitive to the romantic), and from vervain to sweat and excrement (from the romantic to the realistic); and, finally, to complete the circuit, from excrement he returned to new-mown hay. ... And a man like Perkins is able to make the circle of his sensory experience approach the infinite" (35-36).

The biological cycle, the historical cycle, the artistic cycle—all these are manifestations of the cyclical unity of life as perceived by Perkins' nose. This was also the subject of Balso's opening song. Perkins carries his mania for systematization even into his intimate life. He marries a woman solely for the sake of categorizing her smells: " 'He told me that he had built from the odors of his wife's body an architecture and an aesthetic, a music and a mathematic. Counterpoint, multiplication, the square root of a sensation, the cube root of an experience—all were there. He told me that he had even discovered a politic, a hierarchy of odors, self-government, direct . . .' " (36). This is too much for the healthy-minded Balso. He deals Miss McGeeney a blow in the abdomen.

West reduces to absurdity scholarship, the feminine ideal, and the belief in an ordered, coherent unity. If a person trusts that he can perceive the universe in a grain of sand, he must also be able to perceive it in a wart, a tumor, a pimple, and so forth. The attempt of idealistic philosophies to arrange experience into a system of any sort is as arbitrary as Perkins' nose. One unity exists—matter—and that is a unity without system.

Having escaped Miss McGeeney's clutches, Balso finally perceives the secret of the wooden horse. It "was inhabited solely by writers in search of an audience" (37). Balso resolves that he will not listen to another story. He accelerates his search for the exit to the intestine.

Balso stops at a sidewalk cafe where he falls asleep over his beer. A long dream-within-a-dream sequence ensues. He dreams that he is once again with the harem of his youth, the beautiful girl-cripples who congregate in the lobby of Carnegie Hall "because Art is their only solace, most men looking upon their strange forms with distaste" (37). Even in his sexual tastes, Balso manifests the same antipathy to the Ideal: "Their strange foreshortenings, hanging heads, bulging spinesacks, were a delight, for he had ever preferred the imperfect, knowing well the plainness, the niceness of perfection" (37).

The cripple that Balso singles out for his special passion is an intellectual hunchback, Janey Davenport. She, like Balso, has had to settle for an auto-erotic dream life and for the waking dream that is Art as compensation for natural attractiveness: " 'O Arabesque, I, Balso Snell, shall replace music in your affections! Your pleasure shall no longer be vicarious. No longer shall you mentally pollute yourself. . . .

O deviation from the Golden Mean! O out of alignment!' "
(38). Balso kisses her, eliciting from the narrator a passage of
"True-Romance" prose: "Now she had found a wonderful
poet; now she knew the thrill she had never known before
... had found it in the strength of this young and tall,
strangely wise man, caught like herself in the meshes of the
greatest net human hearts can know: Love" (38). This
burlesquing of hack prose will be one of the principal devices
of *A Cool Million.* Here it helps to diminish the conceptions
of a beautiful mind in an ugly exterior and the most flagrant
of human idealizations, love.

When Balso tries to seduce Janey, he is greeted with a
smokescreen of conventional brush-offs: "Love, with me, Mr.
Snell, is sacred. I shall never debase love, or myself, or the
memory of my mother, in a hallway" (39). Although she
prefers music (and vicarious experience in general), Janey
concedes that she will yield up her body to Balso if he
prosecutes a vendetta against Beagle Darwin, the betrayer
whose child she carries in the hump on her back. Balso agrees
to this charade of courtly love and Janey gives him two
letters from Beagle. He has run off to Paris without her and
the letters are defenses of his action as being in her best
interest. The first projects what would have been Janey's fate
if she had come to Paris.

Janey would have been a misfit, Beagle suggests, a
sentimental bourgeois surrounded by cosmopolitan cynics.
She would have been "pregnant, unmarried, unloved, lonely,
watching the laughing crowds hurry past her window" (41).
With a deft narrative touch, Beagle shifts into the first
person, from her viewpoint: "Of course I can laugh at mother
with him, or at the Hearth; but why must my own mother
and home be ridiculous? I can laugh at Hobey, Joan, but I
don't want to laugh at myself. I'm tired of laugh, laugh,
laugh. I want to retain some portion of myself unlaughed at.
There is something in me that I won't laugh at" (41). And so
forth. Janey has no one to turn to. Her mother is pitiless, like
Beagle. Her father was her great love, but he is dead. Her best
friend is a Lesbian. She tries to break the news of her

pregnancy to Beagle—matter-of-factly so as not to seem
ridiculous. But she bungles the pronunciation of *"je suis
enceinte"* and Beagle goes nonchalantly out to plan a
celebration. Janey meditates suicide. She tries on all the
tragic costumes, but in the back of her mind are always the
taunts with which Beagle would deflate her tragedy. Finally
she half-jumps, half-falls from the window ledge. The last
word she hears is her mother's scolding "Clumsy!"

Beagle's laughter rides roughshod over maternity, the
home, romance, suicide, self-respect—all the inalienable sacred cows that Janey would like to declare immune to
ridicule. There can be no via media between idealism and
cynicism. Beagle's offense is also his best defense, as when he
explains his pessimism: "It's the war. Everybody is sad
nowadays. Great stuff, pessimism" (42). Beagle's laughter
may shield him from others, but it does not quell his own
insecurity. His second letter, in the interests of impartiality,
is a projection of his own reaction to Janey's hypothetical
suicide. He is another of those inoculated by literature
against life: " 'You once said to me that I talk like a man in a
book. I not only talk, but think and feel like one. I have
spent my life in books; literature has deeply dyed my brain
its own color. This literary coloring is a protective one—like
the brown of the rabbit or the checks of the quail—making it
impossible for me to tell where literature ends and I begin' "
(47). Thus, when he comes upon the crowd surrounding
Janey's corpse in the street, his first reaction is relief that he
will not have to arrange an abortion, but his second is that he
will not know how to respond spontaneously to her death,
just as Gilson can only exist beneath his numerous masks.
"Why is it impossible for you to understand, except in terms
of art, her action?" he demands of himself (49). Reviewing
the elegies of the human predicament, he makes a concerted
effort to attain a genuine sentiment. He fails.

The immediate problem remains. How shall he greet his
mistress's death? He decides to feign the madness of Hamlet.
To the revelations of the Carcas crowd he insistently replies,
" 'Bromius! Iacchus! Son of Zeus!' " (53). This elicits

astonished comments, including "Greek god!—does he think
we don't know he's a Methodist?" (53). As his oracles
become more allusive, his literary friends begin to appreciate
them. His masterpiece is a parody of the *"ubi sunt"* laments:
" 'Or quick tell me where has gone Samson?—strongest of
men. He is no longer even weak. And where, oh tell me,
where is the beautiful Appolyon? He is no longer even ugly.
And where are the snows of yesteryear? And where is Tom
Giles? Bill Taylor? Jake Holtz? In other words, "Here today
and gone tomorrow" ' " (54).

His role is a success and encores are demanded. Beagle
responds with a long digression on the impossibility of
bridging the gap between the superhuman—Christ, Dionysus,
and Gargantua—who have been born with the attendance of
heavenly omens, and the merely human—Janey Davenport—
"conceived in an offhand manner on a rainy afternoon." For
the first time in his life he experiences profound emotions;
but the next moment, he turns upon himself and sneers at his
own compassion: "After building up his tear-jerker routine
for a repeat, he blacked out and went into his juggling for the
curtain. He climaxed the finale by keeping in the air an Ivory
Tower, a Still White Bird, the Holy Grail, the Nails, the
Scourge, the Thorns, and a piece of the True Cross" (56).
This is Jamesian narrative complexity with a vengeance. Balso
is dreaming a dream within a dream. He is given the letters by
Janey Davenport, a character from the second level-dream,
one of the many faces of his own personality. The letters are
written by Beagle Darwin, and they contain fictional narra-
tions. In the first he assumes Janey's personality; in the
second he views himself under a microscope. By removing the
reader so many steps from reality, West reduces to absurdity
fiction itself. It becomes a shadow of a shadow of a shadow
of a shadow, so remote that it is only a stylized image of
reality.

One more level is added when, with the opening of the
last chapter, Janey Davenport is changed to Miss McGeeney,
who admits that the letters are part of an epistolary novel
which she is writing in the manner of Richardson. She solicits

Balso's opinion of their contemporaneity. Balso, as willing to prostitute criticism as Gilson was willing to prostitute art, hands down a verdict in the worst tradition of book reviewing: " 'A stormy wind blows through your pages, sweeping the reader breathless ... witchery and madness. Comparable to George Bernard Shaw. It is a drama of passion that has all the appeal of wild living and the open road. Comparable to George Bernard Shaw. There's magic in its pages, and warm strong sympathy for an alien race' " (57). Balso's youth is restored by this new passion. Miss McGeeney, he discovers, is really Mary McGeeney, his old sweetheart. They know what they want. In some bushes outside the cafe, "Miss McGeeney lay down on her back with her hands behind her head and her knees apart. Balso stood over her and began a speech the intent of which was obvious" (58).

Balso does not allow Miss McGeeney's readiness to cheat him out of a long seduction speech which sums up the seduction speeches of the ages. Politically, he advises her, sex is in the interests of Liberty. Philosophically, every agent, as Aristotle has shown, acts for its own pleasure. Artistically, experience is the root of creativity and of appreciation. He concludes with the time-honored argument of *carpe diem.*

Mary, in her turn, runs the gamut of female attitudes: the righteousness of the pioneers and the Renaissance queens, the compromises of the virgin and the jaded, the acceptance of the hard-bitten, the desperate, the passionate. Mary's "no's" blend at last into the rhythmic "yes" of Molly Bloom: " 'Moooompitcher yaaaah. Oh I never hoped to know the passion, the sensuality hidden within you—yes, yes. Drag me down into the mire, drag. Yes! And with your hair the lust from my eyes brush. Yes ... Yes ... Ooo! Ah!' " (61).

It would appear that the Unity of which Balso sang has prevailed:

> The miracle was made manifest. The Two became One. The One that is all things and yet no one of them: the priest and the god, the immolation, the sacrificial rite, the libation offered to ancestors, the incantation, the sacrificial egg, the altar, the ego and the alter ego, as well as the father, the child,

and the grandfather of the universe, the mystic doctrine, the
purification, the syllable "Om," the path, the master, the
witness, the receptacle, the Spirit of Public School 186, the
last ferry that leaves for Weehawken at seven (61).

But sex is not an emblem of spiritual unity, an Oversoul, a
world of forms, a brotherhood of men, or any other
manifestation of idealism. It is rather the victory of the
physical. All the artists of the Trojan Horse have tried to
transcend the physical. Balso, in particular, has quested for
transcendence. When he found all the avenues of spirituality
exhausted, he tried to affirm the physical, to join forces with
it. But the physical does not need the cooperation of the
mind; the mind is its plaything. Matter annihilates mind in
this culminating nocturnal emission, a grotesque twist on the
Elizabethan conceit of the little death:

> His body broke free of the bard. It took on a life of its
> own; a life that knew nothing of the poet Balso. Only to death
> can this release be likened—to the mechanics of decay. After
> death the body takes command; it performs the manual of
> disintegration with a marvelous certainty. So now, his body
> performed the evolutions of love with a like sureness.
>
> In this activity, Home and Duty, Love and Art, were
> forgotten.
>
> An army moved in his body, an eager army of hurrying
> sensations. These sensations marched at first methodically and
> then hysterically, but always with precision. The army of his
> body commenced a long intricate drill, a long involved
> ceremony. A ceremony whose ritual unwound and maneu-
> vered itself with the confidence and training of chemicals
> acting under the stimulus of a catalytic agent.
>
> His body screamed and shouted as it marched and
> uncoiled; then, with one heaving shout of triumph, it fell back
> quiet.
>
> The army that a moment before had been thundering in
> his body retreated slowly—victorious, relieved (62).

The only unity, says West, is matter, and the principle of
personality is disintegration.

The critics have been hard put to agree upon the major
theme or themes of *Balso Snell.* C. Carroll Hollis sees a
special clue to the book in the final passage:

> The death-wish that pervades the whole dream sequence

culminates in this closing passage with its savage paradox that the sex act itself, the blind creative act of life, now becomes in reality the Ancient Mariner's Life-in-Death for modern man. This parallel to Coleridge's version of the Wandering Jew provides an added insight. Life-in-death had West in thrall, although it may be doubted that the "woeful agony" which forced him to begin this tale was sufficiently alleviated in the telling to leave him free. In fact he turned immediately to the writing of his second book.[9]

The book is, therefore, a projection of self-criticism, the rejection of the man without beliefs: "When Nathanael West returned to New York from his two year stay in Paris, he told A. J. Liebling that *The Dream Life of Balso Snell* was written "as a protest against writing books." That it is a protest against writing fiction is clear enough, but its significance is much more in its derisive rejection of himself" (Hollis, p. 398).

For James Light the book is not only a rude awakening from the dream of art, but also a search "for a central Unity, an Over Soul, that will make the meaninglessness of multiplicity into the ultimate truth of some essential one-ness" (Light, p. 53-54). V. L. Lokke dismisses *Balso* as an attack on the "literature boys," the intellectual aesthetes.[10] The novel certainly includes such an attack. Similarly, Norman Podhoretz is on the trail of a partial truth in his observation that "the assault on culture in 'Balso Snell' is really part of West's assault on himself; he is sneering not so much at Western civilization as at his own ambition to become a part of it."[11]

The trouble with these summaries of *Balso Snell* is that they do not put first things first; their criticisms do not reflect the complexity of the novel.

Balso Snell is, above all, a rejection not merely of Art, not merely of West, but rather a rejection of life itself. The implied syllogism is that life is worth living only if man can give life meaning through spiritual activity. But all spirituality is either a sham or reducible to physiological causes. Therefore, life is not worth living. Granted, the novel does constitute a revolt against art and a flagellation of the Self.

But it is also an attack on Catholicism, Judaism, Christian
Science, philosophy, history, music, poetry, scholarship,
courtly love, the home, and patriotism. West launches his
attack on the universal by means of attacks on particulars.

The novel has been criticized as formless. It is not
formless. It does, however, constitute an original form
embodying a nihilism which is, in its extremity, original in
American literature. The principle involved is that of Charles
Olson's projective verse: "Form is never more than an
extension of content," along with its corollary, "That right
form, in any given poem, is the only and exclusively possible
extension of content under hand."[12] The form of *Balso Snell*
cannot be described solely in the terminology of traditional
novel criticism because there is no other novel quite like it. In
the "journey" of this study through the novel, however, I
have tried to point out the major methods employed by
West, and a review of those techniques should clarify the
form of the book.

First of all, West attacks the various manifestations of the
spirit in two ways, by the facetious allusion and by the
Westian dialectic. The first works on the principle of guilt by
association; any name summoned up by one of the grotesques in *Balso* is certain to be diminished by the company
it keeps. The dialectic pits thesis against antithesis and lets
them destroy each other. The most important of these
antitheses are Old World versus New World, Jews versus
Christians, Monism versus Pluralism (in various contexts),
realistic art versus abstract art, health versus mortification of
the body, sanity versus insanity, mind versus body, delirium
(or delusion) versus cynicism, optimism versus pessimism, art
versus "animal acts," the consciousness against itself (reflection), the conventional pose versus the eccentric pose, ideal
unity (system) versus material unity (disintegration), cynicism versus sentimentality, and man versus woman. This
dialectic assures that no positive values will be inferred
mistakenly from West's negativism. It rejects equally the two
halves of human existence, mind and body, and in so doing
rejects their sum—life.

The attack on literature has been overemphasized because West, as young writer and voluminous reader, had the secondary purpose of exorcising his influences and exposing the artificiality which reading induces. Victor Comerchero has best summarized West's case against literature:

> West's protest against writing books is rather a protest against the consequences of reading literature: the artificiality and the sense of unreality, the self-consciousness and poisonous awareness that result from wide reading. . . .
>
> Simply stated, this is the problem: the world of books is an unreal world, and yet at the same time heightens our awareness of the real world around us. The result of the insight is either escapism or a tortured, inhibiting self-consciousness. One becomes so aware of the forces at play upon oneself that one falls, in an attempt to escape from this knowledge, into a treacherous pattern of self-deceit. Wide reading forces us to compare ourselves and others with literary figures. We grow to interpret or misinterpret ourselves solely in literary terms. In an attempt to escape from this fascile [sic] automatic label, we are driven to assume subtle and devious poses. The poses are nevertheless self-conscious, but necessary if one is to preserve one's sense of originality, of the integrity of one's ego. The entire process leads, paradoxically, to distortion rather than clarity of vision; we lose sight of what we and others really are.[13]

James Light has analyzed the way in which West "satirizes his influences while he reflects them," thus granting no immunity to his literary masters (Light, p. 54). The most prominent influences were Surrealism, Joyce, Dostoevsky, and Dada. West borrowed from Surrealism the dream structure and the idea of plumbing the unconscious in search of a reality beyond the facade of the commonplace. But Balso's journey refutes the spirituality of the unconscious. Balso's unconscious is simply the primeval slime. Similarly, West appropriates the journey of Bloom, the artistic idealism of Dedalus, the metamorphoses of Nighttown, the rhetoric and word concern of the Gaelic bards, Molly Bloom's affirmation of the physical, and Joyce's concentration and use of leitmotif. But he parodies these as he employs them. Fyodor Dostoevsky tutored West in man's struggle against himself. But Dostoevsky took his themes seriously, while

West is ambiguous. John Gilson reminds one of Raskolnikov, but he is no great compliment to the creator of that character. Finally, the dadaistic disgust, anti-intellectualism, obscurantism, and glorification of the physical, which Dada purveyed, show up in West. These attitudes are allowed to serve West's nihilism, but are ultimately satirized as pretentious in their own right.

West repays other literary debts in this same coin. A few further targets of his ambivalence are the ennui and sordid imagery of Baudelaire, the metamorphoses of *Jurgen* and *The Waste Land,* the case histories of Freud, the collective unconscious of Jung.

The structure of the book is linear and episodic, but it is also incremental and accelerative. The repeated attacks on artists and on religions, for instance, in various contexts have a cumulative effect. So, too, do the variations on the opposition of monism and pluralism. The acceleration is largely imitative of the progress of the dream towards its orgasm, through the quickened tempo of the later episodes.

All the characters of the novel, including Balso the journeyer, are aspects of Balso the dreamer. No attempt is made at the consistent, rounded characterizations of the ordinary psychological novel. We do not remember John Gilson as an integrated person. However, we do remember his many faces and his literary creations. That is true of all the characters. West expended his skill in memorable caricatures, arranged cubistically. Gilson, the guide, Beagle Darwin, Miss McGeeney, and the rest have more than one face, and their faces are pasted almost arbitrarily to a name. More often than not, the two faces involved in a particular episode are arranged antithetically. And the sum of all the faces in the book is the universalized personality of Balso Snell. Most of West's imagery is exercised in the creation of these faces. The images are conceits, extended, diminishing, and incongruous.

There are many parallels between West's writing and the art of certain painters. The principle of the conceit, discussed above, is the most prominent feature of the paintings of Max Ernst, de Chirico, Dali, (for example, the soft watches), among others. The caricatures are reminiscent of the daily comic page and of the bitter cartoons of George Grosz (although this is even more true in West's later work). I have already called attention to the cubistic arrangement of faces, joined by the accident of space. West's art, like Giotto's, is that of fresco, the art of surfaces, and detail realism, rather than oils, the art of overall perspective and deep emotional textures. The anti-worldly tone of the novel is, paradoxically, medieval. A tendency towards the apocalyptic canvases of Hieronymus Bosch and Breughel is carried to completion in *The Day of the Locust.*

To seize upon the uniqueness of West's nihilism it is helpful to compare his spirit with that of Dada. Dada was nihilistic, but directed its disgust at the past:

> The beginnings of Dada were not the beginnings of an art, but of a disgust. Disgust with the magnificence of philosophers who for 3000 years have been explaining everything to us (what for?), disgust with the pretentions of these artists— God's-representatives-on-earth, disgust with passion and with real pathological wickedness where it was not worth the bother; disgust with a false form of domination and restriction *en masse*, that accentuates rather than appeases man's instinct of domination, disgust with all the catalogued categories, with the false prophets who are nothing but a front for the interests of money, pride, disease, disgust with the lieutenants of a mercantile art made to order according to a few infantile laws, disgust with the divorce of good and evil, the beautiful and the ugly (for why is it estimable to be red rather than green, to the left rather than the right, to be large or small?). Disgust finally with the Jesuitical dialectic which can explain everything and fill people's minds with oblique and obtuse ideas without any physiological basis or ethnic roots, all this by means of blinding artifice and ignoble charlatan's promises.[14]

Dada was destruction, but it was destruction with a better future in mind. "It is aimed," says George Ribemont-Dessaignes, "at the liberation of the individual from dogmas, formulas and laws, at the affirmation of the individual on the plance of the spiritual."[15] West's nihilism encompassed not merely 3000 years of history, but all the possibilities of life itself. For West, the future offered no hope, because neither the body nor the spirit offered meaning or value. West's nihilism was, therefore, absolute, whereas that of the Dadaists, as vigorous as it was, was relative.

West differed from the Dadaists in technique also. Dada placed great importance on chance. If we did not have biographical evidence of the extreme control which West exercised over his work, the complexity of the novel just examined would be sufficient proof of it. West gave his imagination free rein in conjuring up the unusual, but the final product was the result of reworking and creative integration.

As far as the poses of the Dadaists themselves were concerned, it is interesting that one of the earliest made a statement very similar to John Gilson's defense of prostituted art: "It is quite simple: If I write, it is to infuriate my colleagues; to get myself talked about and to make a name for myself. A name helps you to succeed with women and in business. If I were as famous as Paul Bourget, I'd show myself in the Follies every night in a fig leaf and I assure you that I'd have a good box office."[16]

The Dream Life of Balso Snell is an exercise in total nihilism cast in an ingenious nihilistic form. By means of his nihilistic dialectic, the author systematically disposes of the various contestants in the world's intellectual arena. By means of facetious allusions and the satirizing of his own models, he wages battle against literature, nullifying what might have been interpreted as positive elements in his own work. By linking his characters and situations to literary tradition, he exposes "real life" for as great a fiction as the novel itself. His attack is comprehensive and it is at one with the method in which it is carried on. But the book is also a first novel, and, as such, it has a further interest as a proving ground for the talents which account for the eventual success of *Miss Lonelyhearts* and *The Day of the Locust*. West shows in *Balso* that penchant for caricature which he finally developed to a Dickensian fineness. Furthermore, all his later books employ a scenic or episodic technique similar to that of his first novel. His prose is, at the beginning as at the end, vulnerable to analysis only in terms of painting. And his comedy, though it varies somewhat from book to book, never compromises the cold eye of satire that so mercilessly exposes the human condition in *Balso Snell*. West need not have been ashamed of his first novel. It lacks the stature of *Miss Lonelyhearts* or *The Day of the Locust*, but it is an extraordinarily original work, and it is successful on its own terms.

FOOTNOTES

1. Malcolm Cowley, "Introduction" to *Miss Lonelyhearts* (New York, 1959), p. iii.

2. A. M. Tibbetts, "The Strange Half-World of Nathanael West," *Prairie Schooner*, XXXIV (1960), 8.

3. V. N. G., "Books in Review," *Contempo*, I (August 21, 1931), 3.

4. In an interview with Harvey Breit, "Go, West," *New York Times Book Review*, LXII (March 24, 1957), 8.

5. Alan Ross, "The Dead Center: An Introduction to Nathanael West," in *The Complete Works of Nathanael West* (New York, 1957), p. xii.

6. James F. Light, *Nathanael West: An Interpretative Study* (Evanston, Ill., 1961), p. 52.

7. *The Complete Works of Nathanael West* (New York, 1957), p. 2. All further references to West's novels are to this edition and are incorporated into the text.

8. Quoted in Marcel Raymond, *From Baudelaire to Surrealism* (New York, 1950), p. 271.

9. C. Carroll Hollis, "Nathanael West and the 'Lonely Crowd,'" *Thought*, XXXIII (Spring, 1958), 399.

10. V. L. Lokke, "A Side Glance at Medusa: Hollywood, the Literature Boys, and Nathanael West," *Southwest Review*, XLVI (1961), 36-37.

11. Norman Podhoretz, "A Particular Kind of Joking," *New Yorker*, XXXIII (May 18, 1957), 146.

12. Charles Olson, "Projective Verse" in Donald M. Allen, ed., *The New American Poetry: 1945-1960*, (New York, 1960), p. 387.

13. Victor Comerchero, "Nathanael West: The Tuning Fork" (unpubl. diss., Iowa, 1961), pp. 98-99.

14. Tristan Tzara, "Lecture on Dada (1920)," trans. by Ralph Manheim, in Robert Motherwell, ed., *The Dada Painters and Poets: An Anthology* (New York, 1951), p. 250.

15. George Ribemont-Dessaignes, "History of Dada," trans. by Ralph Manheim, in Motherwell, p. 102.

16. Arthur Craven, "Exhibition at the Independents," trans. by Ralph Manheim, in Motherwell, p. 3.

A WORD IS A WORD IS A WORD
By John M. Brand

After being threatened with extinction, a Jew of the first century countered by heralding his lineage: "If any other man thinketh that he hath whereof he might trust in the flesh, I more; Circumcised the eighth day, of the stock of Israel, of the tribe of Benjamin, a Hebrew of the Hebrews; as touching the law, a Pharisee; Concerning zeal, persecuting the church; touching the rightousness which is in the law, blameless."[1] An Apostle, Paul was also a true Jew. His Jewishness counted. Another Jew, this one living in our time, also threatened with extinction, cited the same tradition: " 'Sirrah!' the guide cried in an enormous voice, 'I am a Jew! and whenever anything Jewish is mentioned, I find it necessary to say that I am a Jew. I'm a Jew! A Jew!'"[2]

It is tempting to say, "After the first Jew there is no other." For between the first and the second Jew is the way West. The Jew shuns Christianity. He alters or sheds his Judaism; he becomes European or, in our case, American. Nathan Weinstein, who became Nathanael West, was this Jew in our time. Had he possessed the credentials of Paul, it is unlikely he would have used them. He seemed to retain little of his heritage, and instead tasted the recent culture of Europe and went West in America. In his writings, he usually either ridiculed or ignored the Jew.[3]

But Nathanael West remained Nathan Weinstein. Readers

have noted but seldom explored West's essential Jewishness. Trying to discern what constitutes his art, critics have found many ingredients, and have helpfully cited influences ranging from Dostoevsky to William James. In addition, it has been surmised, there is West's life as a Jew. This, however, has been added parenthetically, as if something to keep in mind while regarding the West who was once Nathan Weinstein. I find it telling that almost no mention has been made of the legacy of Israel, for West has been treated as if the legacy were no more than a minimal part of his consciousness. At the same time, critics have allowed themselves the privilege of describing and interpreting West in terms which are understandable only in relation to the faith of Israel. Victor Comerchero writes of West as "the ironic prophet."[4] He assumes a popular understanding of the term "prophet," and does not draw out of the term its essential Jewishness. Today we think of any person who perceives the hidden drift of events as a "prophet," and are right to think of West in this sense. However, we are in error to ignore the Jewish elements in his prophecy. Randall Reid subtitles his book on West "No Redeemer, No Promised Land,"[5] but gives the Redeemer and Resting Place scant mention. Instead, West's literary antecedents, all taking precedence over the legacy of Israel, receive complete stress. Daniel Aaron titles his article "Waiting for the Apocalypse,"[6] but never really tells us what the Apocalypse is and what it means to wait for it. And critics like Leslie Fiedler have interested us in West's Jewishness without dealing precisely with the Old Testament heritage and how it has been expressed in his writings.[7]

Nathanael West never really doffed his "Hebrew old clothes." In spite of the antagonism he felt against his roots, he nevertheless, in his four novels, gave expression to at least these Jewish concerns: the Word as liberating act (*The Dream Life of Balso Snell*), the New Covenant and the heart's renewal (*Miss Lonelyhearts*), the mission of the Suffering Servant (*A Cool Million*), and the Day of the Lord and reconstitution of creation (*The Day of the Locust*). The task of this essay is to explore—at least partially—West's Jewish-

ness as it is manifested in *Balso Snell*. Not that I am looking
for any degree of affirmation on West's part of this or any
heritage; on the contrary, I find West's art for the most part
negative, so that as he repudiates the Jewish heritage which
he expresses in his works, it is not so he can affirm his new
Western or American heritage. West's art is reductive; he does
not repudiate Israelite man in order to affirm some new man,
yet unlauded. He celebrates the emergence of no new man,
for in his literary world the new is denied, persons seldom
emerge, and little is left to emerge. Human, and not simply
Jewish, possibilities are apparently played out, the self frayed
past the point of recognition. The repudiation of Israel is
therefore but the first step taken by West en route to his
negation of man. This course of reduction commences in
Balso Snell.

Words are cheap in West's first novel. They clog the air,
because Balso's people are always talking. Yet hardly are
these words uttered before they fade and the air is empty;
readers are too, for talk has a way of deadening, especially
talk that is only talk. A word should do more than sound and
vanish; people should too, and do, within the context of
Hebraic faith in the power of the spoken word. An awareness
of this trust in the uttered word should increase our
understanding of *Balso Snell*.

Anticipating the futile striving of the inhabitants of
Balso's world, Pascal wrote, "For it is a wretched thing to
have the wish but not the power."[8] In the biblical accounts
of creation, wish and power are one, and the ease with which
this occurs is dramatized in the words, "And God said, Let
there be . . ." (Genesis 1:3 *passim*). Creation presupposes the
utter sovereignty of God, who exercises sovereignty through
his Word. Creation also presupposes chaos: "And the earth
was without form and void; and darkness was upon the face
of the deep. And the Spirit of God moved upon the face of
the waters" (Genesis 1:2). The created world is here viewed
as a cosmos where there either was, or could be, chaos. But
God is declared the sovereign: when he desires, he acts; when
he says, he does. The Word is a happening, an inevitable
event.[9]

It is far, yet not so far, from the Divine to the human word. Divine and human words, while not coeternal, become coexistent and coefficient, making up what Georges Gusdorf calls an "ontological union."[10] The two words work together, the human word deriving a shaping power from the Divine. Human speech thus participates in God's sovereignty over the world as Adam names the creatures in the Garden (Genesis 2:20). Naming is an exercise in sovereignty, as only a greater can grant a name to a lesser being. Naming is also an achievement of meaning, for the named creatures have conferred upon them a greater degree of reality than before.[11] On the basis of this understanding, Harvey Cox can write, "Thus the world does not come to man already finished and ordered. It comes in part confused and formless and receives its significance from man . . . . Here is a truly exalted view of man. God does not simply insert man into a world filled with creatures which are already named, in relationships and meaning patterns already established by decree. Man must fashion them himself. He doesn't simply discover meaning: he originates it."[12] In naming the animals Adam both indicates and achieves his place in God's design; man's is a place, it might be added, that ought to be achieved even within the wooden horse of *Balso Snell.* Creation is thus seen occurring through the Divine Word and continuing through the mediation of the human word. Speaking is continuous creation. When the Fall happens, creation devolves in the direction of chaos (Genesis 3). This Fall is both expressed in and hastened through the human word. Sin is a manifestation of an inner condition, such as pride; at the same time, sin is compounded through speech. After the Fall, for example, speech is turned into deception and silence when Adam and Eve hide from God. And when Adam blames Eve for the Fall, speech becomes accusation. With the Fall, the word is debased, and in turn debases its speaker. Complete chaos does not occur, for God clothes Adam and Eve before they leave the Garden. This act coincides with Adam's final naming of Eve, so that we can still see the human word occurring within the context of the Divine.

Nevertheless, in attempting to exercise sovereignty over the world, Adam and Eve must labor under the consequences of the Fall. The human word will always be subject to its own undoing. The Namer will become a mere talker, as Balso and his associates will show us.

Following the Fall, other falls begin. Our history begins under the blight of repetition; mortals are caught in a treadmill of repetition, where what they say reveals and causes their plight (Genesis 4:9, 11:4). Fallen history is so repetitive that the experience of Adam, Cain and Babel recurs in the elect society, that very society summoned to counter the effects of the Fall by reenacting the original obedience and dominion of Adam. Prophets are thereby called by God, not only to demand a new creation, but to be that creation in the midst of the old, in short, to be discontinuous with sin. The prophet, of course, shares the sin of Adam and is in this respect one with his people. But when the Divine Word comes to him, he is empowered to transcend just that situation, as the ecstatic nature of the prophetic call indicates (Ezekiel 1, Isaiah 6). As the first man was raised above the lesser beings of creation, and above the supine mass of his original dust, the prophet is now raised above a decaying people. He is endowed with the same Word endowing creation.[13] His word is thus going to be accompanied by God's, just as Adam's was in the beginning (Jeremiah 1:9, Ezekiel 3:4). Through the prophet and his word, as it echoes the saving intervention of God in the processes of history, the continuum of the Fall undergoes a healing rupture, and a new situation is given to the people. As Abraham Heschel writes, "The prophet seldom tells a story, but casts events."[14] The casting of events will bear little resemblance to the moralistic speeches recurring in *Balso.* For the prophet to moralize is to abstract an idea from the continuum of redemption, in which the Word remains active. It is to disengage the human word from its own basis of existence, and to dissolve the union gracing the world from the beginning. What results is the nonredemptive or even irredemptive saying, slogan, or cliché. The false prophets are guilty of reducing prophecy to pleasing slogans and hence receive some of the more scathing indictments in the Old Testament (Jeremiah 5:12, 27:9, Amos 7, I Kings 22:2-28). Their words deliver no one, and further mire people into the repetitive and decreative continuum of sin.

My purpose has not been to write a comprehensive definition of prophecy, but instead to focus attention upon a Hebraic understanding of the power of the spoken word. Because of its original connection with the Divine Word, the human word is co-effectual in the achievement of truly human being, a humanity confronting the world from the posture of generous and lucid mastery. With the Fall, language loses its formative power, history becomes devolutionary, or repetitive, or both, and those longing for change just talk about it. Wretched, they "have the wish but not the power."

I am aware that the distance between the prophets and *Balso Snell* is vast, but it is not as wide as we may suppose. What relates the two is a focus upon the word as a potentially liberating act. The people in this book are forever making speeches. The set speech, uttered pontifically, is recurrent. Small talk is almost absent. With either a prophetic or poetic sense of calling, characters rise to address and defy the repetitive. But in *Balso Snell* the spoken word is allowed to run its course and achieve nothing. As the biblical writers try to authenticate the Divine Word in its human counterpart, West is equally determined to establish its absence. In his world a word is a word is a word, and people talk about but never experience emancipation. Vocal, they nevertheless are in bondage to the routine of the Fall; their words are leaden.

I am therefore suggesting that this work needs to be understood as the lament of a Jew whose time is Wordless. Recipient of a tradition which savored significant events, and avowed that the hum-drum was always susceptible to the discontinuous redemption of God, this Jew comes to view the course of history like the writer of Ecclesiastes, who laments that there is "no new thing under the sun" (Ecclesiastes 1:9). I am not suggesting that West was thoroughly schooled in these traditions, since this is an assertion I cannot at this time make; I am simply suggesting that he expresses a Jew's consciousness of the tedium of things, plus the growing fear that history may be impenetrable to either Divine intervention or eruption.

It should then be clear that what we are going to encounter in the work is the cyclical, a continuum lacking saving events or words. Experience repeats itself, which *Balso* shows both thematically and structurally.[15] In fact, the structure is the theme: one after another, legitimate masters of creation abdicate while making pompous utterances and fail to alter the rhythm of repetition. It may thus be helpful to think of the book as a coil or spiral which extends itself without significant change. Its motions are apparent only. The whole and its parts are the same.[16]

West opens the work on this incongruous note as Balso stands at the ass of the Trojan horse. Here he begins his journey. The beginning and the end are the same; the Alpha and the Omega are found not only in the same place or condition, but are experienced at the same time. The journey thus will go nowhere and eventuate in no new thing. Its direction will be circular, as seekers will be enclosed within the merely repetitive. Balso's initial speech does no more than echo the confinement around him. Viewing the carved words within a heart on a tree, "Balso carved with his penknife another heart and the words 'O Byss! O Abyss! O Anon! O Anan!' omitting, however, the arrow and his initial (4). The circularity of events is caught in the "o" sounds; the numen of the abyss is thinned down through the poet's word play; and " 'O Anon! O Anan!' " sounds curiously like Onan, whose sex life consisted in spilling his seed upon the ground, and whose ineffectual ejaculation is like Balso's wet dream in the burst of creativity closing the book (Genesis 38).

It is fitting that the Jew should guide Balso through the horse, since he is one of the guides of our civilization, and should excel in the journey, especially in one across a wilderness, having no apparent end and demanding endurance. But this Jew is quickly ridiculed, as he is forced to wear a cap embroidered with the label " 'Tours' " (5). He is a poet of sorts, but is no more than a spokesman for the pseudopoetic. He views the viscera of the horse and then shows us the kind of guide he is going to be. " 'First you will please look to the right where you will see a beautiful Doric prostate gland swollen with gladness and an over-abudance of good cheer' " (6). The Jew euphemizes the rough of experience; he superimposes color upon the matter-of-fact. Balso retorts, " 'Exposed plumbing, stinker, that's all I see—and at this late date' " (6). If the guide is pseudopoetic, Balso is depoetic.[17] He has a pseudopoetic tendency, lush and syrupy, which he will exercise, but with no more power than the guide. Here, however, he subjects the pseudopoetic world to a rigid restructuring, so that what was " 'a beautiful Doric prostate gland' " becomes " 'exposed plumbing.' " It is true that the entity being discussed is part of a wooden horse. Even so, if the art of the guide is ridiculously flowery, that of Balso is painfully flat. His words turn the matter-of-fact into the drab, the organic into the metallic. The pseudopoetic guide creates a world of tinsel, whereas Balso creates a world of tin. The depoetic is no more redemptive than the pseudopoetic. Balso and the guide remain where they started, a fact reinforced in their ensuing discussion about art. The guide quotes Picasso, who says, " 'there are no feet in nature . . .' " (8), and adds, citing the circularity of creation, " 'A circle has neither a beginning nor an end. A circle has no feet' " (9). When the guide begins to refer to the mystical, or discontinuous and saving element in routine experience, Balso quotes Cezanne in such a way as to reinforce the cyclical: " 'Everything tends toward the globular' " (9). These two are slaves to the circular, where sameness is all that occurs. The poet thus has run over the treadmill of experience, has spoken, and has either reduced the matter-of-fact to the stale and drab, or, because it is expedient in a world of slaves, has tried to beautify it through strained rhetoric. He is usually depoetic, but can be pseudopoetic; never prophetic or poetic, he has no hand in delivering the captive, no power to "cast events."[18]

With the Gilson episode, the reductive tone we have noted in *Balso* is intensified, for in Gilson-Raskolnikov the repetitive becomes annihilative; tedium eventuates in the evaporation of selfhood. Gilson, for example, is rendered inane from the very first. His diary's first entry stands between two statements, one revealing the author as an eighth-grader, the other referring to a moistened forefinger. Reduced, he is also reductive, as Gilson turns menacingly upon the world around him: " 'If I could only discover the Real. A Real that I could know with my senses. A Real that would wait for me to inspect it as a dog inspects a dead rabbit' " (14). He prefers fixity and rigidity to the flux which apparently repudiates coherent interpretation. He does not, however, speak in fixed terms; metaphor comes alive in his description of his imagination as " 'a wild beast that cries always for freedom,' " (16) but not enough to vitalize Gilson himself. Before being convinced that we are watching genuine passion, we should remember that we are reading the journal of a youth who fancies himself Raskolnikov, while he derives existence solely through the dream life of Balso Snell; scantly delineated, he makes a faint physical appearance; vaporous, his voice alone comes to us, so that words referring to the beast of passion, although more animate than preceding images, are still discarnate. As is the case with most of West's characters, his is the huffing of a stick figure.[19]

The flesh begins to get its due as Raskolnikov describes the intended victim, but the victim's fat, fleshy pink is devitalized by " 'stale tobacco, dry perspiration, clothing mold, and oatmeal soap,'" his neck becomes "'covered all over with tiny blue veins like a piece of cheap marble,' " and the organic act of swallowing becomes " 'a sound like a miniature toilet being flushed' " (18). And through this fusion of skin and stone a " 'beast of laughter' " emerges, and is contagious enough to infect Raskolnikov, (18). Experience thus becomes insular and circular, so that " 'I knew that I must become interested in something outside of myself or go insane. I plotted the death of the idiot' " (19). Deliverance is sought out of a frustrated search for the Real, but the means

by which the search is to be realized are annihilative. The
seeker is generating the passion both underlying and undermining the quest, and baldly exposes himself in words that
may possibly stand as one key to West's art: " 'Because I
want you to believe me, I shall say that in order to remain
sane, I had to kill this man, just as I had to kill, when a child,
all the flies in my room before being able to fall asleep' "
(19-20).

The murder, of course, is degenerative, exposing the
youth who stands before us naked in a mock ritual of
renewal. His nakedness is far from carnal, as his genitals
become " 'tight and hard, like a dog's, or an archaic Greek
statue's—they were as though I had just come out of an
ice-cold bath' " (21). Cold, he is also afraid, his fear being
granted minimal vitality as it is likened to " 'a rapidly
growing child inside the belly of a mother' " (21). He is a
stone-cold progenitor: " 'I opened my mouth wide, but I was
unable to give birth to my fear' " (21). The openness of the
mouth manifests the enfuriating circularity of events, which
even violence has not made discontinuous. The youth thus
undergoes rebirth, changes his sex, generates brief heat, and
returns home " 'sick and cold' " (22).

The interlude between the Gilson episodes gives Balso a
chance not only to appear, but to appear with force, and as
the poet so "cast events" that the hold the repetitive has on
mortals may be broken. He speaks, but as the effusive poet:
" 'Ah youth!' he sighed elaborately. 'Ah Balso Snell!' " (23).
Then he speaks as the moralist: " 'What you ought to do,
child, is to run about more. Read less and play baseball' "
(23). The new is never voiced, so that Gilson is given a chance
to speak again, his second episode both revealing and
hastening the course of deanimation.

In this section, West follows Gilson's search for an
emotion, but in such a way that we must ask if the mission is
not to "search and destroy." What is burlesqued is the very
feeling which is at the bottom of the desire to live fruitfully.
Again we see the combat between the pseudopoetic, in
Saniette, and the depoetic, in Gilson. By her own name, with

its metallic and antiseptic ring, Saniette is diminished. In words that suggest the annihilative nature of West's art, the narrator admits that he always finds it " 'necessary to burlesque the mystery of feeling at its course; I must laugh at myself, and if the laugh is "bitter," I must laugh at the laugh. The ritual of feeling demands burlesque and, whether the burlesque is successful or not, a laugh. . .' " (27). West lets Gilson reduce Saniette, but at the same time is reducing Gilson. Trying to explain his irritation, Gilson says, " 'This evening I am very nervous. I have a sty on my eye, a cold sore on my lip, a pimple where the edge of my collar touches my neck, another pimple in the corner of my mouth, and a drop of salt snot on the end of my nose. Because I rub them continually my nostrils are inflamed, sore and angry' " (28). These images are earthy, yet scabrous images have been superimposed upon a character whose corporal existence is fading away. The sty, cold sore, pimple, and drop of salt snot are circular, the snot resting on the end of Gilson's nose, a circle within a circle. The cyclical thus is becoming synonymous with the discarnate, and the same reduction occurs in Gilson's words about the beast within him. " 'He sits within me like a man in an automobile. His heels are in my bowels, his knees on my heart, his face in my brain. His gloved hands hold me firmly by the tongue; his hands, covered with wool, refuse me speech for the emotions aroused by the face in my brain' " (29). The highly intensified material imagery should not lead us to think that a birth, or incarnation, is about to occur. The case is precisely the opposite, as the flesh within Gilson is going to be quashed by a creature whose own organic life has already become swallowed up in clothing. " 'Can you imagine how it feels to have this cloth-covered devil within one? While naked, were you ever embraced by a fully clothed man? Do you remember how his button-covered coat felt, how his heavy shoes felt against your skin? Imagine having this man inside of you, fumbling and fingering your heart and tongue with wool-covered hands, treading your tender organs with stumbling soiled feet' " (30). Where is man?

The episode closes with an excremental deluge, poured upon Gilson's audience. The deluge, however, is not confined to this audience. Insofar as he must burlesque the mystery of feeling, Gilson has already defecated upon his own art. And since he concludes with no more substantial existence than that of a voice within a dream, we must again raise questions concerning the intensity of West's annihilative feelings.

The course of repetition and deanimation continues in the concluding section of the book. Miss McGeeney and Janey Davenport engage in the pseudopoetic, and are foils for depoetics like Balso and Beagle Darwin. Miss McGeeney uses effusive speech to reanimate the world around her: " 'Charge, o poet, the red-veined flowers of suddenly remembered intimacies—the foliage of memory' " (31-32). Her bondage to the repetitive is revealed in a single line in which the vitality of redness is bracketed by spiritless imagery: " 'Like the gums of false teeth, red are the signs imploring you to enter the game paths lit by iron flowers' " (32). Balso reacts in anger to her and sticks his tongue in her mouth. "But when he closed his eyes to heighten the fun, he felt that he was embracing tweed. He opened them and saw that what he held in his arms was a middle aged woman dressed in a mannish suit and wearing hornrimmed glasses" (32). Miss McGeeney begins to stick in the mind as tweed and hornrimmed glasses, just as Samuel Perkins does as a nose. These two are linked together in the treadmill of scholarship: " 'It seems to me that someone must surely take the hint and write the life of Miss McGeeney, the woman who wrote the biography of the man who wrote the biography of the man who wrote the biography of the man who wrote the biography of Boswell' " (33). She tries to rise above her confinement by reaching the Infinite. Although Perkins himself called the senses a treadmill, she idealizes them, citing their circular movement, and begins her movement towards the Infinite: " 'The circumference of a circle infinite in size is a straight line. And a man like Perkins is able to make the circle of his sensory experience approach the infinite' " (36). Obviously, she says this without transcendence: her rhetoric is expansive, but her experience is fettered to the sense of smell; the soaring imagination is taking the creature no further than the tip of Smeller's nose. Balso stops her flight by striking her. Not having any way of liberating mortals from sameness, he rightly attacks those who would do this with false rhetoric, but the best he can do is either attack with fists or words. Where epiphany has ceased, the best this prophet can do is to silence or mock those still seeking.

Reacting to this story that goes nowhere, Balso counters with one of his own. His story is the dream within the dream, in which he courts Janey Davenport and receives the letter in which Beagle Darwin imagines her response to his rejection. Balso awakens to find McGeeney, whom he thought he had escaped. His dream is found to be no more than a figment of her imagination, just as her existence is derived from his dream world. The narrative is deliberately confusing, as it expresses the diminishing hold the cyclical has over mortals, and moves towards an appropriate fusion of events and voices.

As the dream begins, Balso meets many girl-cripples, and sees only their parts, "their disarranged hips, their short legs, their humps, their splay feet, their wall eyes" (37). If there is "the dearest freshness deep down things," it has a strange way of appearing, since Janey, pregnant by Beagle, bears the new in the hump on her back. Because of his desire for her body, Balso quickly switches roles and speaks in the voice of the flowery Jew, Maloney the Areopagite, Saniette, and Miss McGeeney: " 'O arabesque, I, Balso Snell, shall replace music in your affections! Your pleasures shall no longer be vicarious. No longer shall you mentally pollute yourself. For me, your sores are like flowers: the new, pink, budlike sores, the full rose-ripe sores, the sweet, seed-bearing sores' " (38). A seductive Balso then fades out, while Beagle comes in.

Beagle, like Balso and Gilson, is predatory and insubstantial. Having put the hump on Janey's back, the great lover is now amorphous and talks as from afar: " 'You once said to me that I talk like a man in a book. I not only talk, but think and feel like one. I have spent my life in books; literature has deeply dyed my brain its own color. This literary coloring is a protective one—like the brown of a rabbit or the checks of the quail—making it impossible for me to tell where literature ends and I begin' " (47). Beagle has identity insofar as he gets it from books, and he grants identity by the same pattern, chiding himself, " 'Why is it impossible for you to understand, except in terms of art, her action?' " (49). His narrative is a fade-out in which he loses himself in several poses.

Balso awakens and finds Miss McGeeney. He is back where he started before the dream, and when he sees in McGeeney none other than his childhood sweetheart, the cycle is complete: all has led back to tweed and hornrimmed glasses. Rather than seek some degree of transcendence over this fettered world, Balso repeats the routine of the Fall and seeks to immerse himself in the repetitive flow of things.[20] Seizing the day, he acts to seduce McGeeney and plays the part of an arty book-reviewer: " 'A stormy wind blows through your pages, sweeping the reader breathless . . . witchery and madness' " (56-57). He becomes pseudopoetic, but is cut down by West: " 'Oh!' His mouth formed an O with lips torn angry in laying duck's eggs from a chicken's rectum" (57). Here the anger conceived in relation to the repetitive is voiced directly by West, in an almost pointless intrusion, unless the aim is to disfigure and destroy. West needs no intrusion, however, since his art is so contrived that Balso will handle his own evaporation. Having a voice for all seasons, he becomes direct, like Gilson: " 'So come, Mary, let us have some fun' " (58); literary, like Beagle: " 'In a little while, love, you will be dead' " (59); and gushy, standing in a train of pseudo-poetics: " 'Ah, make the most of what we may yet spend before we too into the dust descend. Into the dust, Mary! Thy sweet plenty, in the dust. I tremble, I burn for thy sweet embrace. Be not miserly with thy white flesh' " (59-60). His love rhetoric is borrowed, abstract and codified, chilling the heart's lust. What else is next to be expected besides a wet dream, Balso's last act of abdicating in favor flux and repetition? Quite telling is the behavioristic and regimental imagery West chooses to describe Balso's orgasm: "An army moved in his body, an eager army of hurrying sensations. These sensations marched at first methodically and then hysterically, but always with precision. The army of his body commenced a long intricate drill, a long involved ceremony" (61-62). With everyone else, the poet relinquishes or is parted from his identity. The circular encloses and ingests the personal. In Balso's world there are "no feet."

After going through *Balso* in this manner, we should see the degree to which both the faith of Israel and the image of man are reduced. Not reduced beyond recognition, they are distorted or diminished enough to force us to strain to see them. If the life that is present in *Balso* could speak, these words of Simone Weil would be fitting: " 'Indeed, for other people, in a sense I do not exist. I am the color of dead leaves, like certain unnoticed insects."[21] West perhaps should not be questioned for failing to see any sign of the eternal in history, but why should he have gone to such great lengths in stripping both the divine and the human from his work? Furthermore, he may have chosen to show us how bad art can be, especially as it does little more than reflect or idealize the chaos around it. Bad art may well have forced the writing of *Balso* upon Nathanael West, but not its peculiarly pernicious form. There is a strong sense in which his art is "the mechanics of decay" (61). Of course, decay presupposes existence, and there is good reason to question the degree of existence found in *Balso Snell*. Like Balso, the occupants of the wooden horse are amorphous and vapid, possessing neither self-consciousness nor manifesting innner conflict. While West does subject them to his reductive style, he is only effacing creatures who have scarcely existed.

It is because of the minimal degree of their existence, coupled with the blatant hilarity of the novel, that we cannot grant *Balso Snell* any remarkable depths. It is true that we are forced to watch creatures fade and begin a lapse into nothingness, but we have not been allowed to see being, and its presence in a person; that is, we have no understanding of a condition from which West's characters begin to make their descent, and find them without beginning, readymade, or better, unmade. Neither do we perceive their end, since we are never allowed a look into the depths which receive them. If we listen long enough to these hollow voices, and let ourselves be caught in the rhythm of their coming and going, we may find arising in us an emotion akin to awe; we are having to watch people as we ordinarily sight flies: without origin, they appear, and within the span of days, are gone. Any semblance of this emotion, however, is soon quelled by the mocking tone of the novel. This, of course, is West's intention from the first, so if he is not trying to evoke awe out of us, he cannot be blamed for not doing so. As his readers, we must keep in mind that spokesman who is compelled to " 'burlesque the mystery of feeling at its source,' " and note how natural it would have been for West to dissipate the emotion of awe.

A final consideration has to do with the voice West uses in the novel. He seldom transcends the voices we hear, and does this by choice. Not as noticeable as his ability to mock the values, feelings, and words of others, but far more profound, is the utter willingness with which he lets his voice merge with and mock theirs. He is a natural at mocking, and with perhaps too much ease surrenders other forms of discourse. The tone he uses may be catching, so that when he chooses to do more than ridicule, as he will for example in *The Day of the Locust*, he may find resistance from both his nature and his practice. The prophets, on the other hand, were able to move from one form of speech to another, and were not above resorting to the mock-prophetic, a prime example of which is found in these verses from Jeremiah: "The word that came to Jeremiah from the Lord saying, Stand in the gate of the Lord's house, and proclaim there this word, and say, Hear the word of the Lord, all ye of Judah, that enter in at these gates to worship the Lord. Thus saith the Lord of hosts, the God of Israel, Amend your ways and your doings, and I will cause you to dwell in this place. Trust ye not in lying words, saying, The temple of the Lord, The temple of the Lord, The temple of the Lord, are these"

(Jeremiah 7:1-4). Jeremiah is as aware of false prophets as West is of false poets, and is as adept in speaking their language, which he indicates in his barbed refrain. But he is not confined to this form of address, as his initial words show. The mock-prophetic stands out in his address because it is but occasionally, and only partially, reductive. The mock-prophetic originates in the far more formative, "Hear the Word of the Lord." The mocking prophet both pronounces and denounces, and is far from being captivated by the habit of mockery. Whether this can happen in the case of Nathanael West is another matter, since in his art distorted personalities are seen, but seldom as a deviation from personality that is whole, and since the mock-poetic is seen, but seldom as a deviation from the poetry that can heal. He may have but one form of speech, and hence but one way of approaching and apprehending the world.

FOOTNOTES

1. *The Holy Bible Containing the Old and New Testaments In the Authorized (King James) Version, Philippians* 3:4-6. (Philadelphia, 1948). Subsequent references will be found in parentheses in the text.

2. Nathanael West, *The Dream Life of Balso Snell,* in *The Complete Works of Nathanael West* (New York, 1957), pp. 7-8. Future references will be made in parentheses in the text.

3. James F. Light, *Nathanael West: An Interpretative Study* (Evanston, 1961), p. 18. I am indebted to Light for his skillful correlation of West's life and work.

4. Victor Comerchero, *Nathanael West: The Ironic Prophet* (Seattle, 1964).

5. Randall Reid, *The Fiction of Nathanael West: No Redeemer, No Resting Place* (Chicago, 1967).

6. Daniel Aaron, "Waiting for the Apocalypse," *Hudson Review,* III (Winter, 1951).

7. Leslie A. Fiedler, *Love and Death in the American Novel* (New York, 1966), p. 487. Also see "The Breakthrough: The American

Jewish Novelist and the Fictional Image of the Jew," in *Recent American Fiction: Some Critical Views*, ed. Joseph J. Waldmeir (Boston, 1963), pp. 84-109.

8. Blaise Pascal, *Pensées and the Provincial Letters*, trans. W. F. Trotter (New York, 1941), p. 126.

9. *A Theological Wordbook of the Bible*, ed. Alan Richardson (New York, 1956), p. 283. Also see Isaiah 55:10, 11.

10. Georges Gusdorf, *Speaking*, trans. Paul T. Brockelman (Evanston, 1965), p. 13. Also see John 1:1-18.

11. *A Theological Wordbook of the Bible*, p. 157.

12. Harvey Cox, *The Secular City: Secularization and Urbanization in Theological Perspective* (New York, 1965), p. 74.

13. Martin Buber, *The Prophetic Faith*, trans. Carlyle Witton-Davies (New York, 1960), p. 64.

14. Abraham J. Heschel, *The Prophets* (New York, 1962), p. 7.

15. Others have made this point. See for example Thomas M. Lorch, "The Inverted Structure of *Balso Snell*," *Studies in Short Fiction*, IV, p. 35.

16. See A. M. Tibbetts, "Nathanael West's *The Dream Life of Balso Snell*," *Studies in Short Fiction*, II, 110. Tibbetts notes that each incident gives us a different view of the same type of person. Also see David D. Galloway, "A Picaresque Apprenticeship: Nathanael West's *The Dream Life of Balso Snell* and *A Cool Million*," *Wisconsin Studies in Contemporary Literature*, V, 117. Galloway notes that people within the horse are "moved without direction."

17. Norman Podhoretz, "A Particular Kind of Joking," *New Yorker*, XXXIII (May 18, 1957), 158. "This novel, then, is a battleground on which West the sentimentalist is pitted against West the cynic, each party asserting his claim to superior wisdom and refusing to concede any value to the other." Podhoretz suggests that writing *Balso* helped West gain control over his feelings. If what I am suggesting is right, West has control over his novel, but may not have control over himself.

18. West's use of an underworld journey, a guide, and numerous circles immediately suggests Dante, whose tour conducted by Virgil is successful, and eventuates in an escape out of hell through Satan's ass. "Now let all those whose dull minds are still vexed by failure to understand what point it was I had passed through, judge if I was perplexed." Dante Alighieri, *The Inferno*, trans. John Ciardi (New York, 1954), p. 286.

19. Robert J. Flavin, "Animal Imagery in the Works of Nathanael West," *Thoth*, VI, ii (1965), p. 30, suggests that West used animal imagery to present man as the beast he is, but overlooks the abstract quality West's figures possess through these novels.

20. Stanley Edgar Hyman, *Nathanael West* (Minneapolis, 1962), p. 12: ". . . Balso is dreaming the schoolboy's dream, and may have become the schoolboy."

21. Simone Weil, *Waiting for God*, trans. Emma Craufurd (New York, 1951), p. 101.

A CONFLUENCE OF VOICES:
MISS LONELYHEARTS

Madden: Miss Lonelyhearts appeared in 1933, the year *Anthony Adverse* was the top best-seller. Also on the list were two by Lloyd C. Douglas, *As the Earth Turns* by Gladys Hasty Carroll, a Galsworthy novel, along with *Little Man, What Now?* by Hans Fallada.

West: [Shrike] practiced a trick used much by motion-picture comedians—the dead pan.

Madden: Miss Lonelyhearts began as a 10 page short story written in the first person and was published in *Contact* in 1932. The story, called "Miss Lonelyhearts and the Dead Pan," comprises much of the first two chapters of the third person novel.

Marcus Smith: The great appeal of *Miss Lonelyhearts* is due . . . to the careful balance West establishes and maintains between ironic and sympathetic norms. The fact that Miss Lonelyhearts is *both saint and fool* has a great deal to do with his contemporary relevancy. In the best sense of the absurd term, he is "absurd" and few writers, in America or elsewhere, have succeeded as well as West in dramatizing the absurd.

West: Like Shrike, the man they imitated, they were machines for making jokes.

Fiedler: [Miss Lonelyhearts] is the final modern turn of the gothic screw: the realization that not the supernatural, the extraordinary, but the ordinary, the everyday are the terrors that constrict the heart.

West: And how dead the world is. . . . a world of doorknobs.

Gogol: [Chichikov] did not approach every landlord but selected those he judged suitable. Then he tried to become acquainted, to gain their friendship, and, whenever possible, to have them transfer dead serfs out of sheer friendship rather than as a commercial transaction.

Herman Melville: Bartleby had been a subordinate clerk in the Dead Letter office at Washington. . . . Dead letters! does it not sound like dead men? Conceive a man by nature and misfortune prone to a pallid hopelessness, can any business seem more fitted to heighten it than that of continually handling these dead letters, and assorting them for the flames? . . . pardon for those who died despairing; hope for those who died unhoping . . . . on errands of life, these letters speed to death. Ah, Bartleby! Ah, humanity!

Hemingway ("One Reader Writes"): Maybe he can tell me what's right to do. . . . In the picture in the paper he looks like he'd know. . . . Every day he tells somebody what to do.

West-Desperate: I was born without a nose.

Evelyn Waugh: The Guru Brahmin was two gloomy men and a bright young secretary. One gloomy man wrote the column, the other, a Mr. Slump, dealt with the letters which required private answers. . . . Mr. Slump, who was a survival from the days of Aunt Lydia and retained her style, usually had the smaller pile, for most of the Guru Brahman's correspondents liked to have their difficulties exposed to the public.

Fiedler: Daniel Fuch's protagonists remain to the end victims and anti-heroes, incapable of any catastrophe more tragic than the pratfall; but this is the traditional strategy of the comic writer. In a more complex way, Nathanael West and Henry Roth manage to achieve at once the anti-heroic and the almost-tragic. In West, the comic butt is raised to the level of Everybody's victim, the skeptical and unbelieved-in Christ of a faithless world. . . .

West: Crowds of people moved through the street with a dream-like violence.

Fiedler: West's novels are a deliberate assault on the common man's notion of reality; for violence is not only his subject matter, but also his technique.

West: In America, violence is idiomatic, in America violence is daily.

William James: Not the conception or intellectual perception of evil, but the grisly blood-freezing heart-palsying sensation of it close upon one, and no other conception or sensation able to live for a moment in its presence. . . . Here is the real core of the religious problem: Help! help! . . . . The lunatic's visions of horror are all drawn from the material of daily fact. Our civilization is founded on the shambles.

West-Shrike: Art is distilled from suffering.

James Hickey: Miss Lonelyhearts uses the human condition as a vehicle for his masochistic play, finds suffering to be a plaything—a drama of guilt and torture in which he can star.

West-Shrike: The Miss Lonelyhearts are the priests of twentieth-century America.

Robert Richardson: Miss Lonelyhearts has a brilliant description of entropy as it commonly appears. . . . Dadaism and films like "Un Chien Andalou" reflect a similar vision.

West: As he followed her up the stairs to his apartment, he watched the action of her massive hams; they were like two enormous grindstones.

Madden: Buñuel violently denounced avant-garde snobs who praised his and Dali's "Un Chien Andalou."

Buis Buñuel: . . . the pack of imbeciles . . . found beauty or poetry in what is, in essence, nothing less than a desperate, passionate appeal to murder.

West: [Miss Lonelyhearts'] tongue had become a fat thumb.

Salvador Dali: Our film ruined in a single evening ten years of pseudo-intellectual post-war advance-guardism. . . .

West: . . . / flowers that smelled of feet.

Paul West: [Miss Lonelyhearts is] an involuntary, jittery cartoon of a novel, sometimes meretriciously slick in style. . . . too jumpy and gaudy to hold one's interest sustainedly and formally.

Madden: Many critics see this cartoon quality as a positive value.

West: [Mary Shrike] always talked in headlines.

Lawrence DiStasi: While the guilty American is practically an archetype in our literature, West adds a dimension which makes Miss Lonelyhearts the prototypical guilty man of the twentieth century. That dimension is media. . . . West responded to media with greater insight than any of his contemporaries. For he saw that not only do media banalize dreams and emotions, causing them to lose their power; equally importantly, they force every man to become a priest tuned in to the suffering of the world, a situation which shears away cultural, social, and ideological resistances to empathy and responsibility.

Dostoyevski-Stavrogin: My . . . feelings consisted of the desire to put some powder under all four corners of the earth and blow everything up at once, if only it had been worth it—however, without any malice, but just because I was merely bored, and nothing else. ... I wanted everyone to stare at me.

West: Miss Lonelyhearts ... was smiling an innocent, amused smile, the smile of an anarchist sitting in the movies with a bomb in his pocket.

Fiedler: ... it is possible to see [West] as just another of our professional tough guys, one of the "boys in the back room" (the phrase is Edmund Wilson's).

Horace McCoy: Then the top of [Dolan's] head flew off, and he fell face downward across the garbage can, trying to get his fingers up to hold his nose.

Thomas Sturak: In 1962 a commentator on the literary scene of the thirties paired Horace McCoy and Nathanael West as novelists of that decade "whose work was important and is still read today," and has "had surprising influence on later writers."

Fiedler: Only the fantasies of post-World War I Germany have reflected (in films like *The Blue Angel*) comparable excesses of male masochism.

Carson McCullers: Mick Kelly and Jake Blount and Doctor Copeland would come and talk in the silent room—for they felt that the [deaf] mute would always understand whatever they wanted to say to him. And maybe even more than that. ... At first he had not understood the four people at all. ... And then after a while he knew what each one of them would say before he began, because the meaning was always the same.

McCullers-Mr. Singer [to Antonapoulos, his feeble-minded, deaf-mute friend]: They all came to my room at the same time today. They sat like they were from different cities. ... I do not understand, so I write to you because I think you will understand.

Truman Capote-Oreilly: I call him Master Misery. Only maybe you call him something else; anyway, he is the same fellow. . . . All mothers tell their kids about him: he lives in hollows of trees, he comes down chimneys late at night, he lurks in graveyards and you can hear his step in the attic. The sonofabitch, he is a thief and a threat: he will take everything you have and end by leaving you nothing, not even a dream. Boo!

James Purdy: That deadly monotony of the human continuity. . . .

Theodore Solotaroff: The first two thirds or so of *Cabot Wright Begins* is a cool, mordant, and deadly accurate satire on American values, as good as anything we have had since the work of Nathanael West.

William Burroughs: NAKED Lunch—a frozen moment when everyone sees what is on the end of every fork.

Flannery O'Connor: He stared out over the empty still pond to the dark wood that surrounded it. The boy would be moving off through it to meet his appalling destiny. [Rayber] knew with an instinct as sure as the dull mechanical beat of his heart that [the boy] had baptized the child even as he drowned him, that he was headed for everything the old man had prepared him for, that he moved off now through the black forest toward a violent encounter with his fate.

AGGRESSION IN *MISS LONELYHEARTS:*
NOWHERE TO THROW THE STONE
By Lawrence W. DiStasi

Nathanael West himself said that "In America violence is idiomatic"[1] and therefore needs little or no explanation. On the contrary, I should like to focus my discussion on West's use of violence in *Miss Lonelyhearts* in the attempt to show that it does in fact bespeak his insight into the fundamental nature of aggression in human intercourse, and his desperation that the dreams and rituals founded on containment of that aggression were dissipating, leaving only naked violence in their place. More than that, it seems to me that West's pessimism concerning the modern world parallels and to a degree objectifies in fiction the pessimism of Freud in *Civilization and Its Discontents.* What Freud was afraid of was that the burden of guilt on modern man, a guilt that he perceived to be intimately bound up with the progress of civilization, was becoming so great as to overwhelm the entire edifice of that civilization. This was due to the fact that the steadily increasing repressions, particularly of aggression, which complex civilization required, were reaching combustible levels. That is, as more aggressions are converted into guilt directed against the self, the self must either succumb or redirect them outward in violence, either individual or collective. West presents Miss Lonelyhearts as the guilty man who cannot avoid the quest for a way out of the Freudian maze. His quest is purposeful, logically consistent and profoundly pessimistic in its conclusion.

While the guilty American is practically an archetype in our literature, West adds a dimension which makes Miss Lonelyhearts the prototypical guilty man of the twentieth century. That dimension is media. Maturing in "that decade (which) saw the real emergence of the tabloids, of feature length films, of radio soap operas—of all those new media,"[2] West responded to those media with greater insight than any of his contemporaries. For he saw that not only do media banalize dreams and emotions, causing them to lose their power; equally importantly, they force every man to become a priest tuned in to the suffering of the world, a situation which shears away cultural, social, and ideological resistances to empathy and responsibility. For the truly sensitive they all but foreclose the possibility of projection of evil, a process which has evolved as an absolute necessity for group cohesion, i.e. civilization. In a world where one's enemies and scapegoats make claims on one's sympathies, there remain no targets for aggression: "If he could only throw the stone. He searched the sky for a target. But the gray sky looked as if it had been rubbed with a soiled eraser."[3] The novel is structured to present the above processes as central elements in Miss Lonelyhearts' quest and ironic integration. Initially, Miss Lonelyhearts perceives that the literary distance which has allowed him to regard the letters of suffering humanity as a joke is no longer operative because unlike the print in fiction, newsprint affords no gap between itself and reality; it is reality. Newsprint (here understood to represent all the media) then, constitutes, in a McLuhanesque sense, a literal extension of all psychic phenomena, particularly guilt, and produces abnormal stress on modern man. West concretizes this for us by dramatizing the interaction between Miss Lonelyhearts and his correspondents, specifically the Doyles. Here the normally tenuous and distilled contact one would expect, and which in fact Miss Lonelyhearts did expect, is breached and replaced by the total physical and spiritual involvement delineated in the novel. That this phenomenon of guilt extension through media exists in contemporary society can be attested to by the almost mythical quality

inhering in some of the place names signifying recent
atrocities: Dachau, Hiroshima, Birmingham, Song My. The
social concern of millions as expressed in civil rights
demonstrations and peace marches is also a function of guilt
through media extension; for clearly, sensitive people feel
guilty and activated by events over which they have little if
any control.

Under the combined pressure of guilt by extension, the
simple increase in abrasive contact in mass society, and the
absence of suitable targets to blame, then, Miss Lonelyhearts
activates two apparently contradictory impulses: a "Christ-
complex" and the protective deadening of his senses. These
processes are contradictory in the sense that the "Christ-
complex" leads to increased contact while the sensory
deadness would appear to lead in the opposite direction.
Both, however, serve the need to eradicate friction in social
relationships by denying the impulses to aggression; paradoxically, both also result in a common impetus toward violence
and aggression. This should not be surprising, however,
because if Freud was correct about the relationship of guilt
to aggression, then reactions which suppress aggression
should mask an aggressive component. In fact, both the
sensory deadness and the "Christ-complex" reveal violence at
their center for Miss Lonelyhearts.

Unable to ignore the suffering of his correspondents,
then, Miss Lonelyhearts turns to the Christ dream, a dream of
relatedness without violence. The problem, however, lies in
his tradition. For unlike the Dostoevskyan brand of Christian
love, Miss Lonelyhearts' Christianity is a peculiarly American
kind:

> His vocation was of a different sort. As a boy in his father's
> church, he had discovered that something stirred in him when
> he shouted the name of Christ, something secret and enor-
> mously powerful. He had played with this thing, but had never
> allowed it to come alive.
> He knew now what this thing was—hysteria, a snake whose
> scales are tiny mirrors in which the dead world takes on a
> semblance of life (75).

The specific American past here evoked is the Calvinist one

strongly oriented to guilt and power. More, the hysteria
which it harbors clearly promises violent outbursts of
repressed emotion (the Salem witch trials come to mind),
precisely the kind of reaction which Miss Lonelyhearts fears.
That this fear is justified is evidenced by some of the religious
rituals, themselves phylogenetic regressions, in which Miss
Lonelyhearts partakes. For they illustrate not only that
regeneration is indeed the psychology of the novel[4] but that
West understood exactly what regeneration involves: killing
and death as well as the rebirth usually emphasized. He
refused to gloss over the fact that active aggression is required
in order to re-enact the primal regenerative act of the race—
the killing of animal prey for food—the action that turned the
antidiluvian desert into a new garden of plenty. Regeneration
is then charged with that memory and Miss Lonelyhearts
knows and fears this condition, for he first tries to re-enact a
symbolic crucifixion in his room: "The walls were bare
except for an ivory Christ that hung opposite the foot of the
bed. He had removed the figure from the cross to which it
had been fastened and had nailed it to the wall with large
spikes" (75). This grotesque but rather literary attempt fails,
however, because he is working with a mere symbol which
has outgrown its significance: "Instead of writhing, the Christ
remained calmly decorative" (75). A real sacrifice involving
real life appears necessary to go beyond meaningless, decorative effects. Regressing still further, but only in the uncen-
sored confines of a dream, Miss Lonelyhearts tries the
sacrifice of the lamb. Again meaningless violence is exposed
beneath the surface of religious ritual. For having banalized
the sacrifice with humor by singing "an obscene version of
'Mary had a Little Lamb' " (77), they lose through dissipa-
tion the power necessary to enact the bloody sacrifice: "The
blow was inaccurate" (77). That is, even in his dreams, man
has lost the cleanliness and one-sidedness upon which pure
sacrifice depends and the ritual degenerates into messy,
sordid violence. It can then be completed only by the bluntly
indiscriminate blow of a stone. Miss Lonelyhearts cannot
perform the priestly function primarily because the pure and
outer-directed aggression required is no longer available to

him, having been repressed and redirected through centuries of culture.

In addition to Miss Lonelyhearts' religious defect there is the added difficulty that in the modern world, particularly America, there has been "an orgy of stone breaking" (100), that is, a leveling or dragging down of ritual and mystery to the level of cynicism and banality. This democratic process of de-mystification pervades Miss Lonelyhearts' world and throughout results in the exposure of violence beneath the emasculated forms. Shrike represents this tendency at its most extreme. In the episode with Miss Farkis, we see Shrike deflating Christian mysteries by associating them with the tawdry aspects of twentieth century reality: " 'I am a great saint, Shrike cried, I can walk on my own water. Haven't you ever heard of Shrike's Passion in the Luncheonette, or the Agony in the Soda Fountain?' " (74). He continues his assault by applying the deflated concept of Christianity to his own sexual needs (the seduction of Miss Farkis), a process which parodies the use of Christian constructs in the tradition of courtly love. Where the latter moved toward non-violence and gentilesse, however, this parody illustrates the counter movement in the modern world. This simultaneous de-mystification of religion and love results in the unbinding of the aggressive component in each of them, leaving only violence in their place: "His caresses kept pace with the sermon. When he had reached the end, he buried his triangular face like the blade of a hatchet in her neck" (74). The final image reverberates not only with the violence which has been exposed but also with traces of the old constructs left behind. Christianity, then, far from providing a relatedness without violence, appears to promise only increasing levels of violence for Miss Lonelyhearts.

Miss Lonelyhearts' sensory deadness proceeds from and results in many of the same conditions concurrently dictated by his "Christ-complex." That is, the increased contact of modern society and the increasing horrors revealed by modern media[5] necessitate a protective deadening of his senses designed to limit overloads of emotional involvement.

The irony, of course, lies in the fact that sense deadening is such a gross reaction that it is primarily in his sexual reactions that he is incapable of any spontaneous response. In his sexual relationships with Betty and Mary Shrike his movements are all automatic, devoid of feeling and character-ized by despair. Romantic situations leave him cold: "the romantic atmosphere only heightened his feeling of icy fatness" (93). That violence or fear of violence is closely related to this deadness is indicated by his brutal realization that "like a dead man, only friction could make him warm or violence make him mobile" (90). The reason for this close relationship of violence and sensual deadness is established in a childhood memory: "Miss Lonelyhearts felt as he had felt years before, when he had accidentally stepped on a small frog. Its spilled guts had filled him with pity, but when its suffering had become real to his senses, his pity had turned to rage and he had beaten it frantically until it was dead" (87). That is, unchecked sensual apprehension of suffering leads to unchecked violence, and it is this that Miss Lonelyhearts fears. Thus it is that his reaction to Betty's cringing is an aggressive one: "She was like a kitten whose soft helplessness makes one ache to hurt it" (81). Again, what West is exposing is the danger in the regression to sensual awakening, due to the fact that phylogenetically earlier reactions to suffering appear to lead to aggression rather than the civilized, Christian ideal of pity. Additionally, of course, it becomes clear that the deadness of his senses is also due to and associated with the prior expenditure of his emotions on literary constructs. Writers and the media have pre-program-med and over-exploited love and all other human emotions to such an extent that the emotional circuits of reflective men are cut off by the knowledge of stock responses. West puts it as follows: "Although dreams were once powerful, they have been made puerile by the movies, radio and newspapers. Among many betrayals, this one is the worst" (115). In the standard romantic scene with Betty, therefore, Miss Lonely-hearts is "Unable to think of anything else to do" (80) than what he has done before and caresses Betty's breast; but having deflated the romance and craving for a true emotion to make him come alive, he resorts to the violence of painfully twisting her nipple. Thus Miss Lonelyhearts finds himself in a circle of ascending violence: to avoid violent responses he becomes sensually dead; to reawaken he must resort to more violence.

Another aspect of this problem is that the sensory deadness is to be understood not only as a contemporary disease; in a larger sense it appears to be a symbol used by West to represent the loss which is sustained by the human organism in its repression-riddled drive toward order and civilization. For in a scene which prefigures much of the later action we see that Miss Lonelyhearts' "almost insane sensitiveness to order" (78), i.e. his need to control his environment, leads him to the related solutions of imposing order by violence and trying to shut out disorder: "If a bird flew across this arrangement, he closed his eyes angrily until it was gone" (78). That is, control of the chaotic life-force has been and can be achieved only through active aggression and the repression of the senses, a conclusion reached by Freud with respect to the repression of the senses of smell and touch.[6] The difficulty for Miss Lonelyhearts is not only that the chaotic elements are increasing as old structural certitudes are eroded, but also that his attempt to renounce violence by adopting the Christ dream forces him to resort to even more exagerrated cutting off of his senses than civilization has dictated.

The violence erupting around Miss Lonelyhearts is concretized in one other way that is related to the demystification of religion and the banalization of emotions already mentioned. In the episode with the "clean old man" we see the puncturing of elaborate manners and societal codes which parallels, in the exposure of violence beneath these rituals, the processes already enumerated. As in the scene with Miss Farkis, a code is parodied; this time manners are degraded to the mannerisms of a homosexual dandy. These vestiges of an outdated code of behavior are confronted and antithesized by the modern culture hero, the scientist: "Scientists have terribly bad manners' " (86). Gates and Miss Lonelyhearts, masquerading as scientists, deflate pretentious manners and the mediating role that they play in social intercourse; but in so doing they pave the way for the eruption of the violence lurking at the core of that intercourse: "When the old man still remained silent, he took his arm and twisted it. Gates tried to tear him away, but he refused to let go. He was twisting the arm of all the sick and miserable, broken and betrayed, inarticulate and impotent. He was twisting the arm of Desperate, Broken-hearted, Sick-of-it-all, Disillusioned-with-tubercular-husband" (88). In addition to exposing the violence beneath social conventions, this episode lends further credence to the theory that it is guilt which impels Miss Lonelyhearts towards his Messiah role. For it is clear here that the under side of his feelings toward his correspondents, all those who demand his pity for their suffering, is hatred and aggression. Social restraints or codes are external manifestations of repression; when they are removed or weakened, guilt often turns outward to become aggression. Guilt still dominates Miss Lonelyhearts' aggression, however, for it is released not with heroic, arm-swinging, therapeutic abandon but with grudging, "twisting" motor movements; and it is directed at the helpless—women and aging homosexuals.

In the face of this mass ungluing of violence Miss Lonelyhearts searches in panic for a way to counteract it. He attempts to re-bind the aggressive component with the force of Eros, the Freudian symbol for the unifying, life-fostering tendency. This is, in effect, an attempt to control outer-directed energies in order to create some kind of objective reality with which to order existence, and is one of the two basic movements in the novel. This attempt is central to the structure of the novel which is, in brief, the alternation of episodic violence with attempts to use love to bind the violence. It has already been suggested that all of the outer-directedness in the novel—projection of evil, sensory awakening, religious awakening—has foundered on the sea of violence. To this list of failures must be added the force of love itself, for it has become dehumanized, mechanized and de-mythicized to such an extent that the aggressive component in it, too, has become unbound. Love itself becomes violence-dominated and unsatisfactory for its broad cultural purpose. Miss Lonelyhearts' search then, becomes a quest for a new erotic or binding force which will be able to bind his steadily increasing encounters with and need for violence and aggression.

The early chapters of the novel illustrate the poles of the conflict outlined above. In the second chapter the Waste Land motif evokes a land of death with no discernible targets for aggression. The erotic pole which should normally counteract this infertility is mentioned only as literary posturing by Shrike (" 'To the renaissance! To the brown Greek manuscripts and mistresses with the great smooth marbly limbs' " [72]) but is realized as the mannish Miss Farkis with results we have already seen. This form of Eros, filled with violence and emptied of significance by its literary quality, must fail to heal the land. The next chapter ends with the violence of the crushed head of the lamb and leads to Miss Lonelyhearts' attempt to bind the violence with Betty's sexuality. This in turn erupts in the violence of the pulled breast, violence toward even those who are loved and helpless. Following this failure is an attempt to evoke a kind of male camaraderie, a platonic love in the bar. Predictably, this too leads to violence, the punch in the mouth which Miss Lonelyhearts receives and the sadistic arm-twisting of the "clean old man" earlier discussed. The next attempt to bind violence is preceded by an image which symbolizes much of what has been said, the image of the stone war monument: "It seemed red and swollen in the dying sun, as though it were about to spout a load of granite seed" (89). Here Eros is devoid of any life-giving quality and has become a monument to war. Even the life-giving seed is rigidified into bullets or instruments of death. The remainder of this chapter is given to the love scene with Mary Shrike, a scene which ends in another kind of violence and despair.

The apotheosis of this sequence is the tryst with Fay

Doyle. She is a central figure in the quest for Eros and in the novel as a whole: she is "a gigantic, living Miss Lonelyhearts letter" (102). She is imaged as the archetypal female: "Her call for him to hurry was a sea moan, and when he lay beside her, she heaved, tidal, moon-driven" (101). She is to be the erotic force to revitalize him: "He thought of Mrs. Doyle as a tent, hair covered and veined, and of himself as the skeleton in a water closet, the skull and cross-bones on a scholar's bookplate. When he made the skeleton enter the flesh tent, it flowered at every joint" (99). But rather than a revitalizing force, she is a voracious vacuum which drains Miss Lonelyhearts and sends him to sick bed. She is the embodiment of de-feminized and de-romanticized sexuality, the opposite of Betty and Mary Shrike. The image which most clearly describes the rigidity and violence implicit in her sexuality pictures her with "massive hams . . . like two enormous grindstones" (101). What she represents as compassion to her crippled husband is degrading and leads inevitably to violence: " 'I wouldn't let no man get away with that so I socked back and he swung at me with his stick but missed and fell on the floor and started to cry' " (103). Her aggression is far less repressed than that of the males in the novel. For as a result of the "stone-breaking" mentioned earlier, the barriers to female independence and aggression are worn away while male aggression is further circumscribed. This results in the imbalance of the male view seen in *Miss Lonelyhearts,* a perception of the female who has reverted to the sexual power of an earth mother confronted by the male whose greatest powers are directed against himself. In order for genital sex to be restorative and energizing, there must be male aggression complemented by female receptivity. The Eros of the female provides the model for binding and enveloping the destructiveness of male aggression and, in the most primitive biological sense, giving it a life-promoting function. On the contrary, Fay Doyle's emasculation of her husband, an impotent cripple, forces him finally to murder in the attempt to re-affirm his degraded masculinity.

Miss Lonelyhearts' tryst in the country with Betty comes

closer to the ideal outlined above. The problem with this, however, is that it is so transparently a throwback to a simpler time of pastoral bliss that it lacks currency in the jaded world of which Miss Lonelyhearts is a part and in which he must function. This withdrawal is akin to sensory deadness in that it is an attempt to select the sensory input supposed to reawaken the primitive awareness of animal being, and it works to the degree that it is a pleasant diversion. But its failure is signified by the patently literary quality of the scene, which, once perceived, exposes the violent prejudice of the proprietor against "yids" and the violence in the natural landscape. And undermining the viability of the erotic binding is the relegation of Betty's sexuality to the "childishly sexual" gesture with which she finally gives herself to Miss Lonelyhearts. This childish innocence is of a piece with manners, traditions and religious mysteries: all have lost their power and currency through degradation and cannot contain the forces now unleashed. More than that, this childish role is insufficient to contain and adequately defuse male aggression, because the role is the female attempt to inhibit that aggression. It is only the adult female receptivity of a maturely sexual Betty that would be adequate to bind the male aggression of Miss Lonelyhearts. The episode then becomes not an idyllic moment[7] in the novel but rather another instance of the failure of Eros in the modern world.

Miss Lonelyhearts' search now turns toward Christianity again in the attempt to perceive the component in himself which has been lacking in his attempt to make the Christian approach viable. He discovers that his failure is caused by "lack of humility" (115). In positive terms this means that his aggressive, self-assertive ego is blocking the way to true Christianity and spiritual re-birth. He tries therefore to reverse himself, to stop trying to impose his order on objective reality, but rather to redirect energies inward again. Humility is, in effect, the degrading of ego and on the same plane as the turning in of violence and aggression. To become humble one must suspend resistance to pain, to in fact invite suffering: "He read it (the letter) for the same reason that an animal tears at a wounded foot: to hurt the pain" (116). In another sense this movement is a suspension of resistance to death forces as Freud saw them,[8] a relaxation which moves in the direction of repressions. It is in the sense that Miss Lonelyhearts' chronologically earlier psychological state (i.e. his early guilt and sensory deadness) is inner-directed also that this later inner movement is seen as a "relaxation." Nor is it to suggest that it is "easy" in the sense that relaxation is normally associated with ease—witness the force necessary to overcome cultural resistances in his encounter with Peter Doyle. This meeting with Doyle is the first step in the final movement of the novel and is followed by sensory deprivation, mystical experience, and death. For it can be seen that sensory deprivation too evolves naturally from the same tendency as humility; cutting off sensory input is a physical manifestation of the turning in of aggression.

In the cyclical movement outlined previously Miss Lonelyhearts tries to make external contact after violence or depression, and it is in relation to that continuum that he meets Peter Doyle. In that roughly repetitive cycle this is the second attempt at male contact, but the differences between the first encounter and this one are significant. For while both are contacts with homosexual bases,[9] the first degenerates immediately into violence while this one evolves toward a more ethereal plane. The dynamics of this encounter are complex, bifurcating into at least two well defined levels. The first is in line with the humility he is cultivating and moves in the direction of self-abnegation through suffering. The extent of this self-abnegation is indicated by the force needed to overcome the resistance to homosexual contact: "He jerked away, but then drove his hand back and forced it to clasp the cripple's" (126). But the suffering is positive, too, in that it is an existence-validating phenomenon.[10] The other level upon which this encounter must be understood is that of liberation from the repressive aspect of genital heterosexual love and toward a platonic union of souls which Christianity professes as its highest goal. The repressive nature of conventional

genital love is exemplefied by the alternative offered by
Betty. For Miss Lonelyhearts to succumb to her suffocating
brand of love with all it implies—the job in advertising and
the house in Connecticut insulated from the suffering
world—would be equivalent to psychic and spiritual death.
On the contrary, the liberation attested to in this encounter
is indicated by the fact that the feeling which it evokes is one
of the few true ones for Miss Lonelyhearts in the novel: "he
was trying desperately to feel again what he had felt while
holding hands with the cripple in the speakeasy" (126). That
is, Miss Lonelyhearts feels the exhilaration of a friendship
above grasping ego or sex; and this feeling indicates to him
and the reader that it is in the desired direction, i.e. toward
liberation and away from the tyranny of the aggressive ego.

But perhaps the more significant aspect of the total
episode is that Miss Lonelyhearts realizes forcefully that this
solution, this method of love with humility, is not workable
either. For the relationships are already sexually loaded and
the implicit sexuality forces them down to the egoic,
sexual-possessive level. That is, as soon as Fay Doyle is
introduced, the encounter becomes a possessive game which
her husband is too weak to resist. She represents a kind of
sexual necessity[11] intruding into the homosexual/utopian
world of Miss Lonelyhearts and Doyle: "What a sweet pair of
fairies you two are" (129). She is implacable in her insistence
that sexless, ego-less friendship cannot remain unchallenged
in the real world. Her insistence is, of course, violent,[12] and it
is against this force that Miss Lonelyhearts once again lashes
out with violence of his own. In the face of this violence
which seems, in spite of everything that he does, to be
growing, he retreats from this necessity and moves to a
withdrawal from the world into his bed.

The final movement of the novel begins with Miss
Lonelyhearts taking to his bed for three days, refusing all
contact with friends, and limiting his sensual intake to the
sparse effects in his room and "eating crackers, drinking
water and smoking cigarettes" (131). This clearly is an
attempt at a kind of sensory deprivation through withdrawal,

and differs from his withdrawal to the country in that here there is no attempt to substitute an earlier and simpler type of sensory awareness for the abrasive modern kind. Here the attempt is aimed at autistic self-arousal or hallucination, an effect which does in fact result from scientifically controlled sense-deprivation experiments. That the hallucinatory state is self-induced and controlled is evidenced by Miss Lonely-hearts' awareness that he has found a magic carpet: "He had only to climb aboard the bed again." This autonomy is indeed the solution that Miss Lonelyhearts has been looking for from the moment that he began his move toward humility, a move that I have characterized as a turning in of all energies toward the self. It results in the solidification of higher psychic processes symbolized by the "rock" image; and the regression of the ego to an earlier state where the bounds between self and other are blurred or indistinguish-able.

The regression of the ego calls to mind the narcissistic stage of development which Freud posited as the origin of the "oceanic feeling." Since this is the prototype for the religious feeling later sought by adults, a regression of this type makes eminent sense for Miss Lonelyhearts in his search for religious reality. The mystical experience which he undergoes is precisely this reversion to an earlier state, an acceptance of oneness with God: "He was conscious of two rhythms that were slowly becoming one. When they became one, his identification with God was complete" (139). What must not be overlooked is that this mystical experience is an inextricable part of the hallucinatory experiences preceding it; the visions and distortions of objects in his room follow upon his sensory deprivation period. That is, the sensory awakening which he experiences is an hallucinatory one which is characterized by the same "process of seeking order where there is no order and attempting to incorporate nonorder into previously existing schemata"[13] as is noted in sense-deprivation experiments. What this means is that while it is true that the regression does activate for him an apparently authentic religious experience, it also suspends his faculties of ego-separateness and self-consciousness, with the result that he is unable to determine the seriousness of the lies that he tells to Betty or the possibility of the threat embodied by Doyle. Clearly this suspension of aggressive resistances between self and other is what Miss Lonelyhearts has been searching for, but the results are disastrous. This "reculer pour mieux sauter" does in fact carry the organism back to an earlier state where the potentialities for dealing with the problem are expanded; but in so doing it suspends the discriminatory feedback from the senses without which the organism cannot survive untended. West's denouement indicates that this particular regression is not viable and can lead only to death.

The solidification of Miss Lonelyhearts' feelings into the rock relates to the concept of sensory deadness discussed earlier, as here too, the process results in a deadening of feeling: "He did not feel guilty. He did not feel. The rock was a solidification of his feeling, his conscience, his sense of reality, his self-knowledge" (138). Paradoxically, having now abandoned the attempt to awaken his senses, they do awaken in hallucination: "He thought of this black world of things as a fish. And he was right, for it suddenly rose to the bright bait on the wall. It rose with a splash of music and he saw its shining silver belly" (139). This accords with the movement inward of the latter part of the novel, for hallucination is the substitution of inner for outer reality. The final concept of Miss Lonelyhearts as a rock beautifully sums up the thematic and structural unity revealed by tracing the rock imagery in the novel. The cluster of values which reverberate around this image are negative ones, invariably implying violence and rigidity. The first mention of the stone image states the problem of loss of targets for aggression and leads inexorably to the final solution of turning the aggression inward to the self, the self as the rock. In between are a series of processes expressed through rock imagery which outline variations and attempts at solutions to this problem. The religious values which are evoked through stones tend to imply rigidity moving toward death as opposed to flexibility and life. The

stone with which Miss Lonelyhearts crushes the lamb's head
in botched sacrifice is a good example of the violence and
rigidity which religious ritual has become for the modern
priest-Lonelyhearts.

The opposite pole to this rigidity of tradition and ritual is
the American "orgy of stone-breaking," which corresponds
to the exposure of violence through banalization pointed out
earlier. The final implication of this "stone-breaking" leads to
the sexual manifestations of the image. For the conclusion of
the stone-breaking sequence is ". . . they knew the stones
would some day break them" (100). If, as I have suggested
above, one aspect of stone-breaking is the release of women
from traditional restrictions, then the stones do indeed break
modern man as imaged in the "grindstone hams" of Fay
Doyle. The stone phallus "about to spout a load of granite
seed" clearly sustains and concretizes the theme of a violent
sexuality about to destroy the world. Certainly it is with this
image of destructive aggression in mind that we are made
graphically aware of the suicidal consequences of Miss
Lonelyhearts' final condition. For the stone with no targets,
the deadly aspects of aggression threatening to explode or
grind everyone into impotent boredom, are all finally
accepted and enveloped by Miss Lonelyhearts. Since the
normal process of objectifying internal strife through projection (the process of creating dualisms such as angels and
devils is an example of this apparently universal need) is
precluded because of his guilt, so is the control which this
objectification fosters. Miss Lonelyhearts is then forced to
internalize and envelop the already objectified symbols of
aggression, i.e. he incorporates the rock in himself. This once
again accords with the overall pattern in the novel of turning
external aggression inward toward the self.

To sum up the final movement, Miss Lonelyhearts has
succeeded in achieving the relatedness and calm he has been
searching for. The price has been a kind of lobotomy of
certain higher processes, a lobotomy performed by turning
the aggressive, outer-directed ego-forces inward to the point
where they are used to freeze the responses which have been

unbearable. In the final scenes he is untroubled by Shrike's drunken heresies, unmoved by Mary Shrike's attempts to rouse him sexually, and unmoved by the pathos of Betty's situation as the expectant mother of his child. Throughout the novel Miss Lonelyhearts has concluded that the resistances or defenses which these situations normally arouse lead to violence in one way or another. His solution is to suspend them. The faculty which mediates for him at the end is pure mind, an entity which appears to be akin to the egoless state described by mystics: "his mind was free and clear. The things that muddied it had precipitated out into the rock" (136). However, without "feeling, conscience, sense of reality, and self-knowledge," Miss Lonelyhearts becomes placidly convinced of the unreality and ultimate oneness of things, and is therefore able to deceive with impunity and unable to distinguish love from danger. Of course, it can be seen that this is only an exaggerated form of the normal state of affairs where this deception and myopia are sanctified by common consent and prevalent myth. Miss Lonelyhearts can thus be ". . . just what the party dress wanted him to be: simple and sweet, whimsical and poetic, a trifle collegiate yet very masculine" (137). Like Dimmesdale in *The Scarlet Letter* he can perceive a neutral or negative event as a positive sign designed solely for his benefit: "God had sent him (Doyle) so that Miss Lonelyhearts could perform a miracle and be certain of his conversion" (139). Here indeed is literary atavism: like his Puritan ancestor, Miss Lonelyhearts has rediscovered the Calvinist God, dispensing signs to his elect. The ironic emphasis is clear: Miss Lonelyhearts' ego is so enormous because untempered by reality that he excludes from his perceptions any signs which do not contribute to his dream. The importance of perceiving those signs is obvious.

FOOTNOTES

1. Nathanael West, "Some Notes on Violence," *Contact* (October, 1932), p. 132.

2. Randall Reid, *The Fiction of Nathanael West* (Chicago, 1967), p. 100.

3. Nathanael West, *Miss Lonelyhearts* in *The Complete Works of Nathanael West* (New York, 1957), p. 71. Subsequent references are to the same edition and are identified by page number in the text.

4. Reid, p. 82.

5. That this process is directly relevant to guilt extension through media is attested to by a recent study by Dr. Edward Opton of the Wright Institute, Berkeley, concerning average reactions to the media-dispensed news of the Song My massacre in Vietnam. It was found that similar to the situation in Germany after World War II, Americans set up screens against intimate involvement or responsibility by employing cognitive structures to distance and defuse emotional content: "When we asked people how they *felt,* they usually told us what they *thought.*" Such responses as "War is hell; things like this happen all the time;" or "It doesn't affect me; after all, you have atrocities in every war" are examples of cognitive responses functioning in the service of emotional disengagement. Though these intellectual constructs are less severe mechanisms of defense than Miss Lonelyhearts' sensory deadness, they are analogous to the constructs discussed below. Because these constructs or stock responses have been so over-programmed and over-exploited, they no longer function for Miss Lonelyhearts as defenses. In addition, the subjects, unlike Miss Lonelyhearts, seemed unaware of their loss in sensitivity, though one informant, a stewardess, was visibly shaken by pictures of the massacre while simultaneously denying her emotional reaction with intellectual justifications: ". . . it just seems to be one of the outcomes of war . . ." (All quotes courtesy of Edward Opton et. al., *Preliminary Report of the Alleged Massacre at Song My: A Study of American Public Opinion and Emotion* (Berkeley, 1970).

6. Freud, pp. 46f and 52ff. Here in two footnotes Freud discusses his theory that "organic repression" appeared to be the forerunner of all the repressions later demanded by civilization. The replacement of smell by sight as the dominant sense is seen to be due to the adoption of the upright stance.

7. Hyman's reading in S. E. Hyman, *Nathanael West* (Minneapolis, 1962) which characterizes this episode as idyllic and Betty as an "Edenic" innocent is, it seems to me, correctly refuted by Reid, pp. 77-78.

8. Sigmund Freud, *Beyond the Pleasure Principle* (New York, 1959), p. 71.

9. Reid is again correct in denying the claims of Hyman and Comerchero that homosexuality is Miss Lonelyhearts' chief problem. But his assertion that homosexuality is "quite irrelevant to the novel's issues" (77) is overstated. It is relevant in the sense that Marcuse (*Eros and Civilization* (New York, 1955), pp. 144-56) uses homosexuality to characterize the demand for liberation from repression symbolized by both Orpheus and Narcissus.

10. Suffering here is not unlike the violence of the street gangs studied by M. Yablonsky, of which he stated: "In instances of extreme alienation, which places the individual on some kind of social continuum where he is almost emotionally dead and totally disaffiliated, he uses violence to validate his existence." Quoted from *Aggression and Defense: Brain Function*, V (Berkeley, 1967), 25.

11. Reid, p. 43, calls her the "personification of the life force."

12. Orpheus, too, incurs the wrath of repulsed women and "was torn to pieces by the crazed Thracian women" (Marcuse, p. 155). Miss Lonelyhearts is, in effect, murdered by the wrath of Fay Doyle.

13. John F. Corse, *The Experimental Psychology of Sensual Behavior* (New York, 1967), p. 578.

THE CRUCIAL DEPARTURE:
IRONY AND POINT-OF-VIEW
IN *MISS LONELYHEARTS*
By Marcus Smith

Criticism of Nathanael West's *Miss Lonelyhearts* seems stymied by the question of whether his protagonist, Miss Lonelyhearts, is sympathetically presented as a viable modern priest or saint, or whether he is merely a demented fool and meant to be regarded ironically.[1] This dilemma seems irreconcilable by appeal to external criteria, such as sources, literary precedents, or moral and philosophic standards of any sort. Indeed, my present view is that the ambiguous effect of *Miss Lonelyhearts* is intentional and I think I can point to the precise technical features in the novel which produce it and the subsequent critical debate.

Miss Lonelyhearts is established as the "center of consciousness" in the novel's opening sentence: "The Miss Lonelyhearts of The New York *Post-Dispatch* . . . sat at his desk and stared at a piece of white cardboard" (65).[2] Thus we are immediately "locked into" Miss Lonelyhearts' "consciousness," and with very few (but crucial) exceptions our vision and experience in the novel are coincident with his. It is through his eyes that we read the grotesque, agonized letters and see a sky that "looked as if it had been rubbed with a soiled eraser" (71). Indeed, the sky *is* soiled because we see it through Miss Lonelyhearts' anhedonic eyes.

Only once does West himself "enter" the novel to comment directly—in the opening chapter when he describes

Miss Lonelyhearts' appearance: "Although his cheap clothes had too much style, he still looked like the son of a Baptist minister. A beard would become him, would accent his Old-Testament look. But even without a beard no one could fail to recognize the New England puritan. His forehead was high and narrow. His nose was long and fleshless. His bony chin was shaped and cleft like a hoof" (69). West's stance here is authoritative and his description establishes the basic flesh-spirit conflict in Miss Lonelyhearts' character. But this solitary passage does little to shape our attitude towards Miss Lonelyhearts, which is determined subsequently by the novel's pattern of events.

At times Miss Lonelyhearts evokes our sympathy and compassion. His response to the letter-writers is humane and moving. Whenever he is with Shrike, for example, he emerges in a much more favorable moral position: Shrike's glib cynicism is a completely irresponsible alternate to the problem of evil in the world established by the letters. Moreover, Miss Lonelyhearts strikes us as a "larger" person than Betty whose "sureness was based on the power to limit experience arbitrarily" (79). We cannot agree with Betty when she suggests that Miss Lonelyhearts settle for a job in an advertising agency; we sympathize instead with his defense:

> A man is hired to give advice to the readers of a newspaper. The job is a circulation stunt and the whole staff considers it a joke. ... He too considers the job a joke, but after several months at it, the joke begins to escape him. He sees that the majority of the letters are profoundly humble pleas for moral and spiritual advice, that they are inarticulate expressions of genuine suffering. He also discovers that his correspondents take him seriously. For the first time in his life, he is forced to examine the values by which he lives (106).[3]

Miss Lonelyhearts, however, is not always so favorably presented. At times West cruelly undercuts him and shows him to be ridiculous and hypocritical. When he visits Betty he abuses her physically and emotionally, just as later he torments the "clean old man" in the speakeasy: "He was twisting the arm of all the sick and miserable, broken and betrayed, inarticulate and impotent" (88). With both Betty and the old man, Miss Lonelyhearts reacts to the evil in the world by sadistically contributing to it. Likewise, Miss Lonelyhearts' sexual adventures with Shrike's wife, Mary, and with Mrs. Doyle, are selfish and bizarre and they are presented to us as such. His handling of Mrs. Doyle's letter is a clear example. The letter is filled with suggestiveness which he instantly picks up: *"I need some good advice bad but cant state my case in a letter as I am not good at letters and it would take an expert to state my case. I know your a man and am glad as I dont trust women"* (97). Miss Lonelyhearts tries to disarm the leering Goldsmith by dropping the letter in the wastepaper basket. As soon as Goldsmith leaves, however, he retrieves it and betrays the thinness of his morality by thinking that "If he could only believe in Christ, then adultery would be a sin, then everything would be simple and the letters extremely easy to answer" (99). But he cannot find any reason for avoiding adultery and so arranges a rendezvous, which leaves him "physically sick" (104).

The question is raised, therefore, very early in the book: just where is the reader supposed to stand in relation to Miss Lonelyhearts? Is the reader supposed to be with him or against him? Is Miss Lonelyhearts meant to be seen as seriously coming to terms with "the values by which he lives" or as a pretentious and deluded fool? To use Wayne Booth's terms it is a question of ironic versus sympathetic "norms."[4]

The dilemma becomes more obvious (and even more irreconcilable) later in the novel when Miss Lonelyhearts decides in favor of the "Christ dream." This occurs when he returns from the trip to Connecticut with Betty. He discovers that he has not been cured of his *angst* and that after all he is capable of "dreaming the Christ dream," which he has failed at previously, "not so much because of Shrike's jokes or his own self-doubt, but because of his lack of humility" (115).

Miss Lonelyhearts, therefore, sets out to become a humble man. But humility is an extremely paradoxical virtue in that it must be achieved without calculation. Thus, a character consciously trying to achieve humility is ripe for the irony caused by "grotesque disparity between word and word or word and deed" (Booth, p. 316). This is Miss Lonelyhearts' situation: he "dodged Betty because she made him feel ridiculous. He was still trying to cling to his humility, and the farther he got below self-laughter, the easier it was for him to practice it" (121). "Humility" for Miss Lonelyhearts means withdrawal into the self, into a state of ultra-self-consciousness. The next time it is mentioned, when he and Doyle are leaving the speakeasy, Miss Lonelyhearts is completely preoccupied with "the triumphant thing his humility had become" (126).

In short, Miss Lonelyhearts' "humility" is false humility —and West seems to intend it to be seen this way, for when Miss Lonelyhearts goes to the Doyles' apartment he launches into a plea to Mrs. Doyle to love her crippled husband. Miss Lonelyhearts' style is bizarre and messianically hysterical: " 'You can take the chill out of his bones. He drags his days out in areaways and cellars, carrying a heavy load of weariness and pain. You can substitute a dream of yourself for this load. A bouyant dream that will be like a dynamo in him. You can do this by letting him conquer you in your bed. He will repay you by flowering and becoming ardent over you. . . .' " (129). Despite the genuine appeal in this exhortation (again a tension between sympathy and irony), the chapter ends in violence. Miss Lonelyhearts rejects Mrs. Doyle's sexual advances and, in frustration, beats her and flees back to his bed.

Miss Lonelyhearts then withdraws even further into himself and becomes an impersonal "rock" in the sea of humanity. When Shrike appears, he is merely a "clumsy" gull "trying to lay an egg in the smooth flank" of the rock. And Betty is merely a "little wave" splashing at his feet (132-133). Shrike drags Miss Lonelyhearts to his apartment to play a game: "Everyman his own Miss Lonelyhearts." Shrike has taken a batch of letters from the files and distributes them to the assembled drunks. Miss Lonelyhearts, the rock, is unmoved by all this: when Shrike hands him a letter he drops it to the floor without reading it and when

Betty leaves he goes after her. West, however, maintains the party scene. This is the only instance in the novel when Miss Lonelyhearts is not dramatically present, not the "center of consciousness."

There is an important reason for Miss Lonelyhearts' departure at this point, for the letter which Shrike handed him is from Peter Doyle. Shrike picks it up from the floor:

> He took the letter out of its envelope, as though he had not read it previously, and began: " 'What kind of a dirty skunk are you? When I got home with the gin, I found my wife crying on the floor and the house full of neighbors. She said that you tried to rape her you dirty skunk and they wanted to get the police but I said that I'd do the job myself you. . . . So that's what all your fine speeches come to, you bastard, you ought to have your brains blown out' " (135).

Shrike continues his drunken ramble for another two paragraphs, but West has already clearly set up the dramatic irony of the novel's ending by having Shrike read Doyle's threat. The reader knows what Miss Lonelyhearts does not know, that Peter Doyle is out to kill him. Two chapters later when Miss Lonelyhearts gets out of bed and sees Doyle climbing the stairs he thinks he will perform a miracle: "He would embrace the cripple and the cripple would be made whole again. . . ." (139-140). The reader, however, knows that Miss Lonelyhearts will get his "brains blown out."

If West had maintained the ironic distance established by Doyle's letter, then despite his previous engagement of our sympathies the novel would have ended on a bitter but clearly ironic note. West, though, draws us closely into Miss Lonelyhearts' "religious experience" just before he is shot. It is difficult to focus ironically on the description of Miss Lonelyhearts' conversion:

> "Christ! Christ!" This shout echoed through the innermost cells of his body.
>
> He moved his head to a cooler spot on the pillow and the vein in his forehead became less swollen. He felt clean and fresh. His heart was a rose and in his skull another rose bloomed.
>
> The room was full of grace. A sweet, clean grace, not

washed clean, but clean as the inner sides of the inner petals of
a newly forced rosebud.

Delight was also in the room. It was like a gentle wind, and
his nerves rippled under it like small blue flowers in a pasture.

He was conscious of two rhythms that were slowly
becoming one. When they became one, his identification with
God was complete. His heart was the one heart, the heart of
God. And his brain was likewise God's (139).

This passage (only a page before Miss Lonelyhearts'
death) can be read ironically, as the hysterical ravings of a
megalomaniac. But its lyricism does not compel our ironic
response. Instead, it erases the ironic distance established by
Doyle's letter in the previous chapter. Thus the reader's final
emotion is extremely complicated. His sympathy for Miss
Lonelyhearts wars with the irony of Miss Lonelyhearts'
death, his compassion is mingled with his awareness of Miss
Lonelyhearts' folly.

While the discussion above has described the reason for
the ambiguous effect of *Miss Lonelyhearts,* we must ask
whether such an effect is warranted. A neo-Aristotelian such
as Wayne Booth would perhaps conclude that *Miss Lonelyhearts* is a flawed work because it does not control its irony
and establish clear and consistent (or at least ultimate) norms
for the reader's response.

In *The Rhetoric of Fiction,* Booth argues that the
modern novel's tendency towards "objectivity" through
"impersonal narration" (especially the third person "center
of consciousness" method which West employs in *Miss
Lonelyhearts*) leads frequently to confusion of effect and
unintentional ambiguity. The "deep inside view of the center
of consciousness" method tends, because of the very closeness of the "center" to the reader, to make the intelligent
character appealing: as Booth says, "inside views can build
sympathy even for the most vicious character" (377-379). At
the same time, the modern writer's penchant for irony (and
the modern reader's responsiveness to it) creates difficulties,
for when an author selects an impersonal narrative method
and does not directly establish ironic norms for the reader,
then the author must resort to "grotesque disparity between

word and word or word and deed" to warn his reader that irony is intended (Booth, 316-317). A problem arises, however, when we follow Booth into the arena of judgment. "In most works of any significance," argues Booth, "we are made to admire or detest, to love or hate, simply to approve or disapprove of at least one central character, and our interest in reading from page to page, like our judgment upon the book after reconsideration, is inseparable from this emotional involvement" (129-130).

Booth's argument would seem to apply to *Miss Lonelyhearts,* and from a purely descriptive standpoint his insights are extremely useful. Yet I am unable to agree with the implied censure which would seem to follow when dealing with West's novel. In the first place, after careful reconsideration, I find that the great appeal of *Miss Lonelyhearts* is due precisely to the careful balance West establishes and maintains between ironic and sympathetic norms. The fact that Miss Lonelyhearts is *both saint and fool* has a great deal to do with his contemporary relevancy. In the best sense of the absurd term, he is "absurd" and few writers, in America or elsewhere, have succeeded as well as West in dramatizing the absurd. Another objection to Booth's demand for an ultimate "norm" in fiction is that, while this sounds like a good thing, to take this seriously would result in remaindering many of the best works of modern fiction. What is the ultimate norm in, say, *Lord Jim, Portrait of the Artist as a Young Man, Lord of the Flies* or *The Magus*? Do the protagonists of these works emerge as ultimately sympathetic or ironic? I would argue neither side, but would propose that our proper response is an unresolved tension between the two emotions. The reason for this (I cannot justify it aesthetically) lies in the modern reader himself and in the dilemmas of his time.

FOOTNOTES

1. West himself merely described Miss Lonelyhearts noncommitally as "A priest of our time who has a religious experience." "Some Notes

on Miss Lonelyhearts," *Contempo*, III, no. 9 (15 May, 1933), p. 1. Arthur Cohen (*Commonweal*, 15 June 1956, p. 277) says that Miss Lonelyhearts' "Christ complex is precisely a complex, not a belief in specific documents of faith, not faith in any order of sacrament or scheme of salvation. It is a complex, a fixation of the mind." James Light in *Nathanael West: An Interpretative Study* (Evanston, 1961) argues that Miss Lonelyhearts is a "Christlike man who preceives that love and faith are the only answers in a universe he cannot understand" (86-87). W. H. Auden in "Interlude: West's Disease," *The Dyer's Hand* (New York, 1962), implies that Miss Lonelyhearts is sick, "absolutely self-centered. A selfish man ... who satisfies his desires at other people's expense" (238-245). Stanley Edgar Hyman in *Nathanael West* (Minneapolis, 1962) argues that Miss Lonelyhearts has "a true religious vocation or calling, but no institutional church to embody it" (16). Victor Comerchero, *Nathanael West: The Ironic Prophet* (Syracuse, 1964), is, as his title suggests, an irony-hunter. Of Miss Lonelyhearts' concern for the letter writers, Comerchero says "The ironic depth of this joke is fearful, for Miss Lonelyhearts is not a godless man seeking faith: that search is altogether too trivial and trite. He is a fallen man who would seek a reassuring word from God" (78).

2. References to *Miss Lonelyhearts* are given parenthetically and are keyed to *The Complete Works of Nathanael West* (New York, 1957).

3. Both Shrike and Betty establish "norms" for which their apparent "flatness" of caricature is an advantage. Shrike withdraws from the world's evil into cynical mockery and there is no suggestion that he can ever emerge as a humane person. Betty is uncomplicated and untroubled by evil; she is derived from William James' "Simple" or "Once Born Soul" (see my paper, "Religious Experience in *Miss Lonelyhearts*," *Contemporary Literature*, IX [1968], 172-188). But West does attempt some "rounding" of both Shrike and Betty. Shrike, underneath his cynical, sadistic exterior, is tormented by sexual impotency. And Betty's benign, circumscribed reality is blasted by the novel's ending, which has her witness the murder of Miss Lonelyhearts, the father of her unborn child. None of this, however, affects their normative function *vis-à-vis* Miss Lonelyhearts.

4. *The Rhetoric of Fiction* (Chicago, 1961), 187-189, *et passim.*

FREUDIAN CRITICISM
AND
MISS LONELYHEARTS
By James W. Hickey

If there is a reluctance to accept psychoanalytic theory as a tool to interpret literature, it is not so much the fault of Freud as it is of the would-be critical analyst whose slip-shod approach insults both the science and the piece of art in question. Too often, Freud's theories have been diluted and/or manipulated to advance a thesis which, while possibly being a brilliant application of psychology, does little to increase our appreciation of the studied work. Thus, most Freudian criticism has been labeled extraneous conjecture, to be replaced by strictly contextual analysis of appropriate—which is to imply, literary—considerations.

A contextual analysis is possible, however, with the aid of Freudian theory if such theory seems to comprise a significant position in the studied work itself. A case in point is Nathanael West's concentrated novel *Miss Lonelyhearts*[1] which explores the moral and mental disintegration of a male lovelorn-columnist during the Depression.

The best known such study is that of Stanley Edgar Hyman, who uses Freudian theory to substantiate the idea that the central character is a latent homosexual. He most directly makes clear his interpretation of Miss Lonelyhearts in his study of the character's relationship with the frigid wife of his editor, Willy Shrike.

Terrified of his stern religious father, identifying with his
soft loving mother, the boy renounces his phallicism out of
castration anxiety—a classic Oedipus complex. In these terms
the Shrikes are Miss Lonelyhearts' Oedipal parents, abstracted
as the father's loud voice and the mother's tantalizing breast.
The scene at the end of Miss Lonelyhearts' date with Mary
Shrike is horrifying and superb. Standing outside her apartment door, suddenly overcome with passion, he strips her
naked under her fur coat while she keeps talking mindlessly of
her mother's death, mumbling and repeating herself, so that
Shrike will not hear their sudden silence and come out. Finally
Mary agrees to let Miss Lonelyhearts in if Shrike is not home,
goes inside, and soon Shrike peers out the door, wearing only
the top of his pajamas. It is the child's Oedipal vision perfectly
dramatized: he can clutch at his mother's body but loses her
each time to his more potent rival.[2]

Hyman's observations are fine so long as he confines himself
to that specific incident and does not attempt to apply the
premise to the rest of the novel. Even so, he must stretch his
literary "symptoms" to make his case hold.

Randall Reid's thorough study rejects Hyman's exploitation of Freudian analysis on a number of valid grounds. Reid
cites Hyman's paragraph in its entirety, then observes:

This sounds plausible enough, but it contains a disconcerting
number of inventions, misstatements, and omissions. From the
novel, we know only that Miss Lonelyhearts' father was a
minister, not that he was stern or loud-voiced or that Miss
Lonelyhearts was terrified of him. The only evidence that Miss
Lonelyhearts even had a mother—hard or soft, loving or
cruel—is the fact of his own existence. Further, Miss Lonelyhearts is not "suddenly overcome with passion." Instead, he is
trying "to work this spark [of desire] into a flame," (p. 91)
trying "desperately to keep the spark alive" (p. 92). Mary is so
far from being the object—maternal or otherwise—of his desire
that his sexual response is an effort of the will, not a
passionate act . . . And if we want to identify homosexuals, I
suggest that Shrike is a far more obvious suspect than Miss
Lonelyhearts.[3]

While Reid correctly dismisses Hyman's shallow attempt to
force *Miss Lonelyhearts* into a common Freudian mold, he
should not dismiss so flippantly the issues which Hyman's
theory has raised. He has rightly observed that ML is trying

to fan a spark of passion into desire, but, in his rejection of
Hyman, Reid has made no attempt to explain ML's motivation—psychological or otherwise—for the spark. If Shrike
plays perverse games with his wife—"Do you know why he
lets me go out with other men? To save money. He knows
that I let them neck me and when I get home all hot and
bothered, why he climbs into my bed and begs for it" (93);
"If he doesn't hear us talk, he'll know you're kissing me and
open the door. It's an old trick of his" (95)—he probably
does so because of her frigidity. In any case, we and ML hear
only her side of the situation. What is important is that their
relationship is barbed with frustration and perversion; if such
conduct does not necessarily brand Shrike as a latent
homosexual neither does it make him the potent rival which
Hyman would have us accept. What's more, it seems a pity
that Hyman should maintain that Shrike's harping attacks
against ML are little more than an abstracted loud voice.

   Although Hyman does raise the issue of ML's sexual
abnormality, his Oedipal theory does not work. It seems
especially contrived when we consider that in a subsequent
chapter ML voluntarily makes love to his girl friend Betty in
the country (114). This would seem to cancel out Hyman's
notion that ML is a latent homosexual, despite the contextual evidence to the contrary. In any event, if Freudian
analysis is a feasible approach to *Miss Lonelyhearts,* it
certainly has not been tested very successfully by the
overzealous Mr. Hyman or the skeptical Mr. Reid.

   In the essay "Some Notes on Miss Lonelyhearts," West
himself adds to the confusion: "Psychology has nothing to
do with reality nor should it be used as motivation. The
novelist is no longer a psychologist. Psychology can become
something much more important. The great body of case
histories can be used in the way the ancient writers used their
myths. Freud is your Bullfinch; you cannot learn from him."[4]
Victor Comerchero, one of Hyman's more irresponsible
defenders, tries to justify the role of psychology as a mode of
criticism by interpreting West's words to mean that *Miss
Lonelyhearts* is no less than an artsy embellishment of

Oedipus' case history.[5] Of course, it is just such a reading
which West is trying to avert by his assertion that, Hyman's
thesis to the contrary, the function of the novel is not merely
to illustrate Freudian theory. As such, West reveals that he
did not write *Miss Lonelyhearts* as a fictional case history of
objectified behavior patterns; it is, rather, a subjective
chronicle of ML's conscious and semi-conscious thoughts. All
too aware of the pitfalls of Freudian faddists, West wishes to
protect his novel from shallow exploitation by those literary
critics who—like many psychoanalysts, for that matter—
interpret subjective material as impersonal data and formu-
late absolutes under the guise of objectivity. The novelist,
says West, is not a clinical secretary, but he may use the
lessons of psychology so long as they are a *means* of
expression rather than the motivating principle of the work.
We are not intended to "learn" about psychology from the
novelist, but we may find mythic patterns through this
science that may enhance our literary experience.

Reid interprets West's statement as an undeniable repudiation of "psychology—any psychology—as a system of
revealed truth" and goes on to contend that West's stand
("Psychology has nothing to do with reality") negates any
attempt of the Freudian critic to make any "real" contribu-
tions to literary interpretation (Reid, p. 73). Granted, the
Hyman-Comerchero analysis falls ridiculously short of its
mark. However, in his eagerness to besmirch Freudian
criticism, Reid himself fails to grasp what West is actually
saying. West's passage is clearly and solely concerned with the
relationship between psychology and the novelist. Neither
analysis nor writing is truly concerned with reality *per se.*
The sociologist, the economist, the phenomenologist and the
chemist may be said to study reality; the psychologist studies
man's subjective interpretation of his own reality. Thus it
follows that West, as psychological novelist, does not—should
not—attempt to pass off his characters' perceptions as
necessarily objectified expressions of their experiences. It is
rather the business of the writer—at least in *Miss Lonelyhearts*—to capture the imagined reality of ML's fantasy. West

is not ML's analyst; the novel is not a case history but an intensely compelling projection of a disintegrating mind.

As an extension of ML's consciousness, *Miss Lonelyhearts* records ML's exaggerated and often perverse perception of reality. The Shrike we see through ML's eyes is not the "real" Shrike of some objective "real" world; he is an extension of the relentless, merciless Shrike of ML's psychotic imagination. What is revealed to us is not so much intensified by Shrike's actual personality but by those aspects of Shrike which most affect ML. Such a technique permits West to exaggerate the personalities of ML's adversaries without letting them become the two-dimensional caricatures of his first and third novels, *Dream Life of Balso Snell* and *A Cool Million.* In this way, *Miss Lonelyhearts* has nothing to do with the alleged reality of, say, Howells or even Joyce.

At no point does West confirm Reid's dismissal of psychology as an approach to his novel. Indeed, his remarks indicate that such an approach has been anticipated, albeit with an uneasy awareness that such a tool might be abused. It should be noted that West directs his remarks to the role of the novelist—not the critic: accepting the writer's relationship to Freud the myth-master, the critic is presumably free to turn to Freud so long as he does so with candor and a carefully literary perspective. If the novel is in fact approached as a record of ML's thoughts, Freudian criticism seems not only desirable but mandatory to decipher the problems which have been raised by Hyman's thesis. With Freud as our Bullfinch—not as our Trilling—we should be equipped to understand more fully that misery which ML can only uncomprehendingly relate.

In this essay I will defend, through example, the legitimate place of Freudian theory as a tool of literary criticism and establish, through application of that theory, some new, constructive insights about the main character and central issues of Nathanael West's *Miss Lonelyhearts.*

It is hoped that the findings suggested by our Freudian approach to the novel will dispel Hyman's less disciplined use of Freudian theory and, less directly, show how Light's theory of genuine religious rebirth must be either re-evaluated or totally rejected. Finally, the bulk of this essay is a response to the attacks of Randall Reid, with the intention of settling those issues which have been raised by the three major West critics (Hyman, Light and Reid himself) that defy solution without some acknowledgement of Freud's relevance.

Frederick J. Hoffman defines the correct application of Freudian criticism in Appendix I to his book *Freudianism and the Literary Mind:*

> However inadequate this may be as a sketch of Freud's superbly exact descriptions, I introduce it here as a preliminary to examining its usefulness as a perspective upon literature. The two have in common what we may call a necessary language—language as the instrument of description becomes in the course of my discussion language as a system of strategies. Language is necessary at first to label and define; next, to put phenomena in order; then to characterize the nature of incentives for labelling and ordering; finally, in the most remarkable of its ranges of use, to effect changes in meaning, to represent situations as more complex than they might be or are or ought to be. In the mind of a person endowed with every resource of language, the phenomena of psychic tension, conflict, drive, repression, are articulated and represented in a discourse at once psychologically just and remarkably subtle. I should like to suggest, therefore, that literature may be viewed and analyzed in terms of the verbal and metaphorical equivalents of the psyche and its behavior. Literature possesses a greater metaphoric freedom than psychology, or perhaps it has the license of its own audacity. But it is actively engaged in providing verbal and metaphorical equivalents of and elaborations upon the simply described behavior of the id, ego, and superego in their dynamic relationships. I can scarcely go on from here, to insist upon exact equivalents; it is perhaps as unwise to find iddities and egocentricities in literature as it is to accept literally biographical peculiarities as definitive explanations of achieved works of art. To locate an author's id, ego, superego, etc., in either characters or lines is to violate the subtlety of their necessary arrangements. My purpose is, instead, to explain the complexities of literary work as the results of symbolic actions which report and reflect on a high level of linguistic articulateness and subtlety the basic tensions, balances, imbalances, repressions, and compensations of psychic energies within a system such as Freud has described.[6]

As a guideline for the productive application of Freudian criticism, the statement closely parallels my interpretation of West's own observations on the proper (and improper) uses of Freudian theory. It is generally within these limits that this study of *Miss Lonelyhearts* will be carried out.

If we are to maintain the position that the text of *Miss Lonelyhearts* be treated as a written record of ML's consciousness, it follows easily and of necessity that we regard the themes of the book with more than mere literary appreciation, as symptoms of ML's disturbance. As such, they stress those objects and opinions with which ML is psychically involved—just as these motivations, abstracted as themes, define the issues of the novel. For our purposes, this approach does not demand that we exclude non-psychological interpretation on a more obviously literary level; rather, it is merely a means of more easily revealing the contextual relevance of Freudian theory.

Since we have already raised the question of ML's subjective interpretation of reality, the natural starting place for our study is a definition of his reality. Contextually, West reveals this in the first chapter as ML reads the letters from his lovelorn "congregation." The reality with which ML's ego must deal is filled with chaotic disorder and suffering. Like ML, we are shocked and distressed by the inarticulate pleas of Sick-of-it-all, Desperate, and Harold S. But, in our first reading of the novel, we fail to understand the function of these letters for ML. Surely ML has received letters from girls with pimples or dating problems. Yet he prefers to dwell on the letters from a girl with no nose and a boy whose idiot sister has been raped. There is obviously something about the hopelessness of these situations which ML finds attractive, no matter how much he may deny it consciously. West resolves this incongruity for us immediately: "He stopped reading. Christ was the answer, but, if he did not want to get sick, he had to stay away from the Christ business. Besides, Christ was Shrike's particular joke" (68). With concentrated precision, West thus introduces ML's pathological relationship to "the Christ business." ML has selected these letters because they permit him to indulge in his Christ fantasies. They are prayers for salvation which have been sent to him, the tabloid priest, but which he uses only to confirm his own inability to achieve the Christ identity of his dreams. Past attempts to achieve such a self-image have evidently resulted in emotional and physical illness which ML cannot ignore but refuses to recognize as pathological. It is this tension between ML's craving for the Christ identity and his psychological rejection of it which is at the core of the book's action. The "resolution" of this dilemma in the last chapters finds ML terrifyingly achieving his fantasy.

The above quotation further establishes Shrike's attitude as a sort of alter ego to ML. The novel has already opened with Shrike's shocking parody of the *Anima Christi,* but, more subtly, the parody makes us aware of the role which ML has assumed. Not only does it substantiate ML's perverse relationship to Christ, but it reveals that others are aware of his mania as well. Through his constant jibes, Shrike will not permit ML to escape into the fantasy worlds of art, nature, hedonism or suicide. Although he is treated unsympathetically, Shrike's unrelenting vision of reality is certainly less fanciful than ML's. Shrike, too, is confronted with the misery of humanity, but it is an easy misconception to assume that Shrike's surface callousness negates his despair. Indeed, it confirms Shrike's self-tortured involvement as, like the wounded animal of a later chapter, he tears at the wound to hurt the pain. In this respect, Shrike is interpreted in ML's consciousness as a coalition of ML's alter ego, that which reminds ML that he has not and will not realize his Christ dream. If Shrike is depicted as a jeering, sniveling sadist, it is because that is the way in which ML's demented consciousness perceives him.

The ultimate pathos and, perhaps, nobility of Shrike lies in his own awareness that he too lacks any vision of salvation. He is only too aware of his own futility. When conversing with Goldsmith, a lesser mirror of himself, Shrike observes: " 'Goldsmith, you are a nasty product of this unbelieving age. You cannot believe, you can only laugh. You take everything

with a bag of salt and forget that salt is the enemy of fire as
well as of ice. Be warned, the salt you use is not Attic salt, it
is coarse butcher's salt. It doesn't preserve; it kills' " (122).
Shrike is a man condemned to having few or no illusions
about himself and the world around him; ML is condemned
to having his vision obscured by just such illusions. Podhoretz
suggests that "West regards Shrike's cynicism as a stunted
form of wisdom."[7] In many respects, Shrike thus assumes
the additional role of chorus. Shrike and the newspapermen
at Delehanty's speakeasy, for all their obscene cynicism, are
truly reporters of the "real" reality which ML cannot face,
and we should pay attention to them, even if ML will not. It
is a sordid reality which is as much defined by ML's distorted
fantasies as it is by Shrike's outrageous perspective. West
underscores this disquieting reality by thematically insisting
that we recognize the degree to which fantasy—as corrupting
as it is necessary for survival—constitutes our own vision of
reality.

ML has tried to distract himself from this terrifying vision
by constructing two sub-realities: the Christ business and order.

The brief chapter "Miss Lonelyhearts and the Lamb"
illustrates most completely the extent of his Christ fixation
by describing ML's room and permitting the main character
to lapse into a hysterical dream which recalls a college
experience. The chapter seems to have been written specifically for the Freudian critic.

Within the barren confines of his dark, womb-like room,
ML has spiked an ivory Christ to the wall to make its
suffering more "real," but the desired effect has failed
because he has not nailed Christ (nor himself) to the
wall—merely a hard, unfeeling piece of ivory. The obvious
conclusions to be made here concern not only ML's desire
constantly to fuse his own suffering with the divine passion
of Christ. The ultimate failure of the gesture to achieve
the desired sensational projection confirms his own failure to
experience this fantasy, much less the actual suffering of his
readers. ML will finally accomplish his identification with
Christ once he accepts the self-image of the imperturbable

rock, which is as incapable of suffering and emotion as the ivory statue.

As the chapter continues, we discover that ML blames Shrike for his inability to achieve the Christ dream, thus substantiating the subjective vision of the narrative.

> He realized, even if Shrike had not made a sane view of this Christ business impossible, there would be little use in his fooling himself. His vocation was of a different sort. As a boy in his father's church, he had discovered that something stirred in him when he shouted the name of Christ, something secret and enormously powerful. He had played with this thing, but had never allowed it to come alive.
>
> He knew now what this thing was—hysteria, a snake whose scales are tiny mirrors in which the dead world takes on a semblance of life. And how dead the world is . . . a world of doorknobs. He wondered if hysteria were really too steep a price to pay for bringing it to life (75).

If nothing else, the passage reveals that ML is not entirely unaware of his mental condition. Passing the blame to Shrike, he can admit that his relationship to the Christ business is not "sane." He further reveals that he has been suffering from attacks of hysteria since childhood, but he only feebly rationalizes the condition as something which sets his vocation apart. His hysteria takes the shape of a phallus whose mirror-like scales reflect the dead world which ML apparently perceives. The movement of the phallus-snake permits the world to take on the "semblance of life" while the phallus itself is obscured by the reflection of doorknobs. The doorknobs, which in a subsequent fit he will bring to life as a magician leading prayers, tie in directly with the breast fixation which he and (his interpretation of) the other characters share. The memory, with all its Freudian finery, combines the hysterical vision of the young ML with his father's church. As the child rants Christ's name deliriously, he is establishing for the Freudian reader his view of his relationship with his father.

Tragically, ML has experienced this hysteria so often that he has helplessly made the fit a ritual in itself, telling himself that he is governing it ("He had played with this thing, but he had never allowed it to come alive") whereas in truth it has all but sapped his sanity. ML performs the rite by staring at the obscene crucifix and chanting Christ's name until he is unconscious. West's third-person observation, "For him, Christ was the most natural of excitements," is certainly not a cruel Shrikean joke. It is ML's own rationalization of the act over which he has no control. More importantly, it is the key to ML's impotent relationships with Betty and Mary Shrike. Sex with them and the gross Fay Doyle is unnatural, theatrical to him. His most complete passion is that of and with Christ, an act of narcissistic homosexuality. But even in this fit, he cannot find fruition of his fantasy, for his "performance" of a prayer as a magician recalls Shrike's *Anima Christi*. Again, while ML would blame Shrike for this disruption of ML's dream, it is more clearly ML's own egotism which acknowledges the prayer as being directed to its proper god. Once more, Shrike's apparent irreverence turns out to be a revealed truth. Similarly, in this second prayer, Christ's blood is not transsubstantiated from wine but from boric acid. Such is the destructive essence of ML's Christ.

West uses this prayer and an earlier reference to *The Brothers Karamazov* to establish the religious concept of Christ as the lamb of God. He then shifts the dream to a Freudian nightmare of castration anxiety and self-destruction. The failure to complete the decapitation (castration) of the sacrificial lamb (ML/Christ), the broken sword, the hysterical fleeing, the final crushing of the head with the stone, the swarming flies and altar of flowers—all may be interpreted as both religious and Freudian symbols. A momentary glance at Jung's concept of the rebirth archetype reveals yet another means of fusing the spiritual with the psychological. West manipulates the fantasy like a giant pun as Jud(as) Hume purchases the lamb that is to be slaughtered, as they chant obscene verses of "Mary Had a Little Lamb," as the violent (frenzied) sacrifice takes place on a hill, as the remains of the lamb become Lord of the flies (Beelzebub), and so on. Here, and at the close of the novel, the Jungian rebirth ritual is frustrated in that there is only destruction of a feeble divinity in an atmosphere of omnipresent sterility.

ML's obsession with order is explored in the following chapter. The opening paragraphs of this section offer a different, but equally frightening, form of ML's mental imbalance.

> Miss Lonelyhearts found himself developing an almost insane sensitiveness to order. Everything had to form a pattern: the shoes under the bed, the ties in the holder, the pencils on the table. When he looked out of a window, he composed the skyline by balancing one building against another. If a bird flew across this arrangement, he closed his eyes angrily until it was gone.
>
> For a little while, he seemed to hold his own but one day he found himself with his back to the wall. On that day all the inanimate things over which he had tried to gain control took the field against him. When he touched something, it spilled or rolled to the floor. The collar buttons disappeared under the bed, the point of the pencil broke, the handle of the razor fell off, the window shade refused to stay down. He fought back, but with too much violence, and was decisively defeated by the spring of the alarm clock.
>
> He fled to the street, but there chaos was multiple. Broken groups of people hurried past, forming neither stars nor squares. The lamp-posts were badly spaced and the flagging was of different sizes. Nor could he do anything with the harsh clanging sound of street cars and the raw shouts of hucksters. No repeated group of words would fit their rhythm and no scale could give them meaning.
>
> He stood quietly against a wall, trying not to see or hear. Then he remembered Betty. She had often made him feel that when she straightened his tie, she straightened much more. And he had once thought that if the world were larger, were *the* world, she might order it as finally as the objects on her dressing table (78-9).

Once again, West's understatement in the first sentence of the chapter reflects not so much a lack of awareness on the author's behalf as it does ML's attempt to rationalize his irrational behavior.

One of the reasons that this mania for order is so perplexing rises from the fact that it is not so easy to discover its cause. Whereas the Christ complex is apparently a manifestation of ML's phrenetically ambiguous relationship to his father, there seems to be no set Freudian formula to explain away this second symptom. Rather than reveal its motivation here, it may be more important to concentrate on its significance at this stage of the novel.

The first point to emphasize concerns ML's reaction to his own irrational behavior. This behavior pattern unobtrusively becomes a theme of the novel itself, despite ML's projection of it as the fault of others. Even when ML is reading the pathetic letters in the first chapter—at which time we share his alleged horror and are most willing to identify with him as protagonist—the action of the sequence is held together by ML's inability to enjoy a cigarette. "The cigarette was imperfect and refused to draw. Miss Lonelyhearts took it out of his mouth and stared at it furiously. He fought himself quiet, then lit another one" (68). The incident passes, presumably induced by ML's distress over the letters. However, in light of the passage on the pages quoted above, ML's furious reaction indicates his total loss of self-control. His irrationality complements perfectly the faulty cigarette which obviously connotes impotence. Similarly, ML maintains that he wishes to be free from the sordid confessions of the masses; yet, when the clean old man refuses to bare his soul, ML attacks him viciously and violently until hit with a chair from behind. This same behavior pattern is evident, to greater or lesser extents, in his recollections of the lamb sacrifice and his fondling of Betty's breasts. If nothing else, it is a physical extension of ML's aberration.

The other important point to be learned from the lengthy description of ML's mania for order concerns his second response. He turns to Betty, his fiancée, whom he regards as the personification, the very embodiment of order. Considering ML's complex sexual attitude, it is important to be fully aware of Betty's role as love-object through ML's compulsion for order.

The chapter continues to reveal that Betty offers little more for ML as a love-object than an outlet for his violent frustration. Looking to her for an escape from his own irrationality, his guilt, frustration and anxiety prevent him from expressing any true emotions to her. Though he and the reader do not at this point of the novel know why,

ML can only relate to Betty with theatricality and sadism. It is only in a more sordid setting that ML liminally indicates the subtle relationship between Betty and ML's mania for order. Rather than discuss Betty's intricate role in ML's demented perception, however, we would do well to probe more deeply into ML's other hysterical confrontations with, literally, mental disorder.

The chapter "Miss Lonelyhearts in the Dismal Swamp" is ambiguous in structure. It begins by stating that, immediately following his seduction of Fay Doyle, ML falls victim to a two-day-long session of vomiting and coma, culminating in an elaborate fantasy. ML imagines himself in front of a pawnshop window and begins mentally to order the second-hand items he sees there into geometric shapes, beginning with a phallus and culminating with a cross. The pawnshop articles, like his letters, fascinate him because they are "the paraphenalia of suffering" so vital to his psychotic vision. As with the Christ dream, his struggle with order seems a hopeless expression of his own impotent futility. Man's tropism for order is directly opposed in ML's mind to Nature's "tropism for disorder, entropy" (104). "Every order has within it the germ of destruction," ML muses. "All order is doomed, yet the battle is worth while" (104). Again, as with the Christ delusion, there is the association of the symptom's expression with destruction.

ML's fantasies dissolve into a revolting hallucination of a polluted ocean. The image, which Freudians would interpret as a feminine symbol, offers the perfect cue for Betty's timid return to the action of the novel. With chicken soup in hand, his girlfriend offers advice to him, a lovelorn-columnist, and tries to soothe him with stories of her idyllic childhood. With a flash, Shrike suddenly replaces her in a dream ["Betty left without saying good-by" (106)]. Shrike taunts ML with the various forms of futile escapism open to him and predictably concludes with the Christ dream. The whole chapter assumes a sense of non-reality as the images of Betty and Shrike interchange and they recite their philosophies to the hysterical ML. Indeed, it is entirely possible that the chapter is itself complete fantasy, as the reality of ML's delusions take an increasing hold on ML's conscious faculties. Even if the visitors have actually been present—for Betty appears to him every day following this incident—it is important to stress once more that, as interpreted by ML's consciousness through the narrative of West's words, the Betty and Shrike described to us have little relationship to the actual characters as they exist outside ML's consciousness.

Freudian theory offers a helpful insight into the more general explanation of ML's coma and hysteria. While a general theory cannot pin-point the precise motivation for ML's mania for order, it can indicate the pathological future of the patient.

> In estimating the influence of organic disease upon the distribution of the libido ... it is universally known, and seems to us a matter of course, that a person suffering organic pain and discomfort relinquishes his interest in the things of the outside world, in so far as they do not concern his suffering. Closer observation teaches us that at the same time he withdraws libidinal interest from his love-objects: so long as he suffers, he ceases to love. ... The sick man withdraws his libidinal cathexes back upon his ego, and sends them forth again when he recovers.[8]

In the long run, of course, ML is never to recover, but the quotation does shed light on the chapter following this nightmare in which ML and Betty go to the country and make love without any inhibitions one morning. That ML voluntarily makes love to Betty presents a stiff challenge to the theory of ML's alleged homosexuality and, more directly, offers still greater evidence that Betty holds an underestimated role in ML's psychosexual perception of his unique, distorted reality.

The final chapters of the novel disclose how ML's hysteria and organic suffering become fused into total insanity. Describing ML's activity after he has returned to the city and met Peter Doyle, the chapters depend intricately upon Freud's quotation above to illustrate the process of disintegration in ML's mind. It is here that Peter Doyle, the

ineffectual cripple, becomes ML's second genuine love-object.
Just as ML seeks comfort from Betty as a symbol of natural
order, he seeks from Peter Doyle the fruition of his Christ
fantasy and his own ambiguous sex identity.

We do not need Shrike's bitter sarcasm (123) to tell us
that Peter Doyle is a living symbol of the sordid suffering
humanity who seek salvation in ML's lovelorn column. As
such, he offers ML the opportunity to play out his Christ
fantasy with the silent understanding that he, Doyle, be
permitted to indulge in his own role as this crippled symbol.
A piecemeal collage of society's depravity ("He looked like
one of those composite photographs used by a screen
magazine in guessing .contests" (124), Doyle's physical
unfitness is said to excite ML even as the two men stare
silently at each other. West makes it clear that ML is
attracted to Doyle physically and stirred not by his pathetic
sob story on which he cannot even concentrate, but by the
relationship they are mutually sharing.

> When the cripple finally labored into speech, Miss Lonely-
> hearts was unable to understand him. He listened hard for a
> few minutes and realized that Doyle was making no attempt to
> be understood. He was giving birth to groups of words that
> lived inside him as things. . . .
>
> Like a priest, Miss Lonelyhearts turned his face slightly
> away. . . .
>
> Doyle's damp hand accidentally touched his under the
> table. He jerked away, but then drove his hand back and
> forced it to clasp the cripple's. . . . He did not let go, but
> pressed it firmly with all the love he could manage. At first the
> cripple covered his embarrassment by disguising the meaning
> of the clasp with a handshake, but he soon gave in to it and
> they sat silently, hand in hand (124, 126).

The scene has obvious sexual overtones and establishes for
ML a means by which he may express his libidinal frustration
through his Christ complex.

Again, the scene in the country with Betty raises some
difficult problems. How does she fit into this new homosexual relationship? Why does ML reject aggressively—in an
almost manly fashion—the new advances of Fay Doyle? With
the development of his relationship with Peter Doyle, how

can ML rationalize his plans to marry Betty? And where does the reinforced Christ business fit into ML's new psychological position?

Clearly, some of the answers lie in ML's final attack of hysteria. When presumably counseling Peter and Fay Doyle, ML tries his God-is-the-answer pitch "by becoming hysterical" (129). Although it fails to work when he would wish it to, the hysteria does manifest itself once ML has escaped from Fay's attempt to seduce and rape him. As before, he falls into a three-day coma (the Christian reference is obvious) and is completely lost in the "reality-world" of his own hysterical fantasy. "Without dreaming" (131), ML experiences a surreal hallucination and, when interrupted by Shrike and his friends, maintains the psychotic identity of his ivory Christ. A reaction to the fact of his latent homosexuality having come to the surface of his consciousness, ML defensively establishes his identity as an impervious rock which is incapable of emotion of any kind. The battle has been lost and ML's slightest glimmers of sanity have been obliterated by his all-encompassing schizophrenic hysteria. Naturally, the demented consciousness of ML, as revealed by West's words, is not aware of the perverse manifestations of this new identity. Thus it is that, in keeping with the other descriptions of ML's psychotic perception, West never openly states, as ML's consciousness, that there is anything strange or neurotic about ML's condition. In fact, despite West's indirect indications to the contrary, James F. Light accepts, with the demented ML, his long-awaited religious reincarnation.[9] It becomes increasingly obvious that nothing could be farther from the facts of the case.

We are treating West's novel as an extension of ML's consciousness; as ML's thoughts register those details which most fascinate him, it must be observed that the people with whom ML surrounds himself confront him constantly with breasts and breast imagery. Shrike estimates Miss Farkis' intelligence by the size of her busts (72); Mary Shrike recites the plight of her Mother's breast cancer as her own breasts are being fondled by ML in the doorway of her apartment

(96); Fay Doyle's balloon breasts are a notable contrast to Betty's "pink-tipped thumbs" (114); and, when trying to arouse himself enough to phone Mary Shrike for a date, ML concentrates on a pair of painted breasts in a mineral water advertisement—but even this does not work (90). As previously suggested, the breast imagery becomes expressed more subtly in the subconscious fantasies which ML experiences while undergoing an attack of hysteria (75-6). Recalling ML's helpless, almost unconscious submission to a violent expression of his frustration when confronted with the imperfect cigarette and, later, the clean old man, it is interesting to note that ML's dream breasts, doorknobs, symbolize a dead world, and that ML can consider them living, can bring them to life only by making them bleed and thus become something other than doorknobs.

This association of breasts with violence is more directly expressed in his relationship with Betty. Terrified by his hysteria, ML rushes to Betty for comfort and order, but "by the time he got there, his panic had turned to irritation" (79). Unable to talk (his tongue here shares the image West later uses to describe Betty's breasts—that of the fat thumb), ML defensively seeks some means of rationalizing his inability to behave normally with Betty. Unable to project the blame onto Betty, he tries to evoke her contempt so that he *will* be able to. It becomes clear that this is the role ML would have Betty play for him. He has avoided her since she began describing their dream-perfect marriage, suggesting strongly to us that ML has little interest in such a relationship. Nervous and still irritated, ML fondles Betty's breasts for want of anything else to do.

> She made no sign to show that she was aware of his hand. He would have welcomed a slap, but even when he caught at her nipple, she remained silent.
> "Let me pluck this rose," he said, giving a sharp tug. "I want to wear it in my buttonhole."
> Betty reached for his brow. "What's the matter?" she asked. "Are you sick?"
> He began to shout at her, accompanying his shouts with gestures that were too appropriate, like those of an old-fashioned actor.

"What a kind bitch you are. As soon as one acts viciously,
you say he's sick. . . . Well, I'm not sick. I don't need your
damned aspirin. I've got a Christ complex. Humanity . . . I'm a
humanity lover."
  . . . Instead of answering, she raised her arm as though to
ward off a blow. She was like a kitten whose soft helplessness
makes one ache to hurt it (80-1).

The passage suggests that ML's decision to play with Betty's
breasts is not so much out of boredom, itself not particularly
a natural motivation, but to force her to respond violently
towards him. Although she reacts with frustrating kindness,
that she has reacted at all permits ML to act out his anxiety.
His speech reveals that he is consciously aware of his perverse
behavior but that he must blame her for his actions. He
further consciously rejects the notion that his malady is
physically oriented or that it may be helped by wonder
drugs. He even acknowledges his Christ complex in this fit of
rage, but he must quickly associate this condition with a
lesser symptom, one which he can handle objectively and
which permits a favorable self-image. He has, therefore,
disclosed his use of humanity as an overwhelming symbol of
suffering which he can manipulate until he becomes its
victim. By projecting his Christ complex into this grab-bag of
impersonal grievances, ML has created the illusion of objectivity; more correctly, he has escaped the subjective implications of his own neuroses. By identifying himself as a
humanity lover instead of a demented "Christ nut," ML
affords himself a self-image with which he can play more
gratifyingly and on which he may depend when threatened
with anxiety and/or hysteria. However, West interjects that
such an image is merely a performance, which fact ML
liminally knows but cannot rationally accept. The fantasy
which ML is trying to convince both Betty and himself of is
further destroyed by ML's actions as he relates it. While
professing to be a lover of humanity, he is menacingly on the
brink of violence and "aches" with the compulsion to attack
Betty as he has done to the lamb in college, a small frog in his
memory, and the clean old man in Delehanty's.
  The incident serves many purposes in the novel. It

dramatically unifies the themes of Christ complex, order obsession, and hysteria through the sadistic, semi-literal rape of Betty. Furthermore, it defines ML's perverse dependency on Betty as consoler and scapegoat. ML physically acts out his mental disorder and subsequently explains it until he arrives so close to the truth of the matter that he must retreat to a self-image that is becoming less and less acceptable. Sexual ambivalence is also physically and emotionally in evidence. While performing an act of passion, ML is motivated by hatred rather than the common concept of love; while tearing at Betty and verbally rejecting her, ML is confirming his emotional dependence on her.

> "I love you."
> "And I love you," he said. "You and your damned smiling through tears" (81).

The role ML has made for Betty demands an innocence which cannot help but further frustrate ML, thus creating a literal vicious cycle. At this point of the novel, ML's fondling of Betty's breasts permits him to indulge the neuroses that must be expressed while it protects him from any genuine heterosexual experience which could threaten his sexual identity.

Breasts again assume this symbol of frustration and desired non-intimacy when ML takes Mary Shrike to El Gaucho, the nightclub of sordid romanticism. By her husband's admission, Mary Shrike is frigid, yet she uses her breasts to excite ML. In this way, she personifies ML's vision of the dead world of doorknobs. It is revealing that she is not only frigid but that she is the only woman other than Betty who has tolerated ML (89) prior to Fay Doyle. The marriage of these two qualities make Mary a strangely suitable "love"-object for the sexually ambivalent ML.

ML's petting sessions with Mary Shrike are strikingly similar to the one with Betty and ML's interpretation of them substantiates our conclusions about his role with heterosexuality.

> When he kissed Shrike's wife, he felt less like a joke. She returned his kisses because she hated Shrike. But even there

Shrike had beaten him. No matter how hard he begged her to give Shrike horns, she refused to sleep with him.

Although Mary always grunted and upset her eyes, she would not associate what she felt with the sexual act. When he forced this association, she became angry. He had been convinced that her grunts were genuine by the change that took place in her when he kissed her heavily. Then her body gave off an odor that enriched the synthetic flower scent she used behind her ears and in the hollows of her neck. No similar change ever took place in his own body, however. Like a dead man, only friction could make him warm or violence make him mobile . . . .

He tried to excite himself into eagerness by thinking of the play Mary made with her breasts. She used them as the coquettes of long ago had used their fans. One of her tricks was to wear a medal low down on her chest. Whenever he asked to see it instead of drawing it out she leaned over for him to look. Although he had often asked to see the medal, he had not yet found out what it represented.

But the excitement refused to come. If anything, he felt colder than before he had started to think of women. It was not his line. Nevertheless, he persisted in it, out of desperation. . . (89-90).

The first paragraph shows the complex of motivations surrounding their relationship. For both of them, the affair seems to be dominated by a direct defiance against Shrike. As with ML, Mary's performance does not appear to be associated with love making. She seems to ignore ML's advances and to find her own gratification in the grotesque gestures of their embrace. Her sexual identity is one of negation: she achieves her perverse fulfillment through her denial to Shrike and ML and gratifies her ego with the self-image of a tease.

ML uses her aberration to his advantage. His propositions are delivered as lifelessly as are his gestures of affection.

"The way to be gay is to make other people gay," Miss Lonelyhearts said. "Sleep with me and I'll be one gay dog."

The defeat in his voice made it easy for her to ignore his request and her mind sagged with his. . . .

"Sleep with me," he said.

"No, let's dance."

"I don't want to. Tell me about you mother."

"She died leaning over a table. The pain was so terrible that she climbed out of bed to die."

Mary leaned over to show how her mother had died. . .
(94).

He clearly does not expect her to sleep with him, nor is he
unwilling to permit her to become yet another confessor to
him. Mary acts out her mother's death as she relates it, thus
using ML to fulfill her own breast fixation whose roots are
obviously an outgrowth of her mother's breast cancer. Thus,
the two of them share an intimacy of perversions. As Mary
chatters on, ML concentrates on the medal. "He saw that
there was a runner on it, but was unable to read the
inscription" (95). The medal may be interpreted as a symbol
of ML's attitude toward heterosexuality. As with his propositions to sleep with Mary, ML asks to see the medal but has no
real knowledge of it, repeating the pattern of aggression and
non-experience. It is appropriate that the medal, so overtly a
part of their sexual relationship, should depict a runner. Mary
Shrike's breasts, an ambivalent combination of enticement
and malignancy, symbolize the threat of heterosexuality for
ML, much as the deadness of her body complements his own.

West jokes cruelly when he puns on the word "gay" in
ML's proposition to Mary Shrike, but it is with some of the
most remarkable imagery in the novel that West outlines
ML's perverse sexuality. Sitting in the park trying to decide
whether or not he should phone Mary Shrike for a date, ML
stares at a phallic obelisk which his mind brings to life
through an erotic hallucination. "The stone shaft cast a long,
rigid shadow on the walk in front of him. He sat staring at it
without knowing why until he noticed that it was lengthen-
ing in rapid jerks, not as shadows usually lengthen. He grew
frightened and looked up quickly at the monument. It
seemed red and swollen in the dying sun, as though it were
about to spout a load of granite seeds" (89). West's imagery
reveals the way in which ML's mental condition is controlling
his perception of "real" reality, extending poetically and
contextually ML's losing struggle to separate illusion and
actuality. The image not only serves as a projection of ML's
psycho-sexual frustration but it is also a preparation for his
pathological fulfillment of identity through the self-image of

a rock. Elsewhere, West extends ML's sexual attitude through images in the "real" world when, while phoning Fay Doyle, ML stares at a pair of disembodied genitals which have been carved on the wall (99). In both cases, the imagery is masterfully connotative of ML's sexual deadness, the latter more directly alluding to ML's castration anxiety.

As has been suggested, ML's castration anxiety is most apparent in the chapter "Miss Lonelyhearts and the Lamb." The lamb sacrifice parallels, directly and by implication, that of a child performing an ancient totem ritual, as interpreted by Freud: "It is true that in the case of little Arpad . . . his totemic interests did not arise in direct relation with his Oedipus complex but on the basis of its narcissistic precondition, the fear of castration. . . . The same part is played by the father alike in the Oedipus and castration complexes—the part of a dreaded enemy to the sexual interests of childhood. . . . His attitude towards his totem animal was superlatively ambivalent: he showed both hatred and love to an extravagant degree."[10] Freud's observations here are important to any literary critic, if only to disprove Hyman's dependency on the Oedipus complex as the motivation of ML's delirium. While accounting for ML's castration anxiety and his ambivalence toward his love-objects, the passage further helps to define ML's relationship to his father. Thus Freud presents us with the key by which we may better comprehend the meaning of ML's hysterical recollection while sifting out the symptoms which are at the core of his neurosis. It becomes increasingly apparent that ML's latent homosexuality, overt narcissism, delusions of grandeur, and desire to emulate his father's identity have driven him to augment an abnormal religious obsession to the complete withdrawal of a catatonic Christ complex. Imagining himself to be a rock, he reverts to the symbol of castration with which he has destroyed the sacrificial lamb—symbolically, Christ, his father, and himself. It must be acknowledged that, while the above statement permits us to disregard the Oedipus complex, it does not completely rule out the possibility of the importance of this or any other incestuous psycho-relationship.

There are many indications of sexual ambivalence in *Miss
Lonelyhearts,* not the least of which lies in the irony of the
title. That ML has little or no masculine identity is most
apparent in his attempt to identify himself over the phone to
Fay Doyle:

> "This is Miss Lonelyhearts."
> "Miss who?"
> "Miss Lonelyhearts, Miss Lonelyhearts, the man who does
> the column" (99).

This ambivalence is completely opposite that of Fay Doyle,
for she has written a proposition not to the columnist Miss
Lonelyhearts but to a man in a blue suit she had "pointed
out" to her at Delehanty's (97). ML's reaction to Fay's letter
is his stock reaction to any woman. Without having seen her,
he imagines what she looks like. "He thought of Mrs. Doyle
as a tent, hair-covered and veined, and of himself as the
skeleton in a water closet, the skull and cross-bones on a
scholar's bookplate. When he made the skeleton enter the
flesh tent, it flowered at every joint" (99). ML's perverse
fantasy portentiously anticipates the relationship he is to
share with Fay Doyle, one in which he is to play the feminine
part and find "a strange pleasure in having the roles reversed"
(101). That he imagines himself as a flowering skeleton
extends one of West's most elaborate feminine symbols. Both
Freudian and poetic, West uses flowering as an extension of
his breast imagery: the magician ML brings dead doorknobs
to life by making them flower; Betty's nipples are, to ML,
rosebuds which he would like to wear; kissing Mary Shrike,
ML's living breast symbol, brings her dead body to life as
indicated by her strong artificial flower scent. The pattern of
deadness blossoming into femininity is clearly most important, therefore, in this expression of ML's sexual ambivalence.

The theme of sexual ambivalence is also manifested in
such minor characters as Miss Farkis and the clean old man.
Shrike introduces the theme in the form of a jibe, directly
related to ML's sexual identity. With cruel accuracy, he
observes: " 'Oh, so you don't care for women, eh? J. C. is

your only sweetheart, eh? Jesus Christ, the King of Kings, the Miss Lonelyhearts of Miss Lonelyhearts. . .' " (72). Shrike's comment not only emphasizes ML's Christ complex but shades it with apt homosexuality. It is at this time that Miss Farkis enters. "She had long legs, thick ankles, big hands, a powerful body, a slender neck and a childish face made tiny by a man's haircut. . . . She acknowledged the introduction with a masculine handshake" (72). For all her masculinity, Miss Farkis is most appreciated, by Shrike, for her large breasts which, as perceived by ML, are just part of a "powerful body." West's description of Miss Farkis, as a catalogue of what ML's conscious notices, proves even more interesting when compared to the description of Fay Doyle. "Legs like Indian clubs, breasts like balloons and a brow like a pigeon. Despite her short plaid skirt, red sweater, rabbit-skin jacket and knitted tam-o'-shanter, she looked like a police captain" (100). The physical masculinity of both women is projected by ML's feelings toward (fear of) them as women. Rather than being a simple condemnation of these "real" people, the descriptions are reflexive, testifying more to ML's sexual ambivalence than to theirs.

George B. Simpson, the clean old man, may be studied in a more sophisticated way. Frightened and hiding in a public men's-room near ML's sterile park, the old man asks only to be left alone. His flute-like voice laugh/cries at ML's accusation that he is effeminate, his mind as diseased as his soul. He is a soft lump that cannot protect himself, armed only with a cane and a pair of gloves to protect his hands from redness. Deprived of his phallic cane, Simpson is encouraged to discuss his inversion with ML and his friend. As the old man sticks his tie in his mouth—another sexual allusion—ML is reminded of a frog he had stepped on when a child. Falling into what has become recognized as a behavior pattern, ML's pity and anguish turn to anger, then to violent irrationality as he feels he must destroy the old man.

George Simpson with cane is a forerunner of Peter Doyle. Both represent crippled humanity and both find an identity with ML. ML attempts to adopt his role (consciously Christ, unconsciously homosexual) to make Simpson conform to the now expected (unconsciously sought) role of suffering confidant. In this way, ML enables himself to share the confessor's anguish and displace his own anxiety. In Simpson, ML seeks a passive love-object with whom he can achieve the subconscious role of aggressor, the omnipotent father. ML puts his arm around Simpson and relies on the theatrical pretense of sympathy in his voice to coax the old man. In a curious way, he is repeating the seduction technique he had used with Betty. Like Betty, Simpson remains unmoved and ML turns violent, attacking the humanity he cannot heal— "the sick and miserable, broken and betrayed, inarticulate and impotent" (88). As with Miss Farkis and Fay Doyle, the characterization of Simpson reveals more about ML's perspective and his own character than that of the clean old man. It is interesting to note that in *The Day of the Locust* West created the bizarre Homer Simpson to share the position of protagonist with Tod Hackett. In both novels, it appears that West has used this device of a physically-split personality to enable the main character to converse with the self he does not want to acknowledge. Much in the way Shrike's caustic appraisal of Goldsmith is reflexive, ML's vision of Simpson is a projection of ML as an old man. ML shares the devastating list of qualities which he attributes to humanity as he beats up the old man. ML is compulsively drawn to Simpson because he recognizes himself within the disgusting portrait of the old man's effeminate weakness. Were it not for the fatal intervention of the other cripple, Peter Doyle, ML would all too likely assume an identity similar to Simpson's; however, ML instead will cast off his protective gloves of semi-rationality and be caught red-handed.

Of course, ML's sexual identity climaxes with his relationship to Peter Doyle. Through Doyle, ML is able to break free from the last bonds of rationality. At the Doyle home, ML may now avoid the advances of Fay and smile beautifully in an attempt to recapture the erotic emotion he had experienced when holding Peter's hand. Doyle's sexual identity is further complicated by the role his wife has forced him to play:

> "Ain't I the pimp, to bring home a guy for my wife?" He darted a quick look at Miss Lonelyhearts and laughed apologetically.
>
> Mrs. Doyle was furious. She rolled a newspaper into a club and struck her husband in the mouth with it. He surprised her by playing the fool. He growled like a dog and caught the paper in his teeth. When she let go of her end, he dropped to his hands and knees and then continued the imitation on the floor.
>
> Miss Lonelyhearts tried to get the cripple to stand up and bent to lift him; but, as he did so, Doyle tore open Miss Lonelyhearts' fly, then rolled over on his back, laughing wildly (128).

The pimping situation mirrors the situation between Mary and Willy Shrike, and ML is again the correspondant. In this case, however, the Doyles fight for the phallus of ML, symbolically represented as a newspaper club. Finally, Doyle's canine pantomime is an acting out of ML's feeble proposition to Mary Shrike: "Sleep with me and I'll be one gay dog." Peter, his very name a crude pun, at length succumbs to a hysterical fit of laughter. The homosexual relationship is so open between Doyle and the Christ-rationalizing ML that the jealous wife later jeers, "What a sweet pair of fairies you guys are" (129). His ambivalence is still indicated when Fay Doyle unsuccessfully attempts to seduce him: "He felt like an empty bottle that is being slowly filled with warm, dirty water" (130). The masculine symbol of the bottle assumes a feminine connotation as it is "violated" by the polluted water West has associated with Fay's gross femininity and with ML's pawnshop hallucination of humanity. Nonetheless, the polar sex roles negate each other in ML's psyche, leaving only the asexual identity of the imperturbable rock.

The destruction of his ego identity is expressed in the fantasy he experiences in a non-dreaming state of delusion. Living on eucharistic crackers and water, ML assumes the identity of a statue holding a stopped clock and a cripple protecting his instrument from the rain. The statue recalls the

ivory Christ which he has become in a demented fantasy
world beyond time. The rock seems to be a hardened
extension of the imagined hump with which he, now one
with his sordid humanity, repels the waters of femininity.
When a mixed crowd of Shrike's friends breaks into the
room, ML makes no attempt to cover his naked body, for he
has lost all modesty in his loss of sexual identity.

As Shrike diabolically tempts ML to join their party, ML
examines his saltine eucharists, acting out his identity of the
rock-Christ. ML agrees to accompany them, for he regards
Shrike's taunting as a divine ordeal. With his rock identity,
ML believes he can now save crippled humanity because he
can now believe the shallow truisms he has been struggling
with for so long. More likely, however, he is now totally
impotent for, with the rock identity, he has lost even the
semblance of compassion. Having foresaken what has
appeared to be an existential commitment to humanity, he is
now more than ineffectual; he is a threat to the humanity he
would save. Shrike anticipates this in his description of ML's
relationship to his readers: " 'You are afraid that even when
exposed to his bright flame, you will only smolder and give
off a bad smell. Be of good heart, for I know that you will
burst into flame. Miss Lonelyhearts is sure to prevail' " (133).
Similar to Shrike's allusion to Attic salt, the metaphor
indicates ML's destructive nature, which only ML will
survive.

The last chapters of the book reintroduce the complex-
ities of sexual ambiguity, however, as Betty discloses to ML
that she is to have his baby and the couple plan their life
together. Although ML still regards Betty as a love-object, he
no longer wants her to permit him to act out his psycho-
neurotic anxiety, for he has made real his Christ fantasy with
the help of Peter Doyle. But for ML, his sexual identity has
not become so much a fruition of latent homosexuality as it
has a denial of sexual commitment altogether. It is this new
asexual identity which permits ML to play house with Betty
at the soda fountain. Robbed of all sexual responses, he feels
no threat to his sexuality from his girl friend. Once aware of

the menace of escapism, ML can now accept any dream for he now considers himself beyond experience.
considers himself beyond experience.

> He did not feel guilt. He did not feel. The rock was a solidification of his feeling, his conscience, his sense of reality, his self-knowledge. He could have planned anything. A castle in Spain and love on a balcony or a pirate trip and love on a tropical island.
>
> When her door closed behind him, he smiled. The rock had been thoroughly tested and had been found perfect (138).

In Freudian terms, West cites ML's condition not as diagnostic theory but as the conscious "reality" of ML. The vision is itself crippling and a pathetic submission to emotional catatonia, but, as perceived through ML's thoughts, it is a vision of salvation.

Thus it comes to pass that ML embraces his mental breakdown entirely and passionately.

> After a long night and morning, towards noon, Miss Lonelyhearts welcomed the arrival of fever. It promised heat and mentally unmotivated violence. The promise was soon fulfilled; the rock became a furnace.
>
> He fastened his eyes on the Christ that hung on the wall opposite his bed. As he stared at it, it became a bright fly, spinning with quick grace on a background of blood velvet sprinkled with tiny nerve stars.
>
> Everything else in the room was dead. . . .
>
> The room was full of grace. A sweet, clean grace, not washed clean, but clean as the undersides of the inner petals of a newly forced rosebud.
>
> Delight was also in the room. It was like a gentle wind, and his nerves rippled under it like small blue flowers in a pasture.
>
> He was conscious of two rhythms that were slowly becoming one. When they became one, his identification with God was complete. His heart was the one heart, the heart of God. And his brain was likewise God's.
>
> God said, "Will you accept it, now?"
>
> And he replied, "I accept, I accept" (138-9).

The rosebud grace in ML's fantasy room suggests the essence of Betty as ML again assumes a self-image of flowering. His emotional and intellectual identities do not so much fuse as dissolve into the abyss of his father's identity. ML's psyche achieves an intellectual form of intercourse with his father through total submission of his ego to that of his father-God. West cruelly permits ML to believe he is having a religious experience.[11]

Thus, Doyle's accidental shooting of ML seems not only ironic but justified. In his attempt to escape ML's grasp, his gun, significantly wrapped in a newspaper, goes off unintentionally. Rather than impose any figurative sexual significance upon the incident, we would be wise merely to view the shooting abstractly as a case of self-defense. It may be only assumed that the gun wound is fatal to ML, for the novel ends with no mention of ML's death. This seems only right, for the novel is truly an expression of ML's consciousness.

My purpose so far has been to investigate the main character of *Miss Lonelyhearts,* both contextually and within the Freudian metaphor, with the proper interrelationship between the two approaches as suggested by West himself. We have seen that the most outstanding literary and symptomatic trait in ML's character is his flight into hysterical fantasy.[12] It would appear to manifest itself in the illusionary state of mind which Charcot refers to as *attitudes passionelles* or hallucinations. To corroborate this assumption, we may again look to Freud:

> We say that the dream-wish is converted into an hallucination and as such commands belief in the reality of its fulfillment. . . .
> The formation of the wish-phantasy and its regression into hallucination are the most essential parts of the dream-work, but they do not belong exclusively to dreams. On the contrary, they are found similarly in two morbid states: in acute hallucinatory confusion (Meynert's "amentia"), and in the hallucinatory phase of schizophrenia. . . . The hallucinatory phase of schizophrenia has been less thoroughly studied; it seems generally to be of a composite nature, but in its essence it might well correspond to a fresh attempt at restitution, designed to restore to the ideas of objects their libidinal cathexis (*Theory*, p. 158).

It is with the application of such a key Freudian statement that the relationship between ML's interpretation of his experience and the psychological nature of the character may be more completely defined. Thus, with Freud as our Bullfinch, we are not seeking a new insight on hysteria by our reading of *Miss Lonelyhearts,* but are using psychological theory to aid us in understanding the main character of the work.

The quotation further substantiates the theory that ML's behavior may be comprehended as that of a schizophrenic. Suggested strongly by his latent inversion and ambivalent suspension between subjectified anxiety and rationalized aggression, the condition grows worse as the novel moves from an openly obsessional neurosis to hysterical catatonia.[13]

Within the literary framework of *Miss Lonelyhearts,* West has provided us with a character whose thinking is not only "complex, overabstract, and autistic" as symptomatic of his schizoid personality, but he has done so within the confines of the narrative form. By definition, the main character will appear complex and autistic as we devote our attention to studying his personality, and the overabstractions are so fundamental to the contextual unity of the narrative that we do not recognize the full significance of their intensity at first reading. From the beginning of the book, ML's hostility and subsequent frustration are made evident, and it is clear that, with the exception of ML's tryst with Betty in the country, his interpersonal relationships have only served to augment this feeling of alienation.

We have seen how the theme of ML's inability to experience genuine emotion, gradually extended as his rock identity, is suggested from the beginning of the novel. ML's fantasy is that he would imagine himself a Christ, a martyr of the unintelligible masses who write to him. However, he is actually a perverse extension of his alter ego, Shrike, in that he uses the suffering of his readers to gratify his fantasies. He laments that he must try to answer the irresolvable problems of his readers, but when the clean old man refuses to accept the role of supplicant, ML reacts with a literal fit of rage. Although ML at first appears to represent an existential prototype, painfully and passionately aware of the futility of the human condition, this, we have seen, is merely a mask for the Christ fantasy. ML's relationship to the existential predicament transcends commitment; indeed, it turns upon itself. ML uses the human condition as a vehicle for his masochistic play, finds suffering to be a play-thing—a drama of guilt and torture in which he can star, performing with self-consciously obvious gestures, with Betty, Mary Shrike, and finally Peter Doyle. Almost in the sexual sense, ML permits—forces—himself to be violated by the misery of his readers. Such a manipulation of role-playing affords him a passive self-image of compassion. The ultimate significance, however, lies in the fact that, when denied this role by Betty or Simpson, ML will do his best to create such a situation. It is only within the blind limits of his own perversion that ML can experience anything whatsoever.

The disintegration of ML's thought processes have been most notable in his surreal dreams and semi-fantasies, again culminating in the rock-Christ. In accordance with the definition provided by Coville, the new identity may be seen to have some elements of both hallucination and delusion. Relating to ML's malady, it would seem more strongly allied to the concept of a delusion (of grandeur), whereas the attacks of hysteria complement the definition of visual hallucinations.

Up to the point at which ML meets Peter Doyle, his condition closely resembles that referred to as "simple schizophrenic reaction."

> The outstanding symptoms are a gradual narrowing of interests, loss of ambition, emotional apathy, and withdrawal from social relations. Personal appearance is neglected, conversation is meager, and there is indifference to the opposite sex. The patient appears to be completely absorbed in his inner world of fantasy. ... Close observation of such individuals often uncovers weak, distorted efforts to make contact with others, as a consequence of the pathetic need for love and affection which these patients experience. Usually, however, it is not possible to maintain any emotional contact with them.[14]

ML's obsession with the anxiety-ridden, anxiety-inflicting

letters reflects his narrowing of interests and serves as a major reason for his inability to work after his return from the country. ML makes three short calls on the city room during the novel but never finishes a reply to a letter satisfactorily, that we may read. The outstanding symptoms are equally apparent when the party crowd invade his room in the last section of the novel; however, ML's delusion, through its isolationism, assumes elements of a catatonic reaction:

> In the stuporous state, the patient loses all animation, remaining motionless and in a stereotyped posture for hours, even days. He refuses food and shows no effort to control bowels or bladder. Extreme negativism is a characteristic reaction. ... Hallucinations and delusions occur in this stuporous state, and they may involve the patient in a conflict of cosmic significance (for example, the forces of Good and Evil may be experienced as at mortal combat in his body). The stereotyped posture and gestures are frequently related symbolically to the patient's fantasy experience (Coville et al., p. 167).

Clearly, ML never reaches the full catatonic stupor in which his body would be frozen in a single position—except at the most extreme states of hysteria.

I have used clinical psychology to explain the nature of ML's behavior; the only task remaining is to discern the cause of his derangement.

Especially relevant to the analysis of *Miss Lonelyhearts* is Freud's definition of "obsessional neurosis":

> Here we are at first in doubt what it is that we have to regard as the repressed instinct-presentation—a libidinal or a hostile trend. This uncertainty arises because the obsessional neurosis rests on the premise of a regression by means of which a sadistic trend has been substituted for a tender one. It is this hostile impulse against a loved person which has undergone repression. The effect at an early phase of the work of regression is quite different from that produced later. At first the regression is completely successful, the ideational content is rejected and the effect made to disappear. As a substitute-formation there arises an alteration in the ego, an increased sensitiveness of conscience, which can hardly be called a symptom. Substitute—and symptom-formation do not coincide here. Here, too, we learn something about the

mechanism of repression. Repression, as it invariably does, has brought about a withdrawal of libido, but for this purpose it has made use of a *reaction-formation*, by intensifying an antithesis. . . .

But the repression, at first successful, does not hold; in the further course of things its failure becomes increasingly obvious. The ambivalence which has allowed repression to come into being by means of reaction-formation also constitutes the point at which the repressed succeeds in breaking through again. The vanished effect is transformed without any diminuation, into dread of the community, pangs of conscience, or self-reproaches; the rejected idea is replaced by a *displacement-substitute*. . . (*Theory*, p. 114).

Within these concepts, Freud provides a rationale for the action of the novel. More pertinent, however, is the way in which the observation relates to the source of ML's trouble.

Freud devotes an entire essay to the relationship between obsessions and religious inclinations, in which he finds several parallels between the strong emotional affinity some people draw from a religion and the emotional character of a psycho-neurotic. Not only does his investigation uncover similarities in emotional states but in origin as well:

The structure of a religion seems also to be founded on the suppression or renunciation of certain instinctual trends; these trends are not, however, as in neurosis, exclusively components of the sexual instincts, though even these, for the most part, are not without sexual element. The sense of guilt in consequence of continual temptation, and the anxious expectation in the guise of fear of divine punishment, have indeed been familiar to us in religion longer than in neurosis.[15]

It seems in perfect accord with the general outline of West's novel that the main character's psycho-religious problems may be better understood in the light of these theories.

It has been an accepted tenet of this essay that ML's religious obsession is closely linked with his relationship to his father. As viewed through the lamb sacrifice, ML assumes his father's role of priest and attempts to express his castration anxiety at the bungled ritual. Again we reaffirm our conclusion that ML's schizophrenia is a manifestation of childhood neuroses of castration and incest complexes.

Just what exactly is known to us about ML's childhood?

We know that his father was a Baptist minister and raised his family in the tradition of New England puritanism. We know that ML had a sister four years younger than himself and are told of his fascination at playing the piano while she danced (84). While in college, ML, by then an agnostic, symbolically crushed his (perhaps ambivalently his father's) head with a rock. At the book's close, ML is again a priest of sacrifice in the psychopathic identity of the rock. There is, as Reid has mentioned, nothing said about ML's mother. It is possible to go outside contextual bounds and suggest that ML's memory of his mother is so guilt-laden that he has suppressed it completely from his conscious, but such a projection is neither fair nor necessary.

Of more revealing interest is the relationship between ML and his younger sister. Drinking at the speakeasy, ML experiences a heightening of sensual awareness and paranoia which subsides into childhood memory:

> He forgot that his heart was a bomb to remember an incident of his childhood. One winter evening, he had been waiting with his little sister for their father to come home from church. She was eight years old then, and he was twelve. Made sad by the pause between playing and eating, he had gone to the piano and had begun a piece by Mozart. It was the first time he had ever voluntarily gone to the piano. His sister left her picture book to dance to his music. She had never danced before. She danced gravely and carefully, a simple dance yet formal. ... As Miss Lonelyhearts stood at the bar, swaying slightly to the remembered music, he thought of children dancing. Square replacing oblong being replaced by circle. Every child, everywhere; in the whole world there was not one child who was not gravely, sweetly dancing (84-5).

Enigmatically, it is the only scene in the novel which is pure, free from sordid suffering, or even completely pleasant. Alone with his sister and conscious of his father's temporary absence, the boy finds delight in the simple act shared by him and his sister. As dream symbols, dancing and playing piano are equated with orgasm in countless Freud articles. West has further stressed the concept of initiation, for it is a new experience for both youngsters. Nor is it coincidental that the young ML is experiencing this symbolic coitus at the age of puberty. His tendency to elaborate the incident into an abstract situation, one in which all the children in the world participate, links the innocent memory to ML's current schizoid condition. His sister's dance further accounts for ML's obsession with order while the father's absence introduces the theme of subconscious sexual rivalry.

Those who question the sister's place in the incestuous picture should again look to Freud:

> All that I have been able to add to our understanding of it [the horror of incest] is to emphasize the fact that it is essentially an *infantile* feature and that it reveals a striking agreement with the mental life of neurotic patients. Psychoanalysis has taught us that a boy's earliest choice of objects for his love is incestuous and that those objects are forbidden ones—his mother and his sister. We have learnt, too, the manner in which, as he grows up, he liberates himself from this incestuous attraction. A neurotic, on the other hand, invariably exhibits some degree of psychical infantilism. He has either failed to get free from the psycho-sexual conditions that prevailed in his childhood or he has returned to them—two possibilities which may be summed up as developmental inhibition and regression. Thus incestuous fixations of the libido continue to play (or begin once more to play) the principle part in his unconscious mental life. We have arrived at the point of regarding a child's relation to his parents, dominated as it is by incestuous longings, as the nuclear complex of neurosis (*Totem*, p. 17).

Despite Hyman's attempt to link ML's neurosis to the best-known incest relationship, the context of the novel obviously negates the Oedipal influence in its affirmation of the more dominant brother-sister relationship.

As ML's incestuous desire for his sister contributes the basis for his neurotic inversion, it also resolves the dilemma of defining Betty's importance in the novel. With thumb-like breasts contributing to her boyish (and, more significantly, child-like) physique, ML sees his sister in Betty. Having relived the terrifying castration ritual, he seeks the order he has associated with his sister's dance and goes to Betty for comfort. But being confronted by the love-object he would repress, he is overcome with a renewed guilt and anxiety. Sado-masochistically, he attempts to force her to punish him—thereby fulfilling his tormented guilt feelings, and, with ambiguous gestures of eroticism, making her share in his uncomprehending frustration. When she asks him to leave, he goes to Delehanty's where the memory of "innocent" love is recalled, momentarily purged of incestuous guilt. Picking up the old homosexual, ML again feels guilty and he releases his hostility on a projection of himself through George Simpson.

Disgusted by Simpson, ML remembers another childhood experience: "Miss Lonelyhearts felt as he had felt years before when he had accidentally stepped on a small frog. Its spilled guts had filled him with pity, but when its suffering had become real to its senses, his pity had turned to rage and he had beaten it frantically until it was dead" (87). As we have already seen, the incident is in keeping with the pattern set by ML's other outbursts of hysterical violence. It is through such a recalled instance that humanity (Simpson) becomes a part of the castration rite, thus assuming a similar role in the guilt pattern associated with the Christ complex. Returning to Freud's catalogue of dream symbols, however, reveals a more subtle implication. "Children and brothers and sisters," Freud observes, "are less tenderly treated, being symbolized by *little animals* or *vermin*."[16] Guilt feelings towards ML's sister are symbolized here in such a way that ML, the aggressor, is the inflictor of pain. Unable to cope with the emotion (a mixture of incestuous desire and guilt) and incapable of tolerating the real experience of pain, he obliterates the problem much in the way he attempted to remove the threat of his father (as the lamb). Now feeling guilt about his own actions, he turns on himself through Simpson. The description of the incident is further a key to the final fate of ML, for it allegorically testifies to the perverse manner in which he perceives and interprets the suffering of others.

"Miss Lonelyhearts in the Country" appears less mystifying once Betty's sister role has been accepted. Initially, ML refrains from aggressive sexplay with Betty out of alleged respect for her virginity. However, when ML sees Betty's naked, child-like body as she hangs out laundry on the line, he is sexually aroused for a "normal" heterosexual union. "He blew her a kiss. She caught it with a gesture that was childishly sexual. He vaulted the porch rail and ran to kiss her. As they went down, he smelled a mixture of sweat, soap and crushed grass" (114). Inspired by her "childishly-sexual" gesture, ML unconsciously makes love not to Betty, but to his sister. Incidentally, it is this same childish naivetee which arouses ML on his date with Mary Shrike. ML has been kneading her body passionlessly until he seems suddenly aroused as she recites the morbid saga of her mother's death "in a brave voice, like a little girl reciting at a party" (96).

The little girl at a party is an image which recurs at the end of the novel as the description of Betty. On the surface, the image could hardly appear less appropriate, for Betty has just told ML that she is pregnant. However, it is especially apt as an extension of ML's consciousness, for ML, now fully immured in his rock identity, need no longer acknowledge Betty's "real" identity. To him, she has lost all actual existence except as a little girl's party dress. Attracted to the adolescent frilliness that is associated with what West calls "her little-girl-in-the-party-dress air" (136), ML begs the dress, not Betty, to marry him. He is so protected from "reality" by his own rock identity that he can seriously contemplate marriage so long as the two of them play as children at a soda fountain—like brother and sister playing house. The irony that this asexual relationship is actually the fruition of ML's sexual repression is coupled with the irony that their psychological roles have been reversed: while Betty had once been the symbol of stability for the vicious ML, ML now regards himself as the embodiment of stability for the irritable and frightened (due to her pregnancy) Betty. Without the incestuous motivation for their affair, Betty's announcement that she is going to have a baby would remain in conflict with the homosexual theme of the novel and seem unnecessary melodrama.

Betty is, for ML, his sister. By the time he has established communications with God and won approval from this psychic-father, the psychic-son of God is prepared for the corrupted miracle of rebirth. It is only fitting that Betty should be present at the miracle, for it is because of her that Peter does not turn back. Psychologically, and physically, she is the barrier which brings about ML's destruction.

FOOTNOTES

1. Nathanael West, *Miss Lonelyhearts* in *The Complete Works of Nathanael West* (New York: Farrar, Straus and Cudahy, 1957).

2. Stanley Edgar Hyman, *Nathanael West* (Minneapolis: University of Minnesota Press, 1962), pp. 23-4.

3. Randall Reid, *The Fiction of Nathanael West: No Redeemer, No Promised Land* (Chicago: University of Chicago Press, 1967), pp. 75-6.

4. Nathanael West, "Some Notes on Miss Lonelyhearts," *Contempo*, III (May 15, 1933), p. 2.

5. Victor Comerchero, *Nathanael West: The Ironic Prophet* (Syracuse: Syracuse University Press, 1964), p. 95.

6. Frederick J. Hoffman, *Freudianism and the Literary Mind* (Baton Rouge: Louisiana State University Press, 1957), pp. 320-1.

7. Norman Podhoretz, "A Particular Kind of Joking," *New Yorker* XXXIII (May 18, 1957), p. 148.

8. Sigmund Freud, *General Psychological Theory* (New York: Norton Library, 1963), p. 164.

9. Light's interpretation of the final chapter is incredibly literal, despite contradictory contextual evidence. "Through his humility Miss Lonelyhearts has become dead to the world," Light contends. "Following Christ's injunction that whosoever would find his life must first lose it, Miss Lonelyhearts can now attain a mystical union with God. Transcending the fevered sickness of his body through a transforming grace of light and perfumed cleanliness, he becomes 'conscious of two rhythms that were slowly becoming one. When they became one his identification with God was complete. His heart was the one heart, the heart of God. And his brain was likewise God's.'

". . . True belief in the Christian answers . . . rests upon the dissolution of the self and the subsequent mystical experience of God's love and grace. Until such experiences (the price of which is alienation from this world), the very name of Christ, as Miss Lonelyhearts had felt before his 'sickness,' is a vanity on the lips of man. After God's lover and grace, the personal ecstasy they bring is a 'reality,' but the reality is incommunicable."

Light's confusion of religious zeal with psychoneurosis is easy to understand, especially in the light of Freud's quotation on page 125 of this book. That Light could be so completely misled suggests that he, like Hyman, is more anxious to establish ML's role in a recognizable pattern (the rebirth archetype) at the expense of literary validity. His ability to trump up so positive a case around ML's alleged religious experience does not detract from West's artistry; rather, it confirms his skill. Put another way, Light's observations, though incorrectly interpreted, serve as an investigation of ML's own perverse rationalization of this very subjective experience.

James F. Light, *Nathanael West: An Interpretative Study* (Evanston: Northwestern University Press, 1961), pp. 86,87).

10. Sigmund Freud, *Totem and Taboo* (New York: Norton Library, 1962), p. 130.

11. Those who side with James F. Light and ML, alleging that the experience is genuinely a religious achievement, should consult Josef Breuer and Sigmund Freud, "Studies on Hysteria on the Psychical Mechanism of Hysterical Phenomena: Preliminary Communications," *Classics in Psychology* (Thorne Shipley, Ed.) (New York, 1961), pp. 678-9, 680, 681, 682, and Walter J. Coville, Timothy W. Costello, Fabian L. Rouke, *Abnormal Psychology* (New York, 1960), pp. 162-5. These passages describe in greater detail the clinical proof that ML is suffering from the apex of hysterical schizophrenia.

12. We may note the close relationship between Charcot's association of the influence of early childhood experience (most notably, traumatic experience) with the cause of hysterical outbursts—described in the passages cited from Breuer and Freud—and Freud's discussion of the importance of childhood experience in the formation of dreams.

13. This process is described in the passages cited from Coville et al.

14. Sigmund Freud, *Totem and Taboo* (New York: Norton Library, 1962), p. 130.

15. Sigmund Freud, "Obsessive Acts and Religious Practices," *Character and Culture* (New York: Collier Books, 1963), p. 24.

16. Sigmund Freud, *Interpretation of Dreams* (New York: Avon Books, 1966), p. 392.

A CONFLUENCE OF VOICES:
A COOL MILLION

Madden: When *A Cool Million* was published in 1934, *Anthony Adverse* was still number one on the best-seller list; *So Red the Rose* by Stark Young and *Good-bye, Mr. Chips* by James Hilton were on the list, too, along with novels by Sinclair Lewis, Mary Ellen Chase, and Alice Tisdale Hobart, and the stories of Isak Dinesen. On the non-fiction list, *Life Begins at Forty* was in its second year, along with *100,000,000 Guinea Pigs*.

John Bunyan: My dark and cloudy words, they do but hold the truth, as cabinets enclose the gold. . . . holy writ. . . . is everywhere full of all these things—Dark figures, allegories.

Anatole France: [The Penguins] did not fear men, for they did not know them.

Verlaine: Take eloquence, and wring its neck!

Martin: The literary analogue to this novel, Poe's "The Man That Was Used Up," makes clear that *A Cool Million* follows in the tradition of grotesque comedy, from Poe and Melville through Kafka and Gogol, rather than in the traditions of social or political satire.

Paul West: [*A Cool Million* creates] the cruel percussive world of Jarry's *Ubi Roi*, Heinrich Mann's *Blue Angel* and Camus's *Le Malentendu*.

Jacques Copeau: [In *Ubu Roi*] the schoolboy Jarry, to mock
a professor, had without knowing it, created a masterpiece in painting that somber and over-simplified caricature . . . in the manner of . . . the puppet theatre. . . . an
epic satire. . . .

West: "The Chamber of American Horrors, Animate and
Inanimate Hideosities". . . . was in reality a bureau for
disseminating propaganda of the most subversive nature. . . . "inanimate" . . . consisted of innumerable objects culled from the popular art of the country. . . .

Horace McCoy-Socks: I want you two kids to get married
here. A public wedding. . . . I'll give you fifty dollars
apiece and after the marathon is over you can get
divorced if you want to. It don't have to be permanent.
It's just a showmanship angle.

West: Like many another "poet," [Snodgrasse] blamed his
literary failure on the American public instead of on his
own lack of talent, and his desire for revolution was
really a desire for revenge. Furthermore, having lost faith
in himself, he thought it his duty to undermine the
nation's faith in itself.

Norman Mailer-Stephen Rojack: I met Jack Kennedy in
November, 1946. We were both war heroes, and both of
us had just been elected to Congress. We went out one
night on a double date and it turned out to be a fair
evening for me. I seduced a girl who would have been
bored by a diamond ring as big as the Ritz.

West-Jake Raven [Indian]: In return for the loss of these
things, we accepted the white man's civilization, syphilis
and the radio, tuberculosis and the cinema.

Fiedler: . . . the instinct of Americans has always been to
avoid the avant-garde, to mock its pretentions, or at least
to find an antidote to it in popular culture. Nathanael
West is . . . an illustrative case, beginning in *The Dream
Life of Balso Snell* with the emulation of European

Surrealism, but turning in *A Cool Million* to a tongue-in-cheek emulation of Horatio Alger. . . . the inventor of a non-style congenial to all minor ironies.

West-Mr. Whipple: Go out into the world and win your way. . . . You have an honest face and that is more than gold.

Russel B. Nye: The standard Alger plot concerns a boy of fifteen or so, usually fatherless, who has to make his own way, often in the city, against heavy financial and social odds. . . . The titles of the Alger books play variations on this theme of self-reliance—*Work and Win, Strive and Succeed, Facing the World, Do and Dare, Adrift in New York, Struggling Upward, Striving for Fortune, Making His Way, Try and Trust, Sink or Swim, Risen from the Ranks.*

Mark Twain-The Man Who Corrupted Hadleyburg: My project was to corrupt Hadleyburg the incorruptible.

West-Lemuel: I'll go off to seek my fortune.

West: Our hero's eyes shone with a light that bespoke a high heart.

Oscar Wilde: Lord Henry: Nowadays people know the price of everything, and the value of nothing.

West-Whipple: Oil wells are still found in people's back yards.

Horace McCoy-Thomas Owen: God was in his heaven and all was right with the script writer.

West: [Lemuel] vowed then and there to go and do as Rockefeller and Ford had done.

Melville-Bartleby: I would prefer not to.

West-Lemuel: It seems like a dream to me, Mr. Whipple. This morning when I was set free from jail I thought I would probably starve, and here I am on my way to California to dig gold.

Thomas Sturak: [McCoy's] *Scalpel* is *Kiss Tomorrow Good-
bye* turned upsidedown. Whereas the latter is a bitterly
black parody of the Horatio Alger myth, the former is a
cynically rosy revival.

West-Whipple: These two archenemies of the American
Spirit, the spirit of fair play and open competition, are
Wall Street and the Communists. . . . The uniform of our
'Storm Troops' is a coon-skin cap like the one I am
wearing, a deer-skin shirt and a pair of moccasins.

T. R. Steiner: Like the Horatio Alger novels. . . . *Cool Million*
frequently purports to be a children's book. As such,
although its literary mode may be parody or mock-
heroic, West's novel is also fantasy, myth, dream-wish
identification, imaginative "redemption" and pure play.

West: The [comic] turn lasted about fifteen minutes and
during this time Riley and Robbins told some twenty
jokes, beating Lem ruthlessly at the end of each one. For
a final curtain, they brought out an enormous wooden
mallet labeled "The Works" and with it completely
demolished our hero.

Paul West: [*A Cool Million*] could have been a savage
Gatsby-reduced-to-absurdity; but . . . the result is burlesque. . . . West theatrically, impatiently simplifies: farce
is his natural mode of expression, being at once a
supreme form of irresponsibility and a version of pessimism.

West-Lemuel: I am a clown . . . but there are times when even
clowns must grow serious. This is such a time. I . . .

West: Lem got no further. A shot rang out and he fell dead,
drilled through the heart by an assassin's bullet.

Wilde: We live in an age when unnecessary things are our only
necessities. . . .

West-Whipple: Lemuel Pitkin . . . was dismantled by the

enemy. His teeth were pulled out. His eye was gouged
from his head. His thumb was removed. His scalp was
torn away. His leg was cut off. And, finally, he was shot
through the heart. . . . All hail, the American boy!

Voltaire-The Old Woman: ... A Mohammedan priest ...
preached a beautiful sermon to the soldiers persuading
them not to kill us outright. "Cut just one buttock off
each of these ladies," he said, "and that will provide you
with a delicious meal; if you find you need more, you can
have as much again in a few days' time. Allah will be
pleased at such a charitable action, and the seige will be
relieved."

West: What kind of a pretty boy was this that came apart so
horribly?

Martin: [*A Cool Million*] not only reveals the deceptions of
the American dream; it is in every way a precise reversal
of the very literary form in which that dream had been
best expressed.

WEST'S LEMUEL AND THE AMERICAN DREAM
By T. R. Steiner

Nathanael West's *A Cool Million* remains the least appreciated of his works, to a large extent because it has not been read properly. Its mode of operation is only partially understood at best; hence readers' responses are at the same time not serious enough and too serious. Like the Horatio Alger novels, on which it is based (and in a way like *Gulliver's Travels,* from which it draws the name of its hero, Lemuel Pitkin), *Cool Million* frequently purports to be a children's book. As such, although its literary mode may be parody or mock-heroic, West's novel is also fantasy, myth, dream-wish identification, imaginative "redemption" and pure play. Because of this important "latent content," the book much more resembles *The Dream Life of Balso Snell* and *Miss Lonelyhearts* (called a modern myth by Victor Comerchero) than one might first have suspected.[1] Its great difference from these earlier works is that they are more arty—a quality toward which West manifested much ambivalence.

I do not deny that the book has "serious" social and political content, and clearly shows West's anxiety that a Hitlerian dictatorship may come to Depression-fragmented America. But this content is trite: demagoguery and the blind force of mass-man had been staples of cultural and political analysis since de Tocqueville, Burckhardt and Nietzsche had outlined them as particular dangers of democracy. West

157

seems not so much interested in the fact of these monstrosities as in the popular imagination which makes it easier for them to thrive. That, rather than Nathan "Shagpoke" Whipple, is the arch-villain of his book. As overt pulp-magazine fiction, *Cool Million* is a mirror of the popular imagination—an early piece of pop art, like Rauschenberg or Lichtenstein, using American cultural materials to comment on them, chanting American themes in a skewed, that is to say, "true," fashion. Here, the novel insinuates, is the landscape of the American psyche, which needs and creates Horatio Alger, racial stereotypes, pulp pornography. If we required yet another foil to make the mode of *Cool Million* clear, it would be the many commentators on mass culture from Freud to Robert Warshow and Susan Sontag, but most notably George Orwell in his examination of boys' weekly papers and lewd postcards to get at the common Englishman. For a comparable reason, West consciously wrote a pornographic penny dreadful.[2]

It is, therefore, meaningless to talk of *West's* style in the book since his effort must have been to divest himself of style, to become a scarcely literate and dirty-minded adolescent. West "supplies" only the invisible frame—the skewing of speeches, the introduction of super-grotesqueries, the revelation of what happens after the jump-cut, in short, the consciousness which the reader perceives above and controlling the naive materials, the consciousness revealed by the mere fact of West's recognizable name on the book. So, the Alger material becomes very sophisticated and the skeleton for, as well as merging with, a whole series of American motifs, fictions and myths, American Dreams certainly, but also American Nightmares. The American Boy wants to succeed and honorably have the boss's daughter (or at least a clean "white" girl like Fiedler's Blonde Maiden) but he also wants to destroy (in fantasy-roles like the gangster) and to brutally deflower. He wouldn't mind being Tom Baxter piggishly taking frail Betty; he lusts after the international, dark sex of Wung's House of All Nations, and like the American Girl desires exotic experience but preferably with fabricated authenticity. Alger's hero becomes the picaro (the myth tends readily toward this metamorphosis because of American cultural and geographic mobility), touching North and South, mine and corral, farm and frontier. Here are Davy Crockett, Abe Lincoln and the martyr Patrick Henry; here, introduced in one of Whipple's speeches, the great military landmarks—"Remember the Alamo! Remember the Maine!" Here Chingachgook and the comity of American bloods like that in Cooper and Melville. In outline, sketchy, fragmented, jocose form, then, *Cool Million* is the encyclopedia of mythic "America." And West realizes that the Dreams mask horrors and coexist with nightmares—American xenophobia, anxiety, fear of the cultural exotic. Hence the racial stereotypes: cops are always Irish and revel in brutality; Chinese are inscrutable "celestials"; Indians retain the redness of their savagery; Jews, in their craft and cunning, deceive and steal. American populism hates, fears, but also identifies with the foreign, which enables it to have its darker fantasies. It is like Hitler, who (according to Alan Ross and Norman Cohn) turned the Jew into both the dark father whom he strove to destroy and the dark actor who fulfilled his erotic wishes. Although the Deep South riot which West describes could happen, West is least concerned with describing present reality, or predicting the future; the riot is a "sign of the times," a symbolic probability (very much in the Aristotelian sense) given the real nature of the native American psyche. It is a pleasing fiction to that psyche, the inverse corollary to the "constructive" egoism of the Alger myth. West sees, indeed, that whatever their outward manifestation, however much self-control or sacrifice even our good myths demand, they are power-myths either in essence or application, violent by nature as is every page of *Cool Million.*

The dreams of power are analyzed to their archetypes; so is the dream of martyrdom. The essential structure of the book is not the successful life of an Alger protagonist but the creation of a martyr-hero for Whipple's National Revolutionary Party—the life not of J. P. Morgan but a mock-Christ. Strangely, those critics who see West as a symbolist—his

central fictions as quest and sacrifice, and Lonelyhearts as a
modern Christ—have not recognized the underlying fable of
Cool Million. Like Christ but without His consciousness,
Pitkin bears a Revealed New Life, suffers and dies for his
Dream, leaving his "message" to American youth. Lemuel
(the name means literally, "belonging to God") has no
earthly father; we are asked to see him (through the name of
his widowed mother Sarah) as Isaac, Christ's type as
sacrificial victim in the Old Testament. Whipple is his
spiritual father, sending him into the world with a blessing
(and, ironically, like Judas "selling" him to that world with
the loan of thirty dollars). Before the quest—an attempt quite
literally to "save his house"—begins, Lem kills the "furious
animal" which assails the innocent, Betty conquers the
bestial, pig-eyed Tom Baxter, but is tricked by that fraudulent "butcher boy," in an incident prefiguring his future
defeats. Still, Lem tries to live the destined life, is kind,
charitable, self-sacrificing; experiences degradation and pover-
ty for Whippleism (the avatar of the Dream); and is slowly
destroyed by the world his message is trying to "save."
(Modern America here is Sodom, the Cities of the Plain,
Roman Judaea or their modern manifestation, Eliot's Wasteland which West clearly seems to call on.)

At least once, Pitkin is explicitly likened to Christ.
Having been arrested for trying to accuse the powerful
brothel-keeper Wu Fong, he protests: "But I'm innocent. . . .
I'm innocent," repeated Lem, a little desperately. "So was
Christ," said Mr. Barnes with a sigh, "and they nailed Him"
(Ch. 21). And they nail Pitkin, in the mock-crucifixion of the
music-hall scene. Standing between the two comics, Riley
and Robbins (is it far-fetched to see this name as deliberately
evoking the two thieves?), who use his destroyed body as a
comic prop, Pitkin begins the revolutionary speech prepared
for him by Whipple: " 'I am a clown . . . but there are times
when even clowns must grow serious. This is such a time. I
. . .' Lem got no further. A shot rang out and he fell dead,
drilled through the heart by an assassin's bullet" (Ch. 31).
Brilliantly, West prevents Lem from stepping out of his role.

He must be interpreted by Whipple on the national holiday, Pitkin's Birthday, which combines in a socio-religious cere- mony elements of Washington's or Lincoln's Birthday, Armistice Day and Christmas: "Simple was his pilgrimage and brief, yet a thousand years hence, no story, no tragedy, no epic poem will be filled with greater wonder, or be followed by mankind with deeper feeling, than that which tells of the life and death of Lemuel Pitkin .... although dead yet he speaks .... he did not live or die in vain. Through his martyrdom, the National Revolutionary Party triumphed, and by that triumph this country was delivered. . . . America became again American." Pitkin the redeemer; although "dismantled," his mantle has fallen on other shoulders. The book ends with a striking triptych: on the reviewing stand, as thousands of American youth "March for Pitkin," are Pitkin's mother (his Mary), Betty Prail (surely in her prostitution the Magdalene) and Whipple, at once the God, Judas and Pope of Pitkinism.

So, West jocoseriously sees Christ the hero in Horatio Alger, and a large degree of the Alger quality in Christ. The Greatest Story Ever Told has become in this book pulp- magazine uplift, and West realizes that for the popular imagination Christ (or the archetypal questing hero) can function either as victor or victim. The risen "Christ" is an identificatory model; the fallen, a defenseless recipient of our yearning aggression. We worship the powerful, successful "Christ"; we prey on the meek, submissive, idealistic. Indeed, what West seems most responsive to in the Alger myth, and in some of the other American myths he parodies, is that they are exploitative. In the fallen world of modern America, the promises of the American Dream are used to harness the idealism, energy, altruism of the young. The culture myth, in this novel transmitted by Whipple to Pitkin, implicitly says to the child, "The world is your oyster. Go out and succeed." But it does not prepare him for social and political realities; indeed by its lie, disables him in the inevitable competition with knowing adults and boys who have wised up. Yet, the cultural ideal endures, virtually through the destruction of the idealistic child, betrayed promiscuously to sharper, con-man, Indian, Southerner, WASP, Jew. However sympathetic Whipple may be at times, however consciously idealistic, he is the exploiter (already in the first scene bilking the innocent Lem). And however much of a booby Pitkin is, he functions—like Candide or Parson Adams—as the ingenu in satire, establishing—Pitkin obviously without force or validity—an unshakeable blind belief in the right, the good, the committed.

Through his belief in the Dream, Pitkin is not only like the shoddy, sentimental Alger, but also like Clyde Griffiths, Gatsby, and the host of ingenu martyr-heroes of American twentieth-century fiction. But in one very significant way, *Cool Million* differs from the novels of West's later friend Fitzgerald and "Swedes" like Dreiser. It is in that *Cool Million* was written by a Jew and West's Jewishness deepens as well as personalizes this seemingly abstract, shallow book. Although the two-dimensionality may be attributed to aesthetic distancing, I think that it resulted mainly from West's conscious attempt to use a "witty" symbolic mode and his desire, conscious or not, to mythicize his own cultural experience. By the "Jewish" element I do not mean something as simple as West's often cited "anti-Semitism," which we are told led to the unsympathetic portraits of Jews in this book and the others (where are there sympathetic portraits here of any ethnic type?), because I think that West was no more anti-Semitic than many assimilated Jews. (To call the low self-esteem or self-hatred of these people—often resulting from their acceptance of the American Dream— anti-Semitism is ludicrously inaccurate.)

In *Cool Million* West's Jewishness begins to be seen in the intertwining of native American and Christian (and New Testament) with Jewish (and Old Testament) strains. The hero, his mother, his spiritual father, indeed almost every character in the book, has at least one Jewish (or Hebrew) name: Yankees like Nathan Whipple, Levi Underdown, Ephraim Pierce; Indians like Jake Raven and Israel Satinpenny; an Irish Moe Riley; and Jewish Patriarchs like Asa

Goldstein, Ezra Silverblatt, Seth Abromovitz. There is a lot
of incidental fooling with these names—Jake Raven is violent
("raving," "ravin"), Satinpenny's first name reminds us of
the commonplace equation of Red Indians with the Lost
Tribe, two characters "pierce" and "rile," two Jews are
associated with pelf—but I think that their main point is to
posit modern America as a kind of conglomerate ironic
Chosen People, sharing not only names but characteristics
and cultural "artifacts." Thus, Asa Goldstein sells "Colonial
Exteriors and Interiors" and Ezra Silverblatt supplies coon-
skin caps and other accessories to Whipple's Party. (For their
trading in Americana, even at their own expense, Jews are
indeed satirized heavily.) But the Yankees and Indians also
are characterized by their greed and financial rapacity, while
the two lawyers who "get" Pitkin are Seth Abromovitz and
Elisha Barnes. The characteristic which all share is their
violence, whether overt like that of Irish cops, Southern
lynch mobs, and Indians, or disguised like that of Warden
Purdy who has all of Pitkin's teeth knocked out "to prevent
infection." By taking the melting-pot metaphor seriously,
making it one constructive principle of his book, West
suggests that the Hebrew, Christian, and American myths are
interpenetrable, indeed, interchangeable for "explaining" life
in these eclectic United States. All of them talk about one
life, which is man's.

But I think that the cultural interpenetration points to an
experience and a problem more personal for West. Where
could young Nathan Weinstein (or his Jewish contemporaries) find identificatory cultural myths in a nation whose
early heroes are Anglo-Saxon or Nordic, who bear "American" names like George Washington, Abe Lincoln, Ethan
Allen, Nathanael Greene, Patrick Henry, Nathan Hale? If
Jews had come to the United States in great numbers around
the mid-nineteenth century, this might have proved a lesser
problem because of the high esteem of Hebraism within the
Boston-Concord circle. For two centuries Puritan and Quaker
proper names had been consciously and happily chosen from
Old Testament figures, and Melville's great diabolic hero is

named after a King of Israel while the weaker—albeit less
dangerous—men around him are called Starbuck, Stubb and
Flask. By the 1920's with the anti-Semitism that attended
mass immigration there was little if any esteem: our culture
heroes, "Black Jack" Pershing, George Herman "Babe" Ruth,
Charles Lindbergh "the American Eagle," (Horatio Alger may
well stand for all of these), were not Jews, and if they
accidentally had Hebrew or "Jewish" names this stood in
ironic counterpoint (as it does in *Cool Million*) to their
frequent anti-Semitism. Thus, in confronting American folk-
heroes and culture myths Jewish youth were at a farther
remove than Hoosier farm-boys: the fictive distance of myth
was there for everyone, but Horatio Alger did not even seem
to be *about* Jews (this was also a problem for Poles, Italians
and Negroes, but West was none of these). Fiction after
fiction said to them: "We're not about you."

I am reminded of a fairly recent one, the Gillette Blade
comic-strip of the 1940's. Its obviously Anglo-Saxon heroes
lived adventurous lives, saved archetypal American Beauties
from horrible fates, and thus met their industrialist daddies.
Then, metamorphosed by an obligatory shower and shave
(the point of the ad), each hero would win both the Girl and
the Job. But hath not the Jew a beard since it can be pulled?
Mordecai Richler has spoken similarly of the dearth of Jewish
identificatory models in sports, and thus can explain the
almost hysterical ethnic responses to Sandy Koufax and
Hank Greenberg (*Commentary,* Nov. 1966). (I remember a
different tactic: in the early '40's identifying with football
players whose first name was the same as mine; hence, sharp
in memory is not only Tom Harmon but the forgotten Tom
Kuzma.) *Cool Million* is implicitly about this problem, and
West, again jocoseriously, says that the American mythic
landscape is about and for Jews if they attend to it closely
enough. Another, a more decisive, way to get into "America"
was to change one's name, and West also did that.

We must not forget that West, for all the protestations of
his non-Jewishness, lived a life so typical culturally that as I
read James Light's brief account of it I frequently lived over

remembered scenes.[3] The son of immigrant parents, he began early to drift away from what little ethnic heritage he had—I would guess, from Light's version, because of the religious indifference of his father and the nominalist conception of Judaism by his mother. After an undistinguished high-school career, he divested all the trappings at Brown, becoming an esthete and Brooks Brothers dandy, writing for the rather avant-garde college literary magazine and making many non-Jewish friends. Still, despite his friendship with members of elite Christian fraternities, he was never pledged by one because of their exclusion clauses; and, later, despite his winning the Christian girl, he never wed her, perhaps in part, as Light suggests, because of "the religious difference." He changed his name at college in 1926 before leaving for France; moreover, he had been playing around with the persona "Nathan von Wallenstein Weinstein" for a long time. I would not do injustice to the complexity of West's life, to his two-year Parisian sojourn, and all of the other experiences which made him other than some pasteboard "fallen Jew," but the skeleton of that life is almost ludicrously exemplary down to the pragmatic and possessive Jewish mother who moved in to serve "lavish meals" at his farm when he was a thirty-year-old practicing writer, and to his happy marriage of seven months—ended by double tragedy—to "My Sister Eileen," surely an archetypal American Girl.

So, *Cool Million* is also symbolic spiritual autobiography—or for those who are wary of "biographical fallacy," an interplay of fictive positions which might have gone on in the head of West or some other second-generation "alien" boy. The novel records confrontation with the American myth. It certainly does not seem coincidental that Alice, the daughter of Levi Underdown, whom Lem saves by a bit of derring-do, echoes in name his New York sweetheart Alice Shepard; nor that this fictional "romantic" young lady, having "misunderstood the incident" at the same time protects and rejects Pitkin: "She smiled kindly at our hero, and led her irate parent from the scene" (Ch. 11). But this is at best window-dressing, an insider's joke, resembling others which seem directed at friends like S. J. Perelman. More importantly, much in the novel suggests that West identified with both his major characters. One, like Proust's Marcel and Kafka's "K", carries the name of his creator—Nathan Whipple, Nathan Weinstein, Nathanael West. The other is the young hero, the Christ, the American quester. He belongs to God, and he is the Lamb of God, like Christ, like the symbolic "Isaac" sacrificed by Abraham, like the *lemmele* his name suggests. But like Christ, and as his role demonstrates, Lemuel is also the holy fool (in Yiddish, the *lemech*). His last name also provides a range of associations: "kin" of the everlasting "pit" as Comerchero suggests? a relative of the mass audience which sits in the pit? like the flea Saint Puce of *Balso* who lives in the arm-pit of Our Lord? a little bit of damnation himself? Pitkin Avenue, the Fifth Avenue and Champs Elysees of Jewish Brownsville?[4]

The relationship of Whipple and Pitkin is complex: Whipple is adult, practical, experienced, platitudinous, but ultimately successful; Pitkin is child, innocent, without language, a failure, but idealistic. I have already shown Whipple to be the God-Judas-Pope of Pitkinism. The relationship of the two also resembles that between Abraham and Isaac—Whipple "silently communes" with the picture of Abe Lincoln (Ch. 3), obviously his model—but this mythic relation is ironically skewed like all the others as Abraham sacrifices his "son," not a symbol. All of the myths show division and ambivalence in West's imagination: an "adult" cultural voice presents images of success—known to be evil—to the aspiring adolescent, who is destroyed in their pursuit. And the adult self, Nathan, still strangely tied to West's former life, scourges this "American Boy" in him, figuratively "whipping" him for temerity. It is the same kind of near-hysterical punishment of the questing innocent which underlies some of Swift's best satires: "Fool, how dare you aspire to a lot which is not man's? How dare you be other than a vile human." The author seems to be pointing to the probable cost of his having "gone West," in this book very nearly equated with having gone "Whipple," since that worthy allies himself with such American clichés and at one point leads a gold-mining expedition West. "Going West"—opting for a life that mirrors the national dream—may beckon to the adolescent as ideal personal fulfillment; for the adult it means taking the national lie with full comprehension, with little real to compensate for lost innocence, altruism and the particulars of an individual past. The book ends with no resolution of its underlying conflict, no synthesis of impossible innocence and vile experience, no celebration of heroic loss in the face of insuperable odds. Nathan Whipple has only venal success; but Lem Pitkin has died meaninglessly, in fact, in support of Whipple's Know-Nothing Americanism. One cannot live either as Child or Adult.

Cool Million also seems to examine the author's artistic decisions and the meaning of going West as a novelist. Near the end of the book, both Pitkin and Whipple are constantly before audiences and show two presentational styles: Pitkin is the straight-man, boffoing the audience by his deformities (are there echoes of *Balso Snell* here?), witlessly feeding their destructive lust, but never in control of his own act; Whipple is in control, lulling or inciting them with flatulent pieties, but totally wrapped in an inhuman rhetoric. Lem is killed just as he is about to speak seriously in his own person; and Whipple gets the girl, Lem's proud mother (West's wanted him to go into a more successful line than writing) and power. To command the audience of a hundred thousand, however, he debases the materials of Lem's passion into the heroic inanities of Americanism. Might this not have seemed the danger if Nathanael were to go all the way West?

The reader may be sympathetic to my analysis of the book so far, but I could never convince him—nor would I try—that he was reading anything but a low burlesque, a piece of slapstick. The tone is little like that of other "serious" books, unlike that of *Balso,* which is self-consciously artistic and derivatively literary, unlike *Gulliver* or the learned wit of *Gargantua,* most I suppose like the black comedies of our time. How do we explain this crude tone? What is West saying by it? Apparently, that if our

Dreams derive from the popular imagination they inevitably embody and reflect the quality of that imagination. American life may be verifiably grotesque, incredibly destructive in its effects, but in the average mind it registers in a form banal, slightly titillating, clichéd, impossible to take seriously. The mass—for whatever reasons, not the least of which is the seduction of fantasy—is uncaring of, anesthetized to real experience. In popular apprehension, rape, for example, is not the brutal and painful forcing of a real woman, but something histrionic, played out in an "ideal" world of fancy, somehow detached from rapist and rapee—therefore, potentially ludicrous: "In the half gloom of the cabin . . . the Pike man [was] busily tearing off Betty's sole remaining piece of underwear. She was struggling as best she could, but the ruffian from Missouri was too strong for her. . . . At the sight of poor Lem weltering in his own blood, Betty fainted. In no way disturbed, the Missourian went coolly about his nefarious business and soon accomplished his purpose" (Ch. 26). On one hand, this event is made meaningless; on the other, it shows West can write better soft-core pornography than the professionals. The rape of Betty exemplifies two key effects of *Cool Million*: while deliberately pandering to the American predilection for lust and violence, it drains, through the even-tempered mechanicalness of its language, all human significance from its events. West forces the reader to see the artificiality of this language, but seems in no way to comment on it. That is, he does not posit—even by indirection—a more humane or moral use of language, certainly not an "art" use. (Indeed, the pretension of art is one of the balloons he pricks repeatedly from *Balso Snell* on.) And once again, West uses the medium to comment pessimistically on his own writing. He seems to be saying, "Look how well I write in these trashy American forms." Another in the line of American apocalyptists, closer to loving pornography and violence than hating them, West seems to point to the degree which American Dreams and the mass psyche have penetrated his own imagination.

Cool Million, then, is about the American power-success-violence ethic and how much it has corrupted even its satirist. Surely West with his knowledge of Spengler recognized that by taking his new name he was identifying himself with the decline of a doomed civilization. In *Day of the Locust* he comes to the farthest American Abendland, California, where the refugees from the nation's great heart have come to die. "Going West" becomes synonymous with the death-wish, and we have been told that of all humanity which West hated, he hated himself most. In this context, the epigraph of the book, "John D. Rockefeller would give a cool million to have a stomach like yours," is ambiguous and frightening. Clearly it points to the psychosomatic danger of following the American Dream in its real nature, since Rockefeller and Henry Ford are, for Whipple and the book, types of Horatio Alger. But who is the "you" to whom the epigraph is addressed? Is it the reader (the "cool million," the "hypocrite lecteur," West's *semblable* and *frere*) who can live in that world and read the fantasy-record of its degradation without flinching? Or is it the author himself, in one of his persons so inured to horror and filth that he can treat it lightly, so much of—or aloofly above—degraded mankind that he does not retch as he records?

It may be late in the day to speak of any important American writer, much less Nathanael West, as a Jewish writer, and to involve one's own experience of Jewishness in a discussion of him. To do so invites scorn and misunderstanding. To do so, now that the Jews have made it very nearly to the center of the White Establishment, and other groups are suffering even more intensely their traditional fate of exclusion, runs the risk of seeming dated. Yet Leslie Fiedler in a recent *Partisan* (Summer 1967) called West for *Balso Snell* the first of the modern American Jewish writers, and he is right—at least as far as *Balso* and *Cool Million* are concerned. It is valuable, even necessary, to approach West with some understanding of the Jewish cultural milieu, if only to counteract the effect of his near-convert's fascination with Christ in *Miss Lonelyhearts* and to open up the body of Jewish-Hebrew reference in his books. It may be helpful, although certainly not necessary, for the critic to be personally familiar with the particular cultural shocks which West seems to have been an heir to, however much he tried to avoid or deny them. For whatever degree of universality there is in West's fictions about the American scene, I am convinced that he was an intensely personal writer, with a Freudian's heightened awareness that an author, by indirections, talks of his own wishes and fears, and that his symbols plot his own inner landscape.

FOOTNOTES

1. *Nathanael West: The Ironic Prophet* (Syracuse, 1964).

2. West seems to have been always interested in techniques of the popular arts. Comerchero and others have demonstrated his approximation in *Miss Lonelyhearts* of the comic-strip frame and of cinematic scene and montage.

3. *Nathanael West: An Interpretative Study* (Evanston, 1961). This essay was submitted before the publication of Jay Martin's detailed biography, *Nathanael West: The Art of His Life* (New York, 1970). On some aspects of *Cool Million* my conclusions and Martin's are similar, but his reading of the novel appears to me to have a narrower focus. I would make no significant change on the basis of this biography; I have corrected, however, two minor details about West's life. Martin's chapter on *Cool Million* may be an encouraging mark of the sympathy growing for a book that West thought would be "better than 'Miss Lonelyhearts' " (Martin, 241).

4. A final point on West's names: in the metamorphosis of Nathan Weinstein he "converted" himself from a Hebrew prophet into a disciple of Christ. West's ambivalence about the shadow or substance of names pervades his career. "What a pity childish associations cling to beautiful words such as hernia, making their use as names impossible. Hernia! What a beautiful name for a girl! Hernia Hornstein! Paresis Pearlberg! Paranoia Puntz! How much more pleasing to the ear (and what other sense should a name please?) than Faith Rabinowitz or Hope Hilkowitz" (*Balso Snell*, Ch. 1).

A CONFLUENCE OF VOICES:
THE DAY OF THE LOCUST I

Madden: When *The Day of the Locust* appeared in 1939, Steinbeck's *The Grapes of Wrath* was the number one best seller. Rachel Field's *All This, and Heaven Too,* Daphne du Maurier's *Rebecca,* Ethel Vance's *Escape,* Marjorie Kinnan Rawlings' *The Yearling,* and Sholem Ash's *The Nazarene* were also on the list, along with novels by Marquand and Christopher Morley. *Mein Kampf* by Adolph Hitler was a nonfiction best seller.

Oswald Spengler: The present is a civilized, emphatically not a cultured time-period . . . we have to reckon with the hard cold facts of a *late* life. . . . Of great painting or great music there can no longer be, for Western people, any question.

Madden: As I continued to search for a title for this collection, these possibilities occurred to me: "The Cheat of the West"; "Nathanael West: The Cheaters and the Cheated"; and "Nathanael West and the Confidence Game." The original title of *The Locust* was *The Cheated.*

J. K. Huysmans: Over the whole of Paris . . . there stretched an unbroken network of confidence tricks. . . .

W. C. Fields: Never give a sucker an even break.

171

P. T. Barnum: There's a sucker born every minute.

Warwick Wadlington: Because West's characters are still urgently trying to have life, to redeem the promise of which they have been swindled, they are gaudy and violent, like Melville's more accomplished masqueraders. The elaborate exactness with which West catches their grotesquerie is a skill that manages to be at once extravagant and austere. It is that of a practiced liar dealing with people whose lives are lies.

Wilde-Lord Henry: It is only shallow people who do not judge by appearances. The true mystery of the world is the visible, not the invisible. . . .

Donald Torshiana: In allowing Tod to see through the eyes of Goya, Daumier, Magnasco, Rosa, Guardi, and Desiderio, West has permitted us to view the local chaos of Hollywood as a timeless image, a subject worthy of man's meditation, and a symptom crying for Biblical allusion and the utterance of prophetic art.

Fiedler: Apocalyptics was his special province; and for the sake of a vision of the End of Things, he was willing to sacrifice what his Communist mentors had taught him was a true picture of society. Once out of his books, he felt obliged to apologize for his vision (writing to Jack Conroy, for instance, "If I put into *The Day of the Locust* any of the sincere, honest people who work here and are making such a great, progressive fight . . . [he is talking about Hollywood] the whole fabric of the peculiar half-world which I attempted to create would be badly torn."

James M. Cain (responding to the charge by scriptwriters that the studios want only the worst a writer can do): No doubt they pity themselves handsomely, but I'll tell you why their effort was turned down. It was no goddamn good.

Raymond Chandler: No doubt I have learned a lot from Hollywood. Please do not think I completely despise it, because I don't. The proof of that may be that every producer I have ever worked for I would work for again, and every one of them, in spite of my tantrums, would be glad to have me.

F. Scott Fitzgerald: [Hollywood is] a strange conglomeration of a few excellent overtired men making the pictures, and as dismal a crowd of fakes and hacks at the bottom as you can imagine.

Faulkner: My general impression of Hollywood is that of a very wealthy, over-grown country town. . . . I know very few actors, but the ones with whom I did come in contact were normal, hard-working people, leading much saner lives than we are led to believe.

Fitzgerald: . . . all gold rushes are essentially negative.

Edmund Wilson (to West): Why don't you get out of that ghastly place? You're an artist and really have no business there.

James Agee: I see a lot of people [in Hollywood] and like most of them. Compared with most of the intellectual literary acquaintances I avoid in New York (who are—wrongly—my image of New York) they are mostly very warmhearted, outgoing, kind, and happy and unpretentious—the nicest kind of company. . . .

Martin: [West] spoke to a Republic producer of wanting to adapt C. S. Forester's *African Queen*—later adapted by James Agee—and Crane's *Red Badge of Courage*.

★ ★ ★ ★

Martin: [West's] case was special . . . his talent for script-writing was so different from his novelistic skills that the one never interfered with the other. West always recognized the differences between the two forms. . . . Most of

West's films during 1939-40 were ... inspired by his responsiveness to the mass, collective dreams of the age. ... The very titles of West's pictures hint both at their quality and at their character.

Madden: Beauty Parlor (1933) was about a manicurist; *Ticket to Paradise* (1936), West's first produced picture, based on a *Cosmopolitan* story, is about a business man who has amnesia; *Follow Your Heart* (1936), based on an original story by Dana Burnett, is about a well known singer; *Gangs of New York* (1938), with Charles Bickford and Ann Dvorak, is about a police officer; *Jim Hanvey— Detective* (1937), with Guy Kibbee, was based on a *Collier's* story; *Rhythm in the Clouds* (1937), with Warren Hull, is about a struggling female song writer; *Ladies in Distress* (1938) is based on a *Liberty* story; *Bachelor Girl,* about the scion of a department store family, ended up in the dream-dump; *Born to Be Wild* (1938), the first story on which West worked entirely alone, is about a truck driver; *Orphans of the Street* (1938) starred Robert Livingston; *Osceola* was an ill-fated original about the Indian problem; *The Squealer* was an unfinished script about an old time gangster in conflict with new style gangsters; *Five Came Back* (1939), with Chester Morris and Wendy Barrie, is about a plane crash among savages, with an anarchist among the passengers (Dalton Trumbo worked on the script); *Flight South* was an ill-fated original about the slaughter of waterfowl; *The Spirit of Culver* (1939), with Jackie Cooper and Freddie Bartholomew, about life in a military academy, evoked a sense of the Depression; *I Stole a Million* (1939), starring George Raft and Claire Trevor, about a man who robs a bank but then settles down to a normal life, was one of the best received of West's scripts (he received sole credit); *Before the Fact* was perhaps his best script, but it was rewritten by Hitchcock's staff and released as *Suspicion; Men Against the Sky* (1940), with Richard Dix, Edmund Lowe, and Wendy Barrie, was very well done and West received solo credit; *Stranger on the Third*

Floor (1940) starred Peter Lorre; *A Cool Million: A Screen Story* was never filmed; *Bird in Hand* was about a young stockbroker; *Amateur Angel* is about a geography professor involved with gangsters. These scripts were written for Columbia, Republic, and RKO.

Martin: Only in two . . . pictures was West able to express on film aspects of his personal commitments. . . . [In *The President's Mystery*] West indulged himself in the mass dream of a political utopia. . . . [It] was highly praised by liberal reviewers. . . .

Meyer Levin: [It is] the first Hollywood film in which a liberal thesis is carried out to its logical conclusion.

Martin: West editorialized even more in a movie of 1937, *It Could Happen to You*. This was the Republic Studio's version of *A Cool Million* mixed well with Sinclair Lewis's *It Can't Happen Here*.

Madden: The day has come when West's image in *Balso Snell* of excrement falling on the audience is reversed in a Hollywood movie, *The Magic Christian*, in which characters willingly dunk themselves in a vat of crap for money.

Martin: [West] wrote his novels out of the imagination of personal and collective disaster, but his film scripts out of his imagination of fulfillment.

★ ★ ★ ★

Carolyn See: Another sub-genre . . . of popular, formalized fiction is the Hollywood novel, which takes the whole American history and the American dream as its province . . . the form—like the western, the novel of violence, the spy story—speaks over the heads of its creators. It is the property of the public, a popular form which can be mastered by its authors but hardly ever transcended.

Madden: Some of the best Hollywood novels are: Evelyn Waugh's *The Loved One*; F. Scott Fitzgerald's *The Last*

Tycoon; Raymond Chandler's *The Little Sister*; James M. Cain's *Serenade*; Budd Shulberg's *What Makes Sammy Run*; Wright Morris' *Love Among the Cannibals*; Norman Mailer's *The Deer Park*.

Agee: Movies about Hollywood have always been better than novels about Hollywood (barring only Nathanael West's) because they are made by people who know the world and the medium they are talking about instead of by people who don't, and who have dropped in only to visit, hack or, in their opinion, slum.

Robert Richardson: Pirandello's *Shoot,* subtitled *The Notebooks of Serafino Gubbio, Cinematograph Operator,* Fitzgerald's *The Last Tycoon,* and Nathanael West's *The Day of the Locust* . . . are certainly the best of the novels that try to realize the significance of the mechanical and industrial aspects of the movies. Pirandello's novel uses film-making as a vast metaphor for the modern condition. . . . it is fiction that is soaked in movie technique. . . . West's [novel] is perhaps the most cinematic of the three.

Pirandello-Gubbio: Already my eyes and my ears too, from force of habit, are beginning to see and hear everything in the guise of this rapid, quivering, ticking mechanical reproduction. I don't deny it; the outward appearance is light and vivid. We move, we fly. And the breeze stirred by our flight produces an alert, joyous, keen agitation, and sweeps away every thought. On! . . . Outside, there is a continuous glare, and incessant giddiness: everything flickers and disappears.

Wright Morris-Horter (Hollywood lyricist): If you lived in a world of clichés, as I do, some of them of the type you coined yourself, you may not realize how powerful they can be. . . . You've got to take what's phony, if it's all you've got, and make it real.

Carolyn See: . . . the hard-boiled attitude as an ethic is implicit throughout *The Day of the Locust*. Claude Estee

. . . controls the artificiality by parodying it. . . . West was so taken by the character and the posture that he first wrote part of the novel in Estee's first person. . . . Estee, like Tod Hackett . . . Philip Marlowe (or Jake Barnes), has a "code" in which manners come first, then philosophy. *You are what you pretend to be*, and enough flippancies, put-ons, sight-gags, and trash-talking will build the armored mechanism that a good man needs to be in order to live in a bad world.

Kingsley Widmer: West's insight was that the basic American repressed character was to merge with the Hollywood counterfeit—as it has in our puritanic decadence—providing the largest masquerade of civilization. Essentially, the historic Hollywood is dead; but just as essentially, America has become Hollywood. The "mock riot," the rehearsal of debacle, properly epitomizes it. . . . West compassionately perceived the insatiable longing for some final masquerade ending negation. Yet the end to a life of masquerade is only a masquerade become all reality. And that is the saddest as well as truest apocalypse of all.

West: [Tod] was amused by the strong feeling of satisfaction this dire conclusion gave him. Were all prophets of doom and destruction such happy men?

Martin: . . . if he could satisfy millions of film viewers, West must have asked himself, why could he reach no more than 1,500 with his novels?

1. Henry Wilcoxon, left, in *The President's Mystery*, Republic, 1936. With permission of National Telefilm Associates.

2. Kent Taylor, Grant Withers, Edmund Lowe, unknown, Wendy Barrie in *Men Against the Sky*, RKO, 1940.

3. Ralph Byrd, Ward Bond, Robert Emmett Keane in *Born To Be Wild*, Republic, 1938. With permission of National Telefilm Associates.

4. Nathanael West photographed against a process shot on a Hollywood set. Jay Martin.

5. Chester Morris, John Carradine, Wendy Barrie, Lucille Ball, Patrick Knowles, woman and child unknown, Aubrey Smith and Allan Jenkins, in *Five Came Back*, RKO, 1939.

6. Stuart Irwin, middle, Douglas Fawley, right, in *It Could Happen To You*, Republic, 1939. With permission of National Telefilm Associates.

7. Freddie Bartholomew, Jackie Cooper in *The Spirit of Culver*, Universal, 1939.

8. Lee Tracy in *Advice To The Lovelorn*, 20th Century, 1933. With permission of Twentieth Century Fox Film Corporation.

9.   Claire Trevor, George Raft in *I Stole A Million*, Universal, 1939.

10. Montgomery Clift, Myrna Loy, Robert Ryan in *Lonelyhearts*, United Artists, 1959.

THE LAST MASQUERADE:
THE DAY OF THE LOCUST
By Kingsley Widmer

In *The Day of the Locust* Nathanael West describes his denizens of the Hollywood tide pools as "masqueraders." As with the anguished dead horse at the bottom of a swimming pool in one scene, they all turn out to be rubber imitation bad jokes. Yet West's sardonic detailing suggests that the masquerade applies not only to his characters and the dream factories but to the houses, the costumes, the relationships, and the sensibilities of all southern California, and beyond.

As I understand West's masquerade, it is no mere metaphor. A decade after West's novel, and the historic Hollywood near its end, I washed up in those same brightly stagnant purlieus. A self-identified writer with some naively larcenous Hollywood ambitions, I temporarily played the roles of free-lance advertising hack, market researcher, and whatever other surrogate arts with which I could connivingly connect. However, I kept up the payments on my new car by pretending a more utilitarian craft, template-maker in a Santa Monica aircraft factory neatly triangulated between my Malibu beach rental and Hollywood. By making metal patterns all night (the graveyard shift) and by foregoing the usual ways of dreaming (asleep), I could afford being a not very successful Hollywood self-promoter during the day and an artist-pretender during the evening: a multiple imitation-person.

Eventually, I discovered that many of my co-workers were also masquerading: an actress pretending to be a time-clerk, an assistant director playing at jig-building, a cameraman hobbying with airframe blueprints, an actor practicing a quaint scene in the tool crib. My benchmate was also a writer, disguised, he explained, as a cam-maker in order to accumulate naturalistic detail for scenarios. Not everyone in the shop seemed to be a counterfeiter. At the next bench, for salutary example, was a scruffily dressed and taciturn middle-aged working man who spent his breaks studying the racing results in the paper. At least, I thought, this sad little tool-maker dreaming of long-shots was for real — until I bumped into him one afternoon as he got out of a new Cadillac in front of one of Beverly Hills' most expensive bistros. As a gesture of noblesse to my peasant shock, he removed his homburg, waved me in past the obsequious headwaiter and, over a double of the best cognac which I imitatingly ordered, he gave me to know that he was a bigtime professional gambler, temporarily forced to counterfeit a trivial trade to display a "visible means of support" to the legal guardians. Just how much of this was costuming I had no way of knowing. And probably, to make a Westean point, he didn't either.

Such imitation lives, like screen images, are often cleverly quick-cut; the gambler-template-maker soon disappeared. His benchmate, who turned out to be a sometime war-hero and actor with alimony problems, could provide no enlightenment. Perhaps the horseplayer had yet other masquerades to template. Or even, perhaps, like myself, he finally understood the point of a farmer-grandfather's warning that "ta sell corn ya got ta have corn," and gave up Hollywood ambitions.

From my experience, then, I see Nathanael West as a sharply sad-eyed documentor of a particular reality. I enter this as a caveat against those who see the author of *The Day of the Locust* as primarily a fantast of the grotesque. West, I agree, is an artful stylist, one of the important American adaptors—along with such as Henry Miller—of the surrealist image and the concretely fantastic disjunction. But they apply to an actual world. West, I would also argue, is to American fiction what Zamiatin is to Russian: the small but brilliant descendent of Dostoyevsky, who very specifically influenced them both in their compulsive victims and ironic crucifixions and mockingly anguished prophecies of suffering and destruction and nihilism. And *The Day of the Locust,* from my reading of about four dozen Hollywood novels, is probably the best of that curious subgenre of the reality of fictional corruption. West achieved distinction in his intense mannerist expressiveness. Some of his descriptions—with dusk a "violet piping, like a Neon tube, outlined the tops of the ugly, hump-backed hills"; with night "through a slit in the blue serge sky poked a grained moon that looked like an enormous bone button"—not only most aptly catch the scene (at least back in the times when you could see the mountains and the moon) but also most pertinently suggest the synthetic fabrication which is part of the larger masquerade theme. Similarly, West's precision catches the fusion of corruption and naivete and of apathy and violence which marks his so American characters.

We can also see West as the progenitor of the bitterly wry laugh at the ornately grotesque and sardonically pitiful which became known as "black humor" in his descendents. That victim's smile, as with his narrating Tod Hackett, covers a desperate ambivalence. As with the writer Tod describes in *The Day of the Locust,* the author, too, played out "an involved comic rhetoric that permitted him to express his moral indignation and still keep . . . [his] worldliness and wit." But the mature West is no Pynchon or Barth—not nearly so clever and uncommitted. For he is—how shall we say it?—more simply suffering and serious about the actual. In the first chapter of *The Day of the Locust* he describes his Hollywood masqueraders and bemusedly reports on the grotesquery but concludes with earnest poignancy that "few things are sadder than the truly monstrous." (For other aspects of his writings, see my "The Sweet and Savage Prophecies of Nathanael West," *The Thirties,* ed. Warren French [Deland, Fla., 1967]. For the Hollywood and literary context, see several of the essays in *Tough Guy Writers of the Thirties*, ed. David Madden [Carbondale, Ill., 1968], especially Carolyn See, "The Hollywood Novel: The American Dream Cheat," who discusses other Hollywood novels and emphasizes a related theme: *"You are what you pretend to be."* For some detailing of West's use of the actual Hollywood, see Jay Martin, *Nathanael West* [New York, 1970], but, as I point out in a review of that book in the *Journal of Modern Literature*, I [Winter, 1970], much of his material requires reinterpretation.)

The masquerades are monstrous, comic and bitter pathetic gestures and roles by which one lives, and dies. The more one pursues West's Hollywood, the more actual rather than merely artful it becomes. I once thought the cockfight scene in *The Day of the Locust* a fancying of the bizarre only digressively related to the rest of the novel by the motif of fraudulent violence. In fact, as news files from the Thirties confirm, that banned sport was widespread—as central to the subculture of California then as the briefer fad of marathon dancing in McCoy's *They Shoot Horses, Don't They?*—and can still be viewed in Latin ghettos such as East Los Angeles or Atascadero. West's cockfight scene may revealingly masquerade the characters' violent fraud but also reports their immediate reality. Just as West sees (in *Miss Lonelyhearts*) human warping and suffering as real, not as something to be explained or ameliorated away, so, in *The Day of the Locust,* he sees the unreality represented by Hollywood as devastatingly real, in an actual time and place. Hollywood simply realizes the destruction of cultural vitality—West's major preoccupation—which Miss Lonelyhearts summarized: "Men have always fought their misery with dreams. Although dreams were once powerful, they have been made puerile . . . . Among many betrayals, this one is the worst."

Thus *The Day of the Locust* might appropriately be related to its special subgenre, the literature of cultural betrayal, the "Hollywood novel" or "Southern California rococco," as long as we do not reduce it to mere literature. The grotesqueries of such fictions belong to the continuing historical reality of California which, of course, becomes the all-American future. The main issue is a desperate meaninglessness.

In probably the most earnest of the Hollywood novels, Budd Schulberg's *What Makes Sammy Run?*, a liberal sociologist (lightly masked as a writer-narrator) concludes, in ultimate self-justification after having capitulated to the unscrupulous producer Sammy: "I saw one of my own jobs [movies], a stinker if there ever was one, but with one scene in it that sang . . . . Hollywood may be full of phonies, mediocrities, dictators, and good men who have lost their way, but there is something that draws you there that you should not be ashamed of." What is that "something" that drew so many American novelists? Is it the one visual image, the single good scene (to which the writer makes only a small contribution) in a stinking bad movie, that provides the total meaning of Hollywood? Like simple greed, that would be a parody of all meaning.

When I asked Budd Schulberg a politer version of the question, after he lectured on the Hollywood of the Thirties to a class of mine, he stutteringly replied, "I guess the something was really politics, hope." Surely the last scene of *The Day of the Locust,* by active leftist Nathanael West, the resentful rioting of the "lower middle class" mob of American fascists, was the politics of the future and a hope that had been lost. Still, the disproportions, the awful and awesome incongruities, not only pervade the genre but almost everything about the historic Hollywood. Never did so many make so much of so little.

Such absurd contrast between material and meaning, appearance and reality, characterized the earliest Hollywood novels, such as *Merton of the Movies*. Harry Wilson's genially elaborate playfulness emphasized the discrepancies between his hero's serious intentions and the comic results. A doggedly simple Iowa boy plays his heart out as the great lover and sterling hero. In the mechanical jogging of early film technique, his moral intensity can come out only as Sennett farce. Given the technology, sincere American idealism provides slapstick. The moral still holds for our culture.

More than a generation later, in *Love Among the Cannibals,* Wright Morris puts his Hollywood songwriter in the Lawrencean love of his life. In the absurdity of the late-Hollywood ethos, his passionate intensity can only create a third-rate popular song. Peeling off the masquerade, like peeling away at Peer Gynt's onion, leaves nothing—"You strip down to / The Essentially / Inessential you," as his song has it. The masquerade is all.

The Day of the Locust appeared midway in time between *Merton of the Movies* and *Love Among the Cannibals,* and seems continuous with them. The mock-heroic comedy, then, goes beyond art to the thing itself: Hollywood. In the initial studio scene of West's novel, we have the filming of the Battle of Waterloo; it ends in the disastrous collapse of the prop—Mont St. Jean—a production judgment ironically analogous to Napoleon's. History itself turns into the mock-heroic. For the novelist, as for the tourist who stared in charmed disbelief at the one-dimensional grandeur of the sets, everything turns into a prop.

The characters in *The Day of the Locust,* as in most of the more perceptive Hollywood fictions, turn out to be the props of artists who fear they have themselves become the properties of an unbelievable and puerile myth. As with West's would-be starlet, Faye Greener, who acquires the money for her father's fancy funeral as a call girl—not as an act of guilt or love but simply as mock-heroic role playing of the devoted daughter—the people are as amoral as the fake scenery. It is all a question, as the writer within the novel says of Mrs. Jennings whorehouse, of "skillful packaging . . . a triumph of industrial design."

Even F. Scott Fitzgerald, who described himself as a "spoiled priest" and always desperately tried to give moral weight to his American success stories, cannot avoid turning a moral scene into a pratfall in Hollywood. The sweet young narrator in *The Last Tycoon* lectures her producer-father on charity. Then she opens a closet door and a naked secretary falls out. Or, in a crucial scene, two women ride on the gigantic statue head of the Goddess Siva in a studio lot flood. Not only is the prop absurd, but, when we later learn that one woman is the heroine and the other a prostitute, so is all symbolic portentousness of the scene.

Thus, almost inspite of themselves, the Hollywood novelists force us to see symbols and morals as merely props to other props. In Norman Mailer's *The Deer Park* the ostensibly love-struck narrator and the beautiful movie queen carry on sexually while she carries on a telephone conversation with someone else. The prop takes over, with the lovely lady fornicating later with someone else in a phonebooth. The incongruities, as with West's scene of a lascivious dwarf and an over-sized prostitute, or Mailer's scene of a producer lecturing his stenographer on morals and then dropping her between his knees for *fellatio,* become subject and norm of the Hollywood material.

When you can't tell phonebooths from boudoirs and prostitutes from heroines and grotesqueries from moralities, then the material may properly be called "Hollywood." By similar twisting, the erotic fantasies become desexed. All but the catatonic audience soon recognize the Manly Hero as really a faggot, the Sweet Innocent Girl as a whore, the Passionate Artist (like West's Tod Hackett) as really an impotent voyeur. The figures of virtue, of course, such as Mailer's power-elite or West's fanatic lower-middle class refugees from the Protestant ethos, use moral assertion as warmup for nasty perversion. It adds up to an inverted morality play, in which the only moral is the inversion.

West elaborates at some length the masquerading of Harry Greener, ex-vaudevillean become silver polish huckster. Harry puts on an obviously phony misery act for sympathy and then suddenly finds himself actually ill and dying. The masquerade has become the reality but the very counterfeiting makes him unable to realize, or know how to respond to, his own reality. A generation later, Allison Lurie in *The Nowhere City* (probably the best of the Hollywood novels of the 1960s), has her prim, repressed and disdainful New

England heroine act-out in Hollywood as a bleached, free-wheeling sex-pot, and then with smooth mockery suggests that as her authentic character. The masquerade, like the Hollywood prop, has taken over.

Even in those drearily tendentious and titillating historical romances of Hollywood, such as Robert Carson's *The Magic Lantern* and Harold Robbins' *The Dream Merchants,* the twisted role-playings often overwhelm the tritely mawkish intentions of the hack authors. An unexpected mockery infuses the patterns of the ups-and-downs in fame and fortune of the naively vicious and shrewdly bathetic figures drawn from the historical record of the movie industry. Such built-in burlesque even shows through in the genteel realism of James Hilton's Hollywood as a "democratic deluxe concentration camp" (*Morning Journey*) or the campy "nice Hollywood" of Laura Hobson (*The Celebrity*) or the exacting literalism of the "corrupted dream" of John O'Hara (*Hope of Heaven*). These are all bad movies, even when unfilmed.

In almost all the stories, when we find intelligence at work in Hollywood it insists upon its impotence. Granted, the tone varies from James T. Farrell's exposing flat sarcasm ("$1,000 A Week") about the irrelevance of the artist through the urbane mannering of exactly the same point by Bemelmans (*Dirty Eddy*). Morris' cynical "ex-cornbelt Shelley," Earl Horter, is no more exempt than Fitzgerald's naively literary Bennington girl, Cecelia Bradley. Yet with hardly any exceptions—we can allow a misplaced touch of it to Schulberg's ponderous melodrama-memoir around Fitzgerald (*The Disenchanted*)—such fictions do not even pretend to be tragedies of the defeated artist but only of artists-as-masqueraders. (I suppose the only real Hollywood defeats of artists would be by exclusion, as with Luis Buñuel, which only properly confirmed that Hollywood and art have little connection.) Placed in the Hollywood scene, each artist-intellectual finally responds like the skeptic in the movie audience in the darkened theatre; he discovers that he, too, is laughing or crying with everyone else because the image has become himself. The artist imitates the Hollywood that imitates the artist.

Tod, West's artist-narrator, finds himself hopelessly loving the vacuous heroine, Faye, whom he must also despise. The degraded muse diabolically attracts, even with her narcissistic egotism, ruthlessness combined with stupidity, and bitch-goddess' call to destruction (Tod reflects that "her invitation wasn't to pleasure, but . . . closer to murder than to love"). The fatuousness, even the very dehumanization, seem the essential appeal. In *The Day of the Locust* no man escapes the yearning—sophisticated writer, primitive Mexican, voracious dwarf, drug-store cowboy, middle-aged puritan, perceptive artist. For each, she is the masturbatory muse.

Dos Passos caught many of the characteristics, though externally, in his relentless portrayal of the rise to stardom out of the energizing pathetic-sordid background of the totally untalented Margo Dowling in *The Big Money*. Within that pattern, of course, appeared some variations, such as whether the bitch was complete sexual exploiter (as with Aben Kandel's Kitty Doone in "You Twinkle Only Once") or was also erratic victim of the sexual mythology (as with Mailer's Lulu in *The Deer Park*). But in most of the fictional figures, as with such semi-real people as Harlow and Monroe, there was little more sensuality than personality in the charade of mechanical libido that for half a century created the muses of America.

Yet the sardonic novelists (West, Mailer, Morris, etc.) grotesquely adore the erotic dieties that the sentimental novelists (Fitzgerald, Bemelmans, the romancers) mawkishly adore. No one, as West dramatically insists, escapes. As with Apulieus and the adoration of Isis, the most painful masquerade comes from *not* worshipping the arbitrary deity. Perhaps the absence of love becomes heightened in its parody and, as with the mystics' sense of deprivation, creates the reality. Certainly most of the Hollywood novels expose the love goddess, but it turns out to be by way of embracement. The more disinterested writers, proper satirists of southern California scenes, such as Huxley and Waugh, lessen the erotic self-enchantment both by snobbery and the insistence on mortality (*After Many A Summer Dies the Swan* and *The Loved One*). But no matter how mocking, we discover the American novelist merging with what he exposes.

As the American novelists record it, the studios did for onanistic images what Ford did for automobiles. The Big Con of Hollywood becomes a penultimate image of American aggrandizement. While a Dos Passos or Schulberg emphasized its social class origin, even Fitzgerald and the historical romancers were driven to economic images of the last frontier and goldrush. Though focusing elsewhere, West, too, repeatedly makes the economic point. Yet, in retrospect, the masqueraders' denuding of selfhood seems rather more crucial. Quite antithetical moralists like Mailer and Morris make essentially the same point, the loss of identity demanded by the luxurious games. Even the novelists of manners, such as Raymond Chandler (*The Little Sister*) and Allison Lurie (*The Nowhere City*), who used the Hollywood decor and absurdity, most essentially see it as an image of the loss of all character. Thus West (and Henry Miller in the Hollywood sketches of *The Air-Conditioned Nightmare*) rightly see the surreal congregations of the dissociated and defeated and deranged as the new America. Nothing fully human can sustain itself behind the poses; the aggrandizement now leads nowhere—the final price of the masquerade.

These Hollywood fictions, however, are not really satires of decadence in traditional senses. Even given the style of a Juvenal describing Rome (less his rigid moral nostalgia), one could not find a fall from Republican *virtu* to Imperial corruption. Hollywood may have helped that happen to the rest of America, but not to itself. Some of the novelists (Fitzgerald, Mailer, even the fatuous Libby Block in *The Hills of Beverley*) take metaphors from the classical satirists of decadence, but they do not persuade that there ever was an authentic tycoon or imperium or even grand style. It was masquerade from the founding. In the words of two of the earlier Hollywood novels: "the art of the motion picture started plumb senile" and what we mean by Hollywood "arose from a swindle and it never changed." Some collectors of Hollywoodiana try to proclaim a decline and fall, as do *littérateurs* turned film critics (James Agee, Dwight MacDonald, even Pauline Kael), and assume the classical three ages: from obscure folk origins (vaudeville, mime comedy, popular melodrama) through the Golden Age of kingly directors (Griffith, Chaplin) into technological decadence (lavish and pseudo-moral). However, authentic cinema art seems to have appeared with intermittent rareness throughout the entire history. And the issues of society and character which most concerned the novelists always turned up the exploitation and corruption and falsity. No rise and fall, no focus, really, for the traditional satirist's savage indignation. West was right, then, in his essential tone—the pathos of the monstrous—and in his technique—the empty masquerading. This is a democratic replay of the grotesques of a Propertius and Trimalchio's feast domesticated in Southern California.

Otherwise put, the Hollywood fictions depend less on satire than on exposé, telling it as it is. As West perceptively realized, telling the story of the purlieus and worshippers of Hollywood rather than that of the industry and its royalty more essentially delineates the masquerade. Its creation was a puerile fraud but its effect was horrendously significant. Exposé often played an important role in the history of the novel—letting the literate middle class in on what was happening—but properly enjoyed a distinctive American emphasis. Whether the subject was the Puritan mind, whaling, war, the Midwestern small town, migrant laborers, bohemians and beats, or blacks and student rebels, or exposures of normative predatory institutions such as advertising and academia and Hollywood, artistry subserves the sense of the actual. No doubt the process served the outraged American innocence which it both revealed and fortified. The exposures, it seems, do not reform the actuality—migrant work, movie making, coal mining, professoring, militarism, go on much the same—but the revelations provide a moral masquerade.

I detect in most of the Hollywood novels, with varying

degrees of consciousness, a desperate effort to find a bedrock reality under the masquerading. Struggling to explain the pseudo-greatness of the Hollywood "giants," the force with which they pursued shadow shows, the novelists are curiously driven to "inexplicable megalomania" or simply "the urge towards total exhaustion." West shows this emptying of sensibility unto madness as the mass effect. It ends in the sex-and-violence exhaustion of fantasy and resentment in an otherwise valueless world. Nothing really happens, nothing is thought or felt, not even the experience of nothing. West's artist reflects, amidst rape fantasies, on the nature of would-be starlet Faye near the end of *The Day of the Locust:*

> Nothing could hurt her. She was like a cork. No matter how rough the sea got, she would go dancing over the same waves that sank iron ships and tore away piers of reinforced concrete. . . . Wave after wave reared its ton on ton of solid water and crashed down only to have her spin gaily away. . . . a very pretty cork, gilt with a glittering fragment of mirror set in its top. The sea in which it danced was beautiful, green in the trough of the waves and silver at their tips. But for all their moondriven power, they could do no more than net the bright cork for a moment in a spume of intricate lace. Finally it was set down on a strange shore where a savage with pork-sausage fingers and a pimpled butt picked it up and hugged it to his sagging belly. Tod recognized the fortunate man; he was one of Mrs. Jennings [whorehouse] customers. (406)

Vintage West, this devastating playfulness: the disparate images ("spume of intricate lace" and "pimpled butt"); the parody of the media processing (the thing of beauty turned into a burlesque of a South Sea scenario); the insights into the total masqueraders (machined prettiness, narcissistic mirror, invulnerability to experience); and yet the artist-author's mixed enthrallment and disgust with the "pretty cork."

As West wrote in *Miss Lonelyhearts,* only in the snake-mirrors of "hysteria" can such deadness "take on a semblance of life." Socially, that hysteria is the mob scene, the day of apocalypse. West's timorously chiliastic artist-narrator, gathering his expressionistic fragments for his masterpiece, "The Burning of Los Angeles," can find reality only in the image of the end. And so with West. Yet we have curious reversals here. "The Burning of Los Angeles" is a highly plausible image—many Angelenos half-expect it to happen each fall, with the frenzied spread of brush fires in the peculiar conditions of the basin, with its greasewood and Santa Ana desert winds. But notice also that West plays with that sense of unreality so obsessive in almost all Hollywood novels. We apparently should see the earlier party scenes as rehearsals for the final scene—one is described as a "mock riot"—but the "real" riot becomes yet another dress rehearsal for the ultimate fantasy of the artist. In three or four senses, the final image is only "another picture"—yet another mock riot, a movie premiere, the artist-narrator's preparatory scenes for his masterpiece of apocalypse, and Nathanael West's riotous mockery, as well as the image of the promised end.

Surprisingly, a similar sense of the end runs, like a fuse, through many of the Hollywood fictions. Even Bemelman's urbane Cassard has a vision of the population fleeing and the fish floating belly-up, though it ends as a random image with no place to go. In the sentimental histories of Hollywood, the fall of a producer, a movie technique, a fortune, or a cliché, suggests similar world sundering significance, but without effect. The reader must feel considerable bewilderment at the vastness of the calamity supposedly contingent on the break-up of a shoddy dream. As in Morris and Carson, the frenzy of disintegration in an alien pleasure land gives a cumulative destructiveness that denies the attempt at comic ease, yet, as with *The Day of the Locust,* much of the scene is essentially comedy. We cannot tell—nor, apparently, can Norman Mailer—whether the demonic pimp of *Deer Park,* Marion O'Faye, can finally create, beyond depravity and violence, "a sin so much greater, so terrible and enormous that God himself must blanch," or whether this comes as just another narcoticizing dream of an aging delinquent—the character and the author. Even in the horrendous ends of masquerades we find the nagging sense of unreality.

Alone and despairing in Los Angeles one New Year's Eve

a generation ago, I drifted about downtown. So did thousands of other young, and not so young, inadequately narcoticized delinquents. The aimlessly circling crowd grew, clotted here and there around a curse that offered a fight or a scream that suggested a rape. There were random bits of violence, several plate glass windows shattered, many dresses furtively torn, a few arrests, a few injuries, but finally nothing, not even an adequate mob scene, could find its form. We were all avid spectators for some image of a promising end but all cheated of even the hysteria for which we longed.

So it is, in spite of the overstatements of some critics, with West's concluding, and quite unZolaesque, mob scene. One stomping, some pressing, ripping, shoving; the sirens going, a few injuries, a half-comic simulated hysteria at the end. But little truly happens. West, yet again, remained faithful to his materials. The desperately bored and cheated crowds of *The Day of the Locust* provide only their own image as the end of life. In historic fact, the mob fascism which West, replaying his own ending to the burlesque *A Cool Million*, half-prophesied, has yet to come to full life in America. Our totalitarianisms slyly develop from other directions. The "lower middle class" mob was tricked into safer and isolating fantasies of the lavish boob tube culture, and so their rages usually end in the mechanized passivity which is the basic, and base, condition of the mass technological society.

The ravaging of the land by the petit bourgeoise locusts, as West saw, rests in the culture of social and individual malnutrition which was Hollywood. In combining his Sherwood Anderson Middle American, Homer, with the cheaters, the technological fantasts, West's insight was that the basic American repressed character was to merge with the Hollywood counterfeit—as it has in our puritanic decadence—providing the largest masquerade of civilization. Essentially, the historic Hollywood is dead; but just as essentially, America has become Hollywood. The "mock riot," the rehearsal of debacle, properly epitomizes it. Rather better than most of the other Hollywood fictionists, West compassionately perceived the insatiable longing for some final masquerade-ending negation. Yet the end to a life of masquerade is only a masquerade become all reality. And that is the saddest as well as truest apocalypse of all.

A CONFLUENCE OF VOICES:
THE DAY OF THE LOCUST II

Richard Chase: [*Sanctuary*] offers ... passages of humor
that give it a place among the modern novels of grotesque
comedy as practiced in their various ways by Conrad,
Kafka, Nathanael West, and others who have brought to
the older comic tradition of Dickens and Dostoevski a
modern or "existentialist" tone.

Kafka: ... the crowd broke up, and no one had the right to
be dissatisfied with what he had seen, no one but the
hunger-artist, always only he.

Fiedler: It is not accidental that both these anguish-ridden
comedians [West and Kafka], as uncompromisingly
secular as they are profoundly religious, should be Jews.

Celine-Ferdinand: 'Broadway' it was called. ... Like a
running sore this unending street, with all of us at the
bottom of it, filling it from side to side, from one sorrow
to the next, moving towards an end no one has ever seen,
the end of all the streets in the world. ... It was pleasant
inside the movie house, warm and comfortable. Immense
organs, as gentle as those in a cathedral, but a warm
cathedral, as rich as thighs. Not a moment lost. You
plunge straight into an atmosphere of warm forgiveness.
You only had to let yourself go to feel that the world had
at last become indulgent.

195

T. S. Eliot: Distracted from distraction by distraction. . . .

Martin: Contented to plug along quietly at Universal after his despair over the failure of his play, West had as his office a bungalow near the cowboy Western sets. Reading over the proofs for *The Day of the Locust* he could, like Tod Hackett, walk straight from his office into this fantasy of sets; he could go from the tough actuality of his novel to the fantasies of the *Culver* script, then out to the lot and the sets where those fantasies were made to seem real. It was an absurd circumstance.

West: A group of men and women in riding costume were picnicing. They were eating cardboard food in front of a cellophane waterfall.

J. K. Huysmans: . . . tired of artificial flowers aping real ones, [Des Esseintes] wanted some natural flowers that would look like fakes.

West: The studio lot was . . . a dream dump . . . no dream ever entirely disappears. Somewhere it troubles some unfortunate person and some day, when that person has been sufficiently troubled, it will be reproduced on the lot.

Martin: Like Faye Greener, West daydreamed his scripts.

West: It was a picture of Faye Greener, a still from a two-reel farce in which she had worked as an extra.

West-Faye: I'm going to be a star some day. . . . If I'm not, I'll commit suicide.

West: All these little stories, these little daydreams of [Faye's] were what gave such extraordinary color and mystery to her movements. She seemed always to be struggling in their soft grasp as though she were trying to run in a swamp. . . . She . . . seemed to think that fantasy could be made plausible by a humdrum technique.

Horace McCoy-Ralph Carston: I should have stayed home.

... I hadn't stayed home, I was here, on the famous boulevard, in Hollywood, where miracles happen, and maybe today, maybe the next minute some director would pick me out passing by. ...

West: Faye's affectations ... were so completely artificial that [Tod] found them charming. Being with her was like being backstage during an amateurish, ridiculous play.

Saul Bellow: It was twenty years since [Wilhelm] had appeared on the screen as an extra. He blew the bagpipes in a film called *Annie Laurie*.

Fiedler: The alienated *schlemiel*-heroes of Saul Bellow surely owe something to West's protagonists.

West: If only [Tod] had the courage to wait for [Faye] some night and hit her with a bottle and rape her.

Madden: Faye's father, Harry Greener, was a failure on the stage—and he knew it. He dies in the midst of a "routine."

West: The casket was open and the old man looked quite snug. ... [Harry] looked like the interlocutor in a minstrel show.

Hart Crane: ... and love / a burnt match skating in a urinal—

West: Mrs. Jenning [whorehouse madam] ... ran her business just as other women run lending libraries, shrewdly and with taste.

Walter Allen: The Grapes of Wrath was published in 1939; in the same year appeared another novel which now seems in some ways a sour comment upon it, or at any rate on the almost instinctive westward drive it celebrates. This is Nathanael West's *The Day of the Locust*.

Sherwood Anderson: Wing Biddlebaum ... did not think of himself as in any way a part of the life of the town where he had lived for twenty years. . . . The story of Wing Biddlebaum is a story of hands.

West: [Homer Simpson] got out of bed in sections, like a poorly made automaton, and carried his hands into the bathroom . . . the forty years of his life had been entirely without variety or excitement . . . . Homer was on the side of the flies.

West-Maybelle Loomis: What's Shirley Temple got that [my little Adore] ain't got? . . . . I'm a raw-foodist myself. . . . . Death comes from eating dead things.

West: [Mrs. Loomis'] self-sufficiency made [Tod] squirm and the desire to break its smooth surface with a blow, or at least a sudden obscene gesture, became irresistible.

Bruce Jay Friedman-Joseph's Mother: Did your mother ever let you down?

Friedman: She gave Joseph an ear kiss that seemed overly wet. . . .

Friedman-Mother: Will you please learn to put your last buck down on this baby?

Fiedler: . . . . West's attitudes and devices have been assimilated into what already seems a new convention: that much-touted Black Humor, with which many of our latest writers seem perforce to begin, and the somewhat older practitioners of which (Bruce Jay Friedman, for example) have come to seem in a very few years established models and guides.

West: [Abe Kusich, the dwarf] looked like a ventriloquist's dummy. Miguel grabbed Abe by the throat . . . shifted his grip to his ankles and dashed him against the wall, like a man killing a rabbit against a tree.

Wilde-Lord Henry: Crime belongs exclusively to the lower orders. . . . I should fancy that crime was to them what art is to us, simply a method of procuring extraordinary sensations.

West: But not even the soft wash of dusk could help the houses. Only dynamite. . . . Few things are sadder than the truly monstrous.

Flaubert: The pontiffs of Moloch walked about on the great flagstone, scanning the multitude. An individual sacrifice was necessary, a voluntary oblation to carry the others along with it.

West: [The Mourners] stared back at [Tod] with an expression of vicious, acrid boredom that trembled on the edge of violence. . . . Every day of their lives they read the newspapers and went to the movies. Both fed them on lynchings, murder, sex crimes, explosions, wrecks, love nests, fires, miracles, revolutions, war. . . . They have been cheated and betrayed. They have slaved and saved for nothing.

John Symons: And so there is a great, silent conspiracy between us to forget death. That is why we are active about so many things which we know to be unimportant.

West: [The Announcer] held the microphone out and those near it obligingly roared for him.

Camus-Meursault: And just then it crossed my mind that one might fire, or not fire—and it would come to absolutely the same thing.

T. S. Eliot: After such knowledge, what forgiveness?

West-A Little Man: This is a riot you're in.

West: [Tod] began to imitate the siren as loud as he could.

Max Apple: West and Isaac Babel, who resemble each other as highly self-conscious literary stylists, are even more closely aligned in their relationship to the past. Both writers are literally cut off from the traditional roots of fiction in time and place. Chaos is everywhere the Red Cavalry moves and in every facet of Tod's life in Hollywood. In Russia men speak to each other in the sterile clichés of the Revolution; in Hollywood the characters banter the disembodied jargon of stale fantasies. No character has a "usable past"; each is "boxed in" by the random violence of a particular moment.

Philip Durham: Chandler later referred to West's [*The Day of the Locust*, published the same year as *The Big Sleep*] as excellent in many ways although hardly more than a suicide note.

Chandler: . . . not tragic, not bitter, not even pessimistic. It simply washes its hands of life.

FROM AMERICAN DREAM
TO PAVLOVIAN NIGHTMARE
By Robert I. Edenbaum

At one point in *The Day of the Locust* Tod Hackett searches for Faye Greener on the lot of the movie studio for which he works. He walks past a canvas ocean liner with real lifeboats, a papier maché sphinx on a desert of real sand, a Wild West saloon, a jungle compound, a Paris street. He thinks of the Sargasso Sea: "Just as that imaginary body of water was a history of civilization in the form of a marine junkyard, the studio lot was one in the form of a dream dump. A Sargasso of the imagination! And the dump grew continually, for there wasn't a dream afloat somewhere which wouldn't sooner or later turn up on it, having first been made photographic by plaster, canvas, lath and paint" (353—page references are to *The Complete Works of Nathanael West*, New York, 1957). The dream dump is the central image of *The Day of the Locust*; it represents the ultimate disorder behind a world of shoddy in which everything and everybody is really something else. Still on the studio lot, Tod watches a nightmare version of Waterloo, one in which the Prince of Orange opposes an assistant director in a battle which is lost because Mont St. Jean is still under construction by property men and carpenters. The scene ends with the collapse of the mountain in a comic chaos of plaster, canvas, lath and paint. But the studio catastrophe and chaos is merely analagous to the catastrophe and chaos incipient in the plaster and lath dream-world-turned-nightmare of Hollywood itself.

201

The Day of the Locust is structured on Tod Hackett's juxtaposition of two levels of existence, of reality, if you will, in his paintings of Hollywood: the world of the grotesques—Abe the dwarf, Faye the would-be star, Harry the has-been (or never was) clown, Earle Shoop the street-corner cowboy from Arizona; and the world of the midwesterners who come to California to die, represented in part by Homer Simpson. This counterpoint becomes a basic structural element in the novel: the midwesterners provide, by allusion and appearance, a constant ground against which the grotesques perform. An additional element is provided by Claude Estee, the successful screen-writer, and by the guests at his party and at Mrs. Jenning's genteel, thirty-dollar call-house. Claude, too, is something of a grotesque, but he and his friends are disqualified for West's purposes: they are successful, and with the exception of Claude himself, West dismisses them after two brief scenes. He retains Claude as a representative of the Hollywood success, but his major concern lies elsewhere.

Hollywood itself is a world constructed—like a sand-castle, with fantastic elaboration but without foundation—by the successful; coveted and unattained by the grotesques; worshipped, hated, eventually to be destroyed by the people who come to California to die. The germs of its destruction are contained within itself. This masquerade world sets the scene for West's violently yoked similes and creates the illusion of objective reality, not surrealist fantasy. West says of Faye Greener's fantasies: "The effect was similar to that obtained by the artists of the Middle Ages, who, when doing a subject like the raising of Lazarus from the dead or Christ walking on water, were careful to keep all the details intensely realistic" (320). The comment holds equally for the Hollywood of *The Day of the Locust.*

The city follows no laws, not even structural laws governing stresses and strains. The usual building materials set their own limits, but plaster, lath and paper can take any form, any shape—Mexican ranches, Samoan huts, Italian villas. The "real" world is uniformly false. As in "The

Chamber of American Horrors" in West's *A Cool Million,*
iron "is grained to look like wood," wood "painted to look
like unpainted wood," paper "oiled to look like parchment,"
machined metal "carefully stamped to appear handforged."
Homer Simpson's house contains a variety of cactus plants,
some real, some made of rubber and cork. But there is no
way to distinguish the real from the synthetic; the word
"real" has little meaning in a surreal world.

Hollywood is a "celluloid civilization" at best, but the
image presented is not of a celluloid studio but a celluloid
world. West indicates something of the inextricability of the
worlds within and without studio gates on the first page of
the novel—as he does later in the Waterloo episode. It opens
with Tod Hackett in his office suddenly hearing the noises of
iron-and-leather-clad horses, of cavalry and infantry, of
hussars and grenadiers chased by "a little fat man, wearing a
cork sun-helmet, polo shirt, and knickers," screaming, "Stage
Nine—you bastards—Stage Nine!" But the scene outside the
gates is as obviously incongruous. A masquerade presupposes
masqueraders, and as Tod leaves the studio he walks among
people garishly clothed in "sports clothes which were not
really sports clothes . . . [but] fancy dress" (261). Nor is
nature excluded from the grotesquerie: "The edges of the
trees burned with a pale violet light and their centers
gradually turned from deep purple to black. The same violet
piping, like a neon tube, outlined the tops of the ugly,
humpbacked hills and they were almost beautiful" (262).
Through Tod's artist's eyes, West can select those elements
which are rooted in the real world yet present a grotesque
aspect. For example, there is a eucalyptus tree outside the
window of Tod's room: "A light breeze stirred its long,
narrow leaves, making them show first their green side, then
their silver one." That is accurate description, but the slight
movement transforms the leaves into another stroke of the
grotesque.

Though these perceptions—and most of the perceptions
in the novel—are Tod's, there are critics who think of Homer
Simpson as the main character in *The Day of the Locust.* But

it is hardly possible to call Homer a center of consciousness, even if the point of view is his for a stretch. Homer is no more capable of judging himself or the world in which he finds himself than is Bénjy in *The Sound and the Fury*. Tod Hackett does not judge either—not explicitly, at any rate— not because he cannot but because he denies himself the right to. As a man and as a painter he is concerned with what is, with what West later calls "a statement of fact." As a painter he can transform even the bizarre and grotesque into artifact: the judgment lies in the work itself. As a man he is not morally superior. He can make distinctions, but he is faced with the pragmatic difficulty that they will not work. When he tries to talk Faye out of going to work at Mrs. Jenning's brothel, he decides that "she wouldn't understand the aesthetic argument and with what values could he back up the moral one?" (346). He finds an argument that does work—in that particular situation with that particular girl: "Disease would destroy her beauty. He shouted at her like a Y.M.C.A. lecturer on sex hygiene." When the appalling mother of the appalling eight-year-old star, Adore, forces the child to sing an obscene song accompanied by obscene gestures—"his buttocks writhed and his voice carried a top heavyload of sexual pain"—Tod's only comment is, "That's a funny woman." But by the end of the book it becomes clear that his quietude is a mask which covers a good deal of moral indignation.

West carefully indicates that, whatever Tod's virtues, he is not completely outside the world he is observing. Graduate of Yale or not, he shows little of the intellectual but what he perceives with an eye to his painting, and his painting in no way sets him apart from the world. He is morally little better, if certainly no worse, than any of the others. He makes as much a fool of himself over Faye Greener as Claude, Earle, Abe, and Homer, and if he is conscious of his folly, so are most men, though few stop because of their knowledge. Homer is the most sterile character in the novel, but Tod is the most frustrated and most fumbling, if only because he tries hardest. He plays the awkward straight man, never quite

sure what the results of his overtures will be. His straight-
forwardness and honesty bring out Abe's belligerance; his
clumsy attempt to comfort Harry brings on the one thing
Tod wants to avoid—Harry's usual elaborate reminiscences;
when he laboriously searches for Faye over the entire length
of the studio lot, he finally finds her waiting for him back at
his office; when he tries in vain to get Homer to explain what
has happened at the party at Homer's house, he succeeds by
blundering on the one thing that will unloose Homer's
torrent of language: he says, "I'm sorry."

This is not to say that there is no difference between Tod
and the others. Tod is capable of growth and change, and
growth at least implies judgment. He is the only character
who so much as notices the existence of the crowds of
midwesterners. Their impact on him is immediate and
lasting, for they hover in the background of his mind and of
the novel; the change in his attitude toward them is the
measure of his growth as a man and as a painter.

Their first appearance is in immediate contrast to the
masqueraders: "Their clothing was somber and badly cut,
bought from mailorder houses. While the others moved
rapidly . . . they loitered on the corners or stood with their
backs to the shop windows and stared at everyone who
passed. When their stare was returned, their eyes filled with
hatred. At this time Tod knew very little about them except
that they had come to California to die" (261). Their initial
effect on Tod pre-dates the beginning of the novel, but that
effect is clearly profound: "From the moment he had seen
them, he had known that despite his race, training and
heritage, neither Winslow Homer nor Thomas Ryder could be
his master and he turned to Goya and Daumier" (261).
Before this change Tod was about to give up painting, afraid
that his growing facility would lead only toward "illustration
or mere handsomeness." His turn away from mere handsomeness is embodied in the conception of "The Burning of Los
Angeles" and in "The Dancers," a series of lithographs on
which he is already working. Thus Tod becomes the liaison
between the two major levels of reality, though he himself,

without accepting the Hollywood scale of values, is one of the figures who dance for the midwesterners; he, too, helps to produce Hollywood's ornate, artificial succubi. Tod and the other dancers change in each lithograph, but the midwesterners remain, the only constant: "The group of uneasy people who formed their audience remained the same. They stood staring at the performers in just the way that they stared at the masqueraders on Vine Street. It was their stare that drove Abe and the others to spin crazily and leap into the air with twisted backs like hooked trout" (264).

Though they occasionally verge on violence, the midwesterners remain passive until the apocalypse. For the moment Tod's involvement outside his painting are with the grotesques, the dancers. I have grouped Harry, Faye, Homer, Abe, Earle, and the rest together as grotesques not only because their world, their activities, and their values are bizarre, but because of the disparity between each of them: the mechanical in the human, the pretended in the real, or perhaps more accurately, the human becoming the inhuman, the pretended becoming the real. To begin with, there is Harry Greener, the clown:

> When Harry had first begun his stage career, he had probably restricted his clowning to the boards, but now he clowned continuously. It was his sole method of defense. Most people, he had discovered, won't go out of their way to punish a clown.
>
> He used a set of elegant gestures to accent the comedy of his bent, hopeless figure and wore a special costume, dressing like a banker, a cheap, unconvincing, imitation banker. . . . His outfit fooled no one, but then he didn't intend it to fool anyone. His slyness was of a different sort (282).

"He used a set of elegant gestures" suggests that Harry is acting a role; but they are the only gestures he uses, and thus are hardly a pretence. "His bent, hopeless figure" is real to begin with, though he pretends that it is a pretence. The irony of the newspaper review of one of his acts which Harry carries around with him is all the more effective when West places it after the above description. Harry is described as coming on stage "clean, neat, and sweet;" "The Flying Lings" kick him and toss him around until he is "tattered and bloody, but still sweet." "The pain that almost, not quite, thank God, crumples his stiff little figure would be unbearable if it were not obviously make-believe" (283-4). Only the negatives in that sentence have to be dropped to make it apply at a later date in Harry's career: it would be bearable if it were obviously make-believe.

Harry's whole life is a series of stage routines, mechanical, impossible to stop once started: the pitchman's line he uses to sell bogus silver polish, the insane laughter he uses to get his daughter to bend to him, the "have pity, folks, on my gray hair" routine he uses in bars. All he needs is an audience, willing or not, and the mechanical gyrations take over from there. When he finally does collapse "like a mechanical toy that has been overwound," uncertain himself whether he is acting or sick, his insane laughter goes out of control, the defense becomes itself the punishment. Harry's gesturing and posturing are his formalized defense against a world which West need not explicitly condemn; Harry's discovery that "most people . . . won't go out of their way to punish a clown" is justification enough for his defenses and for those of the other grotesques.

Since *The Day of the Locust* is centered on the points of view of Tod and Homer, both of whom "love" Harry's daughter, Faye, all matters of love—or of sex, at least—are centered on her. At Homer's house after the cockfight all six male characters—Tod, Miguel, Homer, Earle, Claude, and Abe—surround Faye: the same ratio as that of Miguel's six cocks to the one hen which so disgusts Homer. Faye, like Harry, sets up a highly complicated series of automatic defenses; in her case, though, the defenses become weapons of the offense as well. Her sexuality becomes a weapon with which she hopes to battle her way to stardom. She will love only men who are handsome or in a position to further her career, and she is willing to go to work for Mrs. Jenning to get the money to pay for her father's funeral. The tough talk that Faye slips into when talking about Mrs. Jenning's— "punkola," "cheapies"—is the least of Faye's poses. As with Harry, there are within Faye striking incongruities which define her grotesqueness. Just as Harry is like a mechanical toy whose "hands signal [while] his face denies," Faye has her own pattern of formalized gestures. In her case the split is between gesture and word rather than between gesture and facial expression. For example, the gesture which accompanies the simple enough statement, "Oh . . . and I had a luncheon date": "She turned at the waist without moving her legs, so that her snug dress twisted even tighter and Homer could see her dainty arched ribs and little, dimpled belly. This elaborate gesture, like all her others, was so completely meaningless, almost formal, that she seemed a dancer rather than an affected actress" (304). Or her gesture of running her tongue over her lips to repay a compliment: "It was one of her most characteristic gestures and very effective. It seemed to promise all sorts of undefined intimacies, yet it was really as simple and automatic as the word thanks. She used it to reward anyone for anything, no matter how unimportant" (385). West makes explicit the connection between Faye's gestures and Harry's; hers are another version, "uncontaminated by thought," of his response to the discovery that people "won't go out of their way to punish a clown." "It was as though her body recognized how foolish her words were and tried to excite her hearers into being uncritical."

If Tod is the least successful of seducers, he does find out what is behind the "extraordinary color and mystery" of Faye's movements. He finds out that the matter supporting the "smooth glass wall" of her rhythm is the weakest, flimsiest imaginable—the sheaf of impossible daydreams which Faye leafs through as one would a pack of cards, rejecting the ones that will not do at the moment, finally selecting one and re-telling it for the thousandth time. Tod realizes that even she knows that "her method was too mechanical for the best results," but the method works, to his chagrin; she simply has no need of him or of anyone else. "Her self-sufficiency made him squirm and the desire to break its smooth surface with a blow, or at least a sudden obscene gesture, became irresistible. He began to wonder if he himself didn't suffer from the ingrained, morbid apathy he liked to draw in others. Maybe he could only be galvanized into sensibility and that was why he was chasing Faye" (365).

It takes something more threatening than Faye's self-sufficiency to "galvanize" Tod into violence—the onslaught of the wave- and funeral-watchers. He does not rape Faye and does not strike her; instead he withdraws from the battle by falling back on "a childish trick, hardly worthy of a primitive witch doctor," on a workable salvation. He shuts the portfolio of drawings of her, ties it up, and puts it away. Tod may have to fall back on "childish tricks," but at least he does have some tricks. He can escape, if only temporarily. The very fact that he has made the drawings, and that he is working on the lithographs of "The Dancers" and thinking out "The Burning of Los Angeles," is a still more important trick that assumes an increasingly greater role. But there is one character—Homer Simpson—who has no tricks, no defenses except complete isolation or at the very least mental chastity. Faye's effect on Homer is crucial, for it is the failure of his passivity that sets off the apocalyptic riot at the end.

West is faced with a technical problem in connection with Homer, for Homer cannot at the same time be an anonymous figure in a faceless mob and an individual with whom Tod gets involved. West compromises by giving Homer many of the characteristics of the bored midwesterners who come to Hollywood, but he also makes him significantly different. Homer is neither bored nor anxious. The excitement the wave-watchers crave is the very thing Homer tries desperately to avoid. The episode with Romola Martin, the prostitute in Iowa, had shaken Homer out of his apathy for a moment; since he had never known sexual excitement, he had interpreted as disgust his emotions when confronted by a woman on a bed. The rest of his life is an attempt to subdue the thought of his inevitable frustration, for though Romola Martin's seduction of Homer was interrupted by the ringing of a telephone, it is clear that for Homer there will always be a telephone, that he is impotent emotionally, and presumably, sexually.

Homer's hopelessness is unremitting: he is without the hope of hope. Macbeth's horror at having murdered sleep is doubled for Homer—he is even afraid of sleep because he is afraid he will never wake again. When he does fall asleep, the act of waking is a long struggle towards consciousness, and when he achieves the "victory," he has to reassemble himself methodically, mechanically. Nor are tears an anodyne: his most agreeable sensation is a sadness which is so pleasant that he "prods" it until it turns to anguish, the anguish to misery, the misery to tears, the tears to the final horror, sleep. Harry Greener's hopes—or dreams or illusions—lie in his image of himself in the past; Faye Greener's lie in the future; Homer's lie only in the escape from past and future. He has only one delusion—"he was simple enough to believe that people don't think while asleep"—and that delusion destroys him when, in his sleep, he gives up the battle against succumbing to Faye's charms.

I have been using the word "defenses" to describe the formalized, automatic gestures and the dreams which define the grotesqueness of the characters in *The Day of the Locust*. I have suggested, too, that although the defenses are illusory, they nevertheless perform an essential function, and that therein lies salvation. *The Day of the Locust* represents, after all, not only the prophecies of Jeremiah, but also his lamentations; it comes after the fact. The machine is here and it is mechanizing. The idea is not a new one, but West's conception of the conditioned response acting as defense against a mechanized world is a brilliant irony: it turns Pavlov into Christ. In Homer's case, chastity is the desperate defense against potential destruction. Homer's chastity "served him like the shell of a tortoise, as both spine and armor. He couldn't shed it even in thought. If he did, he would be destroyed." West generalizes here, as elsewhere, in a way which I think justifies Edmund Wilson's praise for his "philosophic-poetic point of view": "[Homer] was right. There are men who can lust with parts of themselves. Only their brain of their hearts burn and then not completely. There are others, still more fortunate, who are like the filaments of an incandescent lamp. They burn fiercely, yet nothing is destroyed. But in Homer's case it would be like dropping a spark in a barn full of hay. He had escaped in the Romola Martin incident, but he wouldn't escape again" (313). West places Homer in a wide frame of reference, and at the same time, justifies his concern with the act and imagery of violence and destruction. The passage insists on the seriousness of the problem of salvaging something of oneself in a world where desires become dreams and where destruction is always imminent. And it succeeds in maintaining the humor of the bizarre last element in a perfectly logical sequence.

There is no need to dwell on the other grotesques and their masks—the three-foot dwarf who pretends to be six-foot and a bully; the six-foot cowboy who pretends to be even taller with five inches of Stetson and three of boot-heel. Most important of the minor characters is Claude Estee. Claude is more intellectual and more articulate than any of the other characters except Tod. His wit draws one of the few explicit statements of moral judgment in the novel; the statement is Tod's and is clear indication that he does judge as well as observe: "Tod liked to hear him talk. He was master of an involved comic rhetoric that permitted him to express his moral indignation and still keep his reputation for worldliness and wit" (276). Tod comes into his own with Claude by choosing to be straight man for a change, by feeding Claude lines and waiting for the "comic rhetoric" to take over in elaboration.

Appropriately, the dialogue between Claude and Tod concerns Mrs. Jenning's brothel, "a triumph of industrial design." Tod picks up the idea, elaborates it slightly—"I don't care how much cellophane she wraps it in . . . nautch joints are depressing, like all places for deposit, banks, mail boxes, tombs, vending machines"; and Claude takes it from there. He personalizes the figure, as it were, running through the entire sequence of probable movements in detail: "Love is like a vending machine, eh? Not bad. You insert a coin and press home the lever. There's some mechanical activity inside the bowels of the device. You receive a small sweet, frown at yourself in the dirty mirror, adjust your hat, take a firm grip on your unbrella, and walk away, trying to look as though nothing had happened. It's good, but it's not for pictures" (276).

Claude plays no essential part in the plot; superficially he has no function that could not be taken over by Tod or one of the others. In West's *Miss Lonelyhearts* the hero's consciousness is the only center; his view of the world is a paranoid one in which the inanimate world rises up in hostility to him. *Miss Lonelyhearts* is a nearly perfect book, but West has gone far beyond it in *The Day of the Locust.* Tod's view of the world is not demented; at least part of Claude Estee's function is to indicate another view of the world as automatic vending machine. His glibness is easy, but his moral indignation is genuine; like Tod, he keeps a straight face, and like Tod, he seems to feel that "It is hard to laugh at the need for beauty and romance, no matter how tasteless, even horrible, the results of that need are. But it is easy to sigh. Few things are sadder than the truly monstrous" (262).

I have already mentioned the immediate change which Tod's first encounter with the midwesterners effects in him. He feels that he must paint them, that his masters must be Goya and Daumier rather than Ryder and Winslow Homer. His interest starts as mere curiosity; when he first sees Homer, he is interested in him because he thinks Homer is one of the people who come to California to die; he discovers that he is wrong, but is still intrigued by Homer as a possible subject. Tod gradually allays Homer's shyness and fear until Homer responds without trying to run away. And Tod comments that "sympathy, even of the most obvious sort, made him articulate, almost garrulous" (286). It should be noted that Tod's sympathy at the beginning *is* of the most obvious sort; it is more curiosity, certainly, than compassion. But the history of his developing attitudes towards his painting is also the history of the growth of his compassion.

In about the middle of the book, Tod is rejected by Faye once again, and he escapes from his frustration into thoughts of "The Burning of Los Angeles." The escape is incomplete, but it is a beginning. At Miguel's camp in the mountains, Tod tries to attack Faye—or at least chases her—falls on his face and once again reverts to thoughts of his painting, cartoons for which are under way. For a moment he doubts his own vision, wonders if he is not exaggerating the importance of the wave-watchers. But the doubt is only momentary, and he returns to his conception of the painting with renewed satisfaction and with a new awareness that the conception is itself prophetic, almost despite himself: "He told himself that it didn't make any difference because he was an artist, not a prophet . . . Nevertheless, he refused to give up the role of Jeremiah . . . . The Angelenos would be first, but their comrades all over the country would follow. There would be civil war. He was amused by the strong feeling of satisfaction this dire conclusion gave him. Were all prophets of doom and destruction such happy men?" (335)

At Harry's funeral, the people Tod is concerned with come into the funeral parlor and into clearer focus: "It seemed to Tod that they stared back at him with an expression of vicious, acrid boredom that trembled on the edge of violence" (347). Soon after, in the Sargasso Seas of the studio dumping ground, Tod almost seems to have pushed people out of the foreground of his painting altogether. He mentions a new range of painters in whom he is interested, Francesco Guardi and Salvator Rosa, "the painters of Decay and Mystery." The landscape is bizarre, surrealist, dreamlike, a fantastic confusion of half-demolished buildings, bridges that lead nowhere, monstrous plants transformed into instruments of torture; it overwhelms human figures and diminishes them to the stature of insignificant puppets. In the chapter immediately following (ch. 19), however, the figures come to the foreground once more, but with a difference.

Tod realizes that he cannot satirize them as Hogarth and Daumier might have. He visits Hollywood's innumerable cults—the Church of Christ, Physical; the Church Invisible; the Tabernacle of the Third Coming, the Temple Moderne—

but his approach to the worshippers has changed radically: "As he watched these people . . . he thought of how well Alessandro Magnasco would dramatize the contrast between their drained out, feeble bodies and their wild, disordered minds. He would not satirize them as Hogarth and Daumier might, nor would he pity them. He would paint their fury with respect . . ." (365-6). The abandoning of Daumier for Magnasco indicates the direction of Tod's development. What starts as curiosity about the midwesterners becomes respect, then fear, then terror—never pity or contempt. The insane religious ecstasy of the man "with countersunk eyes, like the heads of burnished spikes, that a monk by Magnasco might have" is a more serious and more deadly consideration than the foibles of the bourgeois individual of Hogarth or Daumier. The "anarchic power" of a sightless, senseless, undirected horde of the lower-middle classes is the violent blow which galvanizes Tod into action. What starts as mere curiosity about the grotesques turns into a desperate need to get through to them as human beings. And in the last chapter, when the bored mob surges forward in fulfillment of Tod's prophecy, Tod has a function, if only a limited and ambiguous one.

In that final chapter all the strands come together masterfully. All the "cultists of all sorts, economic as well as religious, the wave, airplane, funeral and preview watchers" unite, appropriately, before "Mr. Kahn's Pleasure Dome." A radio announcer with a portable microphone is like "a revivalist preacher whipping his congregation toward the ecstasy of fits"—or like one of the false prophets who "prophesy false dreams" against whom Jeremiah rages. Tod's attempts are frustrated again, this time when he tries to help Homer out of his final, total apathy; the only contact that can hurtle Homer out of that apathy is the stone thrown at him by the child star, Adore. Homer is pushed around violently by the mob and by the police, but his insane, silent rage erupts only when this youngest, most fully perverted product of lies attacks him. The dam holding back Homer's emotions breaks and their full force lands on the boy as

Homer jumps again and again. The no longer controlled hysteria of the mob claims its own as Homer is dragged down as a sacrificial offering to their boredom.

Tod himself, in attempting to get free of the mob, performs two actions of significance: he rescues a young girl from the mad attack of an old man, and kicks off the desperate grasp of a sobbing woman who is pulling him from his perch on a fence. It is impossible for West to make Tod a hero in shining armor; it is "necessary" to sacrifice the second woman, without time for regrets, in order to save himself from destruction. To do otherwise would be to avoid the issue; to leave out the second woman would be to be against evil without recognizing the possibility of an inevitable need to do evil, even if against one's will.

The thought of "The Burning of Los Angeles" finally becomes both Tod's escape from his immediate predicament and his escape into the reality of the mob, into the only reality there is for him—his art. "The way to it in his mind had become almost automatic," and clinging to the fence, he paints the mob with bats and torches, the burning city, the fleeing dancers in the foreground—Faye, Harry, Homer, and the others. Each responds appropriately: Faye runs proudly; Harry stumbles along hanging on to his derby with both hands; Homer seems half-asleep, but his hands move in anguish; Claude thumbs his nose at the mob; and "Tod himself picked up a small stone to throw before continuing his flight" (420). It is a small stone, but it represents a large distinction. In the world of West's novels, violence is the given. Tod Hackett, no less than the people who come to California to die and the grotesques, has been fed on "lynchings, murder, sex crimes, explosions, wrecks, love nests, fires, miracles, revolutions, wars." Since violence is a fact of American life, there is no way *not* to respond to it; turning one's back to it is a response no less than wielding a bat in a riot. But West suggests that you cannot turn your back on it, for, invariably, it chooses not to ignore you. Tod does not choose to be in the riot: his attempt to help Homer drags him into it. He has to react to violence, and less accidentally, "uses" it. The "formula" for Tod runs something like this: a world over-run by the machine produces an automatic defense which must be maintained if the ego is to be saved from destruction; the violence of the world of the machine can be the force which "galvanizes" the automaton into meaningful action; the agent of destruction can become the agent of salvation. The defense itself can be more or less valuable and productive. As to whether Tod's painting produces his "morality" or the morality the painting, perhaps the two are part of an identical process in the face of an impossible world.

Tod does succeed in holding on to his painting throughout. Without trying to read *The Day of the Locust* as an optimistic document, I think Tod's painting and his attempts to help Homer are the small stone he throws that reclaims him from apathy and despair. Perhaps the stone is the same one that Adore throws to start the riot: that would be the final irony.

Isaac Rosenfeld said of the West of *The Day of the Locust,* "There is so much gusto in his satire, so much taste for the very thing he was destroying that he achieved in this book a kind of serenity as a man will when his love and hate work together." I would suggest an additional factor in that serenity. At Harry's funeral, the electric organ plays Bach's "Come Redeemer, Our Saviour." The chorale starts as though inviting Christ "with infinite grace and delicacy" to a lawn fete; then the polite note gradually disappears and there is "a hint of a threat" and "a little impatience;" but finally, "The treble soared free and triumphant and the base no longer struggled to keep it down. It had become a rich accompaniment. 'Come or don't come,' the music seemed to say, 'I love you and my love is enough.' It was a simple statement of fact, neither cry nor serenade, made without arrogance or humility" (349). I would suggest that *The Day of the Locust* is West's simple statement of fact, made without arrogance or humility.

A CONFLUENCE OF VOICES. . . .

John Hawkes: My own concept of "avant-garde" has to do
  with something constant which we find running through
  prose fiction from Quevedo, the Spanish picaresque
  writer, and Thomas Nashe at the beginning of the English
  novel, down through Lautreamont, Celine, Nathanael
  West, Flannery O'Connor, James Purdy, Joseph Heller,
  myself. This constant is a quality of coldness, detachment, ruthless determination to face up to the enormities
  of ugliness and potential failure within ourselves and in
  the world around us, and to bring to this exposure a
  savage or saving comic spirit and the saving beauties of
  language. . . . A writer who truly and greatly sustains us is
  Nabokov.

Martin: [West influenced] younger novelists like James
  Purdy, Joseph Heller, Thomas Pynchon, John Hawkes,
  Flannery O'Connor.

Hawkes: The Duke carefully reached out his hand and the
  boy fairy did not move, while the marquee banged to and
  fro, the projector steamed, and the invisible lost audience
  stamped booted feet and rummaged in box lunches.

Ralph Ellison-Invisible Man: They moved in a tight-knit
  order, carrying sticks and clubs, shotguns and rifles, led
  by Ras the Exhorter become Ras the Destroyer upon a

great black horse. A new Ras of a haughty, vulgar dignity, dressed in the costume of an Abyssinian Chieftain. . . . A figure more out of a dream than out of Harlem, than out of even this Harlem night, yet real, alive, alarming.

William Carlos Williams: West was a big fellow who had had a tryout with the Giants at one time as an outfielder because of his hitting. But he lost interest. That wasn't his line.

Lavonne Mueller: Both West and Malamud portray this *dream dump*—Hollywood and the world of baseball—each of which is a papier-mache structure built on the imagination and hopes of an American public nourished for decades on the peculiarly American Dream that every man is capable of becoming *some one* . . . . that he can somehow become part of a world inhabited by beautiful people who themselves were once just one of the lowly, struggling masses.

Vladimir Nabokov-Humbert Humbert: Some motels had instructions pasted above the toilet (on whose tanks the towels were unhygenically heaped) asking guests not to throw into its bowl garbage, beer cans, cartons, stillborn babies; others had special notices under glass, such as *Things to Do*.

Joseph Heller-Old Woman: 'Why are you chasing us out?' the girls said. 'Catch-22,' the men said. 'What right do you have?' the girls said. 'Catch-22,' the men said. All they kept saying was 'Catch-22, Catch-22.' What does it mean, Catch-22?

Leslie Fiedler: West is finally the key figure, at work still as a living influence in the fictions of writers as young as Jeremy Larner, whose Dell Prize novel, *Drive, He Said* . . . comes from *Miss Lonelyhearts* and *Day of the Locust*.

Jeremy Larner: But yes better to stop and look at the void and make our games from that if we can.

Baudelaire: Anywhere, anywhere, as long as it be out of this world!

MALAMUD AND WEST:
TYRANNY OF THE *DREAM DUMP*
By Lavonne Mueller

The Natural and *The Day of the Locust* lay open the vitals of the American Dream. Bernard Malamud's subject is baseball, our national sport, and Nathanael West's sharp gaze is toward Hollywood; both writers deal essentially with the leisure-time terrors of the "idiot masses." Both writers describe mindless fans who are conditioned into automated spectators and then hoodwinked by illusions, drugged by yellow journalism, the tabloids, and the cinema, and headed almost willingly and happily to certain disaster. Their fundamental restlessness and anxiety is the central theme of both books. The baseball field and the Hollywood sound stage are vivid personal worlds—wastelands, in fact—where illusory heroes must conform to the American code of success and "deliver the goods" to hungry spectators. Malamud and West both take broad, satirical swipes at the Horatio Alger myth and at the eternal middle-class ennui sustained by tasteless, gaudy spectacles.

In the baseball world of Malamud there is a gallery of grotesque people who are like those of West's Hollywood. For example, as soon as Roy arrives in the land of the Knights, Bump tells him: "Welcome to the lousiest team in the world barring none. And this is ol' Doc Casey, the trainer, who has got nobody but cripples on his hands except me."[1] The Knights are indeed "cripples"—including Bump. The world of the Knights which the reader first meets is not the

221

place of champions but rather a dark, despairing place typified by insignificant hangers-on vainly scrambling for recognition. Pop Fisher, a former notorious baseball failure himself, manages the Knights even though admitting that he "shoulda farmed instead of playing wet nurse to a last place, dead-to-the-neck ball team" (45). Roy walked blithely into an already decayed dream. Pop Fisher candidly sees his players as "sick monkeys, broken-down mules, pigeon-chested toads, slimy horned worms, but not real, honest-to-god baseball players" (56). In an ironic and prophetic speech, Pop Fisher touches on the portent of calamity to come: "I am tempted to take pity on those poor dopes who spend a buck and a half to watch you play and trade the whole lousy lot of you away" (56). And the narrator himself tells us directly that the Pirates, unlike the Knights, was "a team that was really a team, not a Rube Goldberg contraption" (176). This is the dream-quest, then, that Roy has chosen. How could the reader expect anything but catastrophe when Roy becomes a part of a "Rube Goldberg contraption?" How can anything but aggression be expected from a crowd that pays for dream fulfillment and is plainly gyped?

> They were a nutty bunch to begin with but when they were losing they were impossible. It was like some kind of sickness. They threw to the wrong bases, bumped heads together in the outfield, passed each other on the baselines, sometimes batted out of order, throwing both Pop and the ump into fits, and cussed everybody else for their mistakes. It was not uncommon to see them pile three men on a bag, or behold a catcher on the opposing team, in a single skip and jump, lay the tag on two of them as they came thundering together into home plate. Or watch Gabby Laslow, in a tight spot, freeze onto the ball, or Allie Stubbs get socked with it in the jaw, thrown by Olson on a steal as Allie admired a lady in the stands (75).

Nathanael West's Hollywood, too, is a land of cripples: has-beens, second rate music hall stars, adolescent starlets, cosmetic cowboys and Indians, loiterers, prostitutes, and random walk-ons like the Gingo's, an Eskimo family brought to Hollywood to make retakes for a picture about polar exploration. The Eskimos, like so many other dream-drugged hangers-on, refuse to return to Alaska. West tells us that they "liked" Hollywood. Everywhere the Hollywood illusion is neon-lighted by the agony of the inhabitants obsessed by dreams of beauty and romance.

> He left the car at Vine Street. As he walked along, he examined the evening crowd. A great many of the people wore sports clothes which were not really sports clothes. Their sweaters, knickers, slacks, blue flannel jackets with brass buttons were fancy dress. The fat lady in the yachting cap was going shopping, not boating; the man in the Norfolk jacket and Tyrolean hat was returning, not from a mountain, but an insurance office; and the girl in slacks and sneakers with a bandanna around her head had just left a switchboard, not a tennis court.[2]

And the garish homes in Hollywood are just as shabby and gross as the people who live in them.

> But not even the soft wash of dusk could help the houses. Only dynamite would be of any use against the Mexican ranch houses, Samoan huts, Mediterranean villas, Egyptian and Japanese temples, Swiss chalets, Tudor cottages, and every possible combination of these styles that lined the slopes of the canyon (262).
>
> On the corner of La Huerta Road was a miniature Rhine castle with tarpaper turrets pierced for archers. Next to it was a highly colored shack with domes and minarets out of the *Arabian Nights*. Again he was charitable. Both houses were comic, but he didn't laugh. Their desire to startle was so eager and guileless (262).

What of the protagonists who enter these two worlds of etiolated dreams? Roy Hobbs emerged from the backwoods with child-like confidence and a determined vow that he will be "the best there ever was" in baseball. Roy is obsessed by an ambition so persistent that it sometimes puzzles him. "Sometimes he wished he had no ambitions—often wondered where they had come from in his life, because he remembered how satisfied he had been as a youngster, and that with the little he had had—a dog, a stick, an aloneness he loved (which did not bleed him like his later loneliness), he wished he could have lived longer in his boyhood" (117). The great American dream of fame and fortune was always there, interrupting any hopes he had for serenity. Roy tells Memo:

"There were times I thought I would never get anywhere and it made me eat my guts, but all that is gone now. I know I have the stuff and will get there" (121).

What critics have failed to take into consideration in viewing Roy is the interesting possibility that Malamud meant him to be not only an unfortunate hero but an artist as well. One should not overlook the important fact that Roy once performed as a clown in a sideshow, decorated with red and white warpaint in order to hide his "sadeyed and unhappy" face. And on one occasion we see Roy performing magic tricks as cleverly as a trained actor; he pulls salami from Mercy's pocket, brings forth silver coins from behind Gus's ear, and conjures a white bunny from Memo's purse. In fact, Roy becomes a rather unusual ball player. He guardedly carries his "instrument"—a baseball bat—with him in a bassoon case. Roy is essentially a creator who lives by his art. "And if he once abandoned Wonderboy there was no telling what would happen to him. Probably it would finish his career for keeps, because never since he had made the bat had he swung at a ball with any other" (144). The bat represents the artist's talent. Wonderboy was created in Roy's youth. When Wonderboy is finally destroyed, Roy begins to strike out. Then, once he has sold out, corruption overtakes his art, and the artist is dead.

Roy—good-bad, ordinary-extraordinary—moves through the novel as a hero caged by his inherent human attributes. On the diamond he is a giant, but outside the ballfield the hero is only a guy looking like "any big-muscled mechanic or bartender on his night off." The hero lusts after home runs, but the man lusts for sex and food. Roy has concern for his team, yet he agrees to "throw" the big game. A toothsome Memo is more important to him than the authenticity of Iris Lemon. Roy is trapped in the empty spectacle of the American Dream. Heroes are men, and men are inevitably susceptible to failure, and this failure reflects not on man but on mankind. As Iris puts it: "Without heroes we're all plain people and don't know how far we can go." The anguished discontent of Roy's defeat is really Everyman's defeat.

Saturated by grandiose fancies, but felled by a stomach which "dredged up unbelievable quantities of bilge," Roy sees himself in true cosmic perspective when he envisions himself to be "a little Roy Dwarf (Hey, mister, you're stepping on my feet)" (192).

West's Tod Hackett is a young painter working at a Hollywood movie studio. Like Roy, Tod has been discovered by a "talent scout." His appearance is as prosaic as Roy's. Tod has a large, gawky body and a silly grin which makes him seem "completely without talent, almost doltish in fact" (260), but we are told that he has talent. Throughout the novel, Tod is preoccupied with his personal vision of Hollywood. He plans an ambitious canvas to be called "The Burning of Los Angeles," showing the city blazing at noon, having been set on fire by a spirited and festive crowd carrying baseball bats and torches. Tod believes that he has a mission in Hollywood—he must paint these people. Never again would he be content with the "fat red barn, old stone wall or sturdy Nantucket fisherman" (261). Tod is an artist intent on presenting his particular perceptions; yet what he sees is confused by a whole complex of fantasies, one inside the other like a nest of Chinese boxes. On one occasion he walks across the studio lot as if on an odyssey.

> Throwing away his cigarette, he went through the swinging doors of the saloon. These was no back to the building and he found himself in a Paris street. He followed it to its end, coming out in a Romanesque courtyard. He heard voices a short distance away and went toward them. On a lawn of fiber, a group of men and women in riding costume were picnicking. They were eating cardboard food in front of a cellophane waterfall. He started toward them to ask his way, but was stopped by a man who scowled and held up a sign—"Quiet, Please, We're Shooting." When Tod took another step forward, the man shook his fist threateningly.
>
> Next he came to a small pond with large celluloid swans floating on it. Across one end was a bridge with a sign that read, "To Kamp Komfit." He crossed the bridge and followed a little path that ended at a Greek temple dedicated to Eros. The god himself lay face downward in a pile of old newspapers and bottles (351-352).

Much like Roy, Tod is not only locked in by his desire to

"succeed" in Hollywood, but he eventually becomes the prey of Hollywood—he literally is trampled by a crowd of "cheated" fans. Tod becomes infatuated with a small-time movie Goddess, Faye, and follows her slavishly through an insane gyp-world of jerks, creeps, cowboys, drunks, fairies, con artists, phallic promoters, and child monsters. In a scene as ludicrous as that in which Malamud described the fumbling Knights piling up on one another like Keystone cops, West describes a filming of the battle of Waterloo:

> The man in the checked cap was making a fatal error. Mont St. Jean was unfinished. The paint was not yet dry and all the struts were not in place. Because of the thickness of the cannon smoke, he had failed to see that the hill was still being worked on by property men, grips and carpenters.
> It was the classic mistake, Tod realized, the same one Napoleon had made. Then it had been wrong for a different reason. The Emperor had ordered the cuirassiers to charge Mont St. Jean not knowing that a deep ditch was hidden at its foot to trap his heavy cavalry. The result had been disaster for the French; the beginning of the end (355-356).

Tod Hackett, then, is caught between two cultural standards—the aesthetic and the popular. His lust for a tinseled Venus results in the loss of his ideals. Lonely, frustrated, and bitter, he plots revenge on Los Angeles by contemplating his canvas that will show the masses of "cheated" ones setting fire to the city. In a moment of true insight, he reflects: "Maybe they weren't really desperate enough to set a single city on fire" (334). But then he rationalizes that it "didn't make any difference because he was an artist not a prophet" (335). In the end, Tod "sells out" as easily as Roy. As he is being crushed in the final mob scene, Tod forgets his art and with cinema-like magic creates his own kind of vengeance. While lapsing into a reverie about his canvas, he enacts his escape by imagining himself in the role of a show-biz director in his own creation: "He had almost forgotten both his leg and his predicament, and to make his escape still more complete he stood on a chair and worked at the flames in an upper corner of the canvas, modeling the tongues of fire so that they licked even more avidly at a corinthian column that held up the palmleaf roof of a nutburger stand" (420).

Both Roy and Tod are the prey of the same kind of beautiful, superficial women, and these are women who are themselves the victims of a way of life shiftily built on material values and the convulsive reach for a veneer culture. In both cases, these women goad their man to a state of near insanity.

Memo Paris is portrayed as an "unlucky" woman. Moody and elusive, she controls Roy by bludgeoning him with the guilt of Bump's death. She punishes him instead of trying to accept him; she stuffs him with food instead of love: "And every mouthful seemed to have the effect of increasing his desire for her. He thought how satisfying it would be to lift that yellow dress over her bare thighs" (184). Memo is Roy's "unlucky fate" and he is a terminal victim of her body. On the one occasion when he sleeps with Memo (a trick devised by Bump), Roy is startled by her deadly impact: "He thought he was still dreaming of the picture but the funny part of it was when she got into bed with him he almost cried out in pain as her icy hands and feet, in immediate embrace, slashed his hot body, but there among the apples, grapes, and melons, he found what he wanted and had it (65). Later, he still longs for her, although the result is even more pain.

Memo, like Tod's Faye, has had a full dose of the Hollywood dream. She tells Roy that she was never really happy except for a year or two with Bump, and earlier when she was nineteen and first went to Hollywood. Like so many others before her, she had won a beauty contest and then developed a strong desire for film success.

> For a few weeks I felt like the Queen of the May, then they took a screen test and though I had the looks and figure my test did not come out so good in acting and they practically told me to go home. I couldn't stand the thought of that so I stayed there for three more years, doing night club work and going to an acting school besides, hoping that I would some day be a good enough actress but it didn't take. I knew what I was supposed to do but I couldn't make myself, in my thoughts, into somebody else. You're supposed to forget who you are but I couldn't (120).

With Hollywood discarded, Memo concentrates on Bump and finally turns to Roy for the kind of future she has in mind for herself. But her plans are at the expense of Roy's ideals, and she steers him to bribery. " 'There's one thing you have to understand, Roy, and then maybe you won't want me. That is that I am afraid to be poor' " (199). Roy, like Tod, is so mermerized by the elusiveness of his tantalizing love object, that he begins to have aggressive thoughts: "Yet she was a truly beautiful doll with a form like Miss America, and despite the bumps and bruises he had taken, he was sure that once he got an armlock on her things would go better" (166). "He trapped her lips, tasting of lemon drops, kissing hard" (121). But Roy finally realizes that the Memo he yearns for is not the real Memo at all. "It later struck him that the picture he had drawn of Memo sitting domestically home wasn't exactly the girl she was. The kind he had in mind, though it bothered him to admit it, was more like Iris seemed to be, only she didn't suit him" (180). Deceived, and yet aware of the deception, Roy is still unable to save himself. In an almost Dostoevsky-like way, Roy is vividly aware of his own impending destruction—the classic victim.

Faye Greener, a girl of seventeen, is tall, beautiful, and has "long, swordlike legs." She is Tod's "unlucky fate." She leads him on a harum-scarum journey through her corrupt environment of swindlers and frauds, distracting him from his true vocation of art. Tod becomes more interested in Faye than in painting. And like Roy, he suffers from a dislocated love affair while fully aware of his strong sexual longing for the wrong woman. "Her invitation wasn't to pleasure, but to struggle, hard and sharp, closer to murder than to love. If you threw yourself on her, it would be like throwing yourself from the parapet of a skyscraper. You would do it with a scream" (271). Although Tod realizes her deadly nature, he nevertheless admits: "If she would only let him, he would be glad to throw himself, no matter what the cost. But she wouldn't have him" (271). Faye, much like Memo, is a product of false and contrived dreams. Tod will not suit her; he has "nothing to offer her, neither money nor looks"

(270). She tells Homer, another victim in her path, that she is "going to be a star some day" (309). Faye is a by-product of the "star build-up" system and glamour publicity aimed at movie-magazine mentalities. Yet Tod cannot resist her, even though he knows her pose of innocence and her persistent strivings for Mammon will destroy his ideals. "Being with her was like being backstage during an amateurish, ridiculous play. From in front, the stupid lines and grotesque situations would have made him squirm with annoyance, but because he saw the perspiring stage-hands and the wires that held up the tawdry summerhouse with its tangle of paper flowers, he accepted everything and was anxious for it to succeed" (316). Trapped by his lust for Faye, Tod, like Roy, recognizes his woman as a portent of his destruction, and yet he is helpless to do anything about it. Also like Roy, he even resorts to images of aggression: "If he only had the courage to throw himself on her. Nothing less violent than rape would do. The sensation he felt was like that he got when holding an egg in his hand. Not that she was fragile or even seemed fragile. It wasn't that. It was her completeness, her egglike self-sufficiency, that made him want to crush her" (320). Constantly stalking and skirting the two illusion worlds of Malamud and West are the fans—the masses, or mobs. Both writers deal with these mobs as being both grotesque and comic. The great swarm of American dreamers file by the thousands into movie houses and ball parks avidly seeking the idols who, as Iris explains, will keep them from being "plain people." But these American Philistines are pathetic because of their inability to accept the humanness of their heroes; they clutch desperately to the hope that men can become Gods.

Roy is quite aware of the absurdities of his fans. He realizes that the stadium often resembles "a zoo full of oddballs, including gamblers, bums, drunks, and some ugly crackpots," and he is also quite aware of their shifting loyalties (76). When he goes into a playing slump, the old timers begin to "heave vegetables and oddments around" (138). They call Roy everything from hero to son-of-a-bitch.

Roy is sensitive to this hostility for he has "rabbit ears" and hears everything.

These baseball fanatics resemble the middle-class mobs of West's world. The police have problems with "the ticketless hordes that descend on them" (176). Riding home from Philadelphia, Roy finds his reception "a bughouse nightmare because the way the fans on the train pummeled players" (176). In a scene as dramatic as the rioting mob at the end of *Day of the Locust*, Malamud described the crowd's behavior on the morning of the big championship game. "On the morning of the game fist fights broke out all over the stands in Knights Field. Hats, bottles, apple cores, bananas, and the mushy contents of sack lunches were thrown around. A fan in one of the boxes had a rock bounced off his skull, opening a bleeding gash. Two special cops rushed up the steps and got hold of an innocent-looking guy with glasses, whose pockets were stuffed with odd-shaped rocks" (212). The first frightening thought that occurs to Roy after he had "thrown" the game is what the mobs might do to him. "He feared the mob would swarm all over him, tear him apart, and strew his polluted remains over the field, but they vanished" (233).

The *Day of the Locust* was originally intended to be called *The Cheated*. West wanted his novel to be basically about the bored and bitter middle-aged who swarm to California seeking a kind of end-of-the-road nirvana. These people were not meant to be harmless or passive. West saw the lower middle classes as a frightening, pugnacious mob of cheated people—victims of America's dream world.

> New groups, whole families, kept arriving. He could see a change come over them as soon as they had become part of the crowd. Until they reached the line, they looked diffident, almost furtive, but the moment they had become part of it, they turned arrogant and pugnacious. It was a mistake to think of them as harmless curiosity seekers. They were savage and bitter, especially the middle-aged and the old, and had been made so by boredom and disappointment.
>
> All their lives they had slaved at some kind of dull, heavy labor, behind desks and counters, in the fields and at tedious machines of all sorts, saving their pennies and dreaming of the leisure that would be theirs when they had enough. Finally

that day came. They could draw a weekly income of ten or
fifteen dollars. Where else should they go but California, the
land of sunshine and oranges? (411)

The natives of Hollywood—the "cheaters"—have no more
identity than the "cheated." Living in their "Samoan huts,
Mediterranean villas, Egyptian temples, Swiss chalets, Tudor
cottages," the "cheaters" represent a national hoax.
Together, the *cheaters* and the *cheated* feed on each other
and propagate their sordid culture. The masses, starved for
the sunshine and freedom of California, descend like locusts
upon the city to revenge themselves for having been bilked
by a popular myth that provides only disillusionment and
frustration. Tod, caught in the melee, is swept along
helplessly, a cheated one himself. "The crowd in front of the
theatre had charged. He was surrounded by churning legs and
feet. He pulled himself erect by grabbing a man's coat, then
let himself be carried along backwards in a long, curving
swoop. He saw Homer rise above the mass for a moment,
shoved against the sky, his jaw hanging as though he wanted
to scream but couldn't. A hand reached up and caught him
by his open mouth and pulled him forward and down" (415).

The most grotesque character in both novels is a dwarf.
In *The Day of the Locust,* Abe Kusich appears, momentarily,
as a perfect replica of dwarfdom in his "high green Tyrolean
hat." However, he is not exactly pathetic or typically
puckish. He carries a copy of the *Daily Running Horses* under
his arm and is pugnacious and glib. Eventually, he erupts into
the role of a murderous little creature who squeezes Earle's
testicles until Earle collapses. In *The Natural,* the dwarf Otto
Zipp is equally hideous. Otto's face is "like a pancake with a
cherry nose," and he is about as gross and abrasive as Abe,
reappearing "like a bad dream with his loud voice and pesky
tooter venomously hooting Roy into oblivion" (138). Otto
yells: "Carrion, offal, turd—flush the bowl" (223). In the
end, after Roy strikes out, it is Otto who comes down from
the stands and hits an "illusionary" home run. These two
truncated humans, one might conclude, are Man cut down to
his right size—both the answer and conclusion to Man's
absurd role as a hero.

Both Malamud's and West's *cheaters* and *cheated* violate society and represent an America that Daniel Aaron depicts as being "carried to its logical conclusion."

> The tormented, hungry, violent people who end up at the edge of the western ocean and who finally riot in the eerie conclusion of the book are the products of middle-America, the degraded descendents of the Populists, with no further frontiers to conquer. They are the locusts, mindless and numberless, who, like their Biblical namesakes, have turned a once beautiful country into a desert; they are impelled by forces they can neither understand nor control. They may even be the instruments of God's wrath. West observes them humorourly but also with wonder and fear as they scream imprecations in their "New Thought" temples and swarm aimlessly through the streets waiting for the apocalypse.[3]

According to West, the dreams of America finally come to rest in a "dream dump"—a graveyard of worn-out props and moving picture artifacts. He sees the history of civilization ultimately coming to this—a mighty heap of hopes and aspirations thrown into a back lot like twisted auto bodies. West compared this image to Janvier's "Sargasso Sea"—a cultural history that is only an imaginary body of water in a marine junkyard. "A Sargasso of the imagination! And the dump grew continually, for there wasn't a dream afloat somewhere which wouldn't sooner or later turn up on it, having first been made photographic by plaster, canvas, lath and paint. Many boats sink and never reach the Sargasso, but no dream ever entirely disappears. Somewhere it troubles some unfortunate person and some day, when that person has been sufficiently troubled, it will be reproduced on the lot" (353). Both West and Malamud protray this *dream dump*— Hollywood and the world of baseball—each of which is a papier-mache structure built on the imagination and hopes of an American public nourished for decades on the peculiarly American Dream that every man is capable of becoming *some one,* that he can occupy any level of society; and, furthermore, that he can somehow become part of a world inhabited by beautiful people who themselves were once just one of the lowly, struggling masses. It is the fantastic lure and excitement of these two worlds that have fed the eager imaginations of so many Americans for so long, and, according to Malamud and West, have lured so many to destruction on the commercial, cardboard rocks of Hollywood and the baseball arena. Both authors imply a prophecy in their writings, as if they felt a need to warn others of the impending disaster. West warns us not to be carelessly sucked into the maelstrom of the "Sargasso Sea." Tod sees the danger as being "ingrained, morbid apathy" (365). The dilemma is most clearly defined by Malamud himself: "It is, in the end, the fact of being alive that shuts you off from life."[4]

It is interesting to speculate on how both writers would have viewed their subjects at this time in history. Today, would West consider Hollywood as having "grown up"? Is Hollywood more professional, authentic, closer to realism in what it tries to portray on the screen? Are its fans soberer, more aware of the humanness of the people who perform before the cameras? Or would he view Hollywood as being even more insidiously evil, in that—like today's Mafia mobster—it wears conventional clothing, goes to work every morning with a newspaper under its arm, and plays the role of conservative, middle-class, salt-of-the-earth suburbia? And what would Malamud say of athletics today? Are its fans *more* hysterical, more prone to antics of mob behavior? Or like the recent trend in sportswriting, are a growing number of sports fans judging athletes in proper perspective—as very human and error-prone performers who work at something that is really quite simple but do it just a little better than anyone else?

Either way, both writers—then *or* now—surely would indict the masses, and the mass media that feed on them, for so blatantly distorting what should remain as rather harmless, diversionary games. And, like true gamesmanship, one should be able to immerse oneself, and then when the game is over, emerge from it all with a whole skin and soul. West and Malamud quite plainly view with horror the fact that Hollywood and the baseball world seem to subvert so many people so totally and irreversibly. And, in an artistic sense, both are implying that when one lingers too long in the bewitching atmosphere of a dream dump, he is likely to stay forever. Perhaps West and Malamud might wish us to heed the advice of Marshall McLuhan who urges Americans "to turn off the TV for three years so we can restore our psychic balance."

FOOTNOTES

1. Bernard Malamud, *The Natural* (New York: Farrar, Straus & Giroux, 1968), 54. Hereafter, only the page numbers will appear after the quote. It is ironic to note that even Pop's hands are "crippled." His fingers are loosely bandaged since he had had the misfortune to catch athlete's foot on his hands. It is only when Pop gets in the spirit of winning that his hands, we are told, heal. Success, it would seem, is a cure-all. Also interesting is the fact that West uses the image of "hands" to dramatize Homer in *The Day of the Locust*. Every part of Homer, we are told, is awake except his hands. West uses "strange aquatic" hands to symbolize Homer's repressed yearnings for sex and success.

2. Nathanael West, *The Complete Works of Nathanael West* (New York: Farrar, Straus & Giroux, 1966), 261. Hereafter, only the page number will appear after the quote.

3. Daniel Aaron, "Writing For the Apocalypse," *Hudson Review*, (Winter, 1951), 635.

4. Frank Kermode, "Bernard Malamud," *New Statesman* (March 30, 1962), 452.

HISTORY AND CASE HISTORY IN
RED CAVALRY AND *THE DAY OF THE LOCUST*
By Max Apple

There are many immediate comparisons between the works and careers of Isaac Babel and Nathanael West. Babel writing primarily in the 1920's, West in the '30's, both died without making a great impact on the literary world. Each was "promising" in his day, yet lived to be neglected, and each has been fully "resurrected" by the literary tastes of the 1970's. The "figure" of Isaac Babel, growing silent under the Stalinist regime he helped to create, is perhaps more familiar than Babel's stories, although a collection of his early works and other literary fragments is at this moment close to the top of the best seller lists. From the back cover of *The Lonely Years,* an earlier anthology of fragments, Babel's round, joyless face looks out of steel rimmed glasses in a thousand American bookstores. Babel, who finally could not "program" his genius to Soviet demands, is a kind of hero to contemporary Americans who select his works from the lists of their book clubs. Not really a "great," Babel has become in paperback America one to be reckoned with. The popularity of the resurrected West novels is more confined. *Miss Lonelyhearts* and *The Day of the Locust* are more likely to be found on freshman reading lists than on a New York *Times* chart.

The most immediately striking similarity between the Russian's short stories and the American's short novels is the precision of their syntax and the imagistic speed of their sentences. "Forget the epic," West wrote. "In America fortunes do not accumulate, the soil does not grow, families have no history. Leave slow growth to the book reviewers, you have only time to explode." ("Some Notes on *Miss Lonelyhearts," Contempo,* May 15, 1933, p. 2.) Yet West's novels do not crash upon the senses to numb by sheer clatter of bombast. The "explosions" are not the "bombs of those realists" whom Nabokov characterizes as typing "powerful and stark" novels with their thumbs. West and Babel are masters of the power of "containment." Even in dispassionate understatement their events and images threaten sentence by sentence to burst into the wild rhetoric of a Dostoyevsky or a Faulkner. They do not. The effect is virtually the opposite of those grandiose periodic sentences of a Dr. Johnson which ramble gracefully, ironies in hand, toward a solemn conclusion. West and Babel drop periods like knives, using speed to avoid the "explosions" of sentiment. Yet these are not the kind of short sentences which everyone associates with Hemingway. West and Babel draw their "styles" not from the banality of the world as Hemingway does, but from the contrast between the physical awesomeness of events and the paltry resources of language. In a two and one half page story, "With Old Man Makhno," Babel presents a heroine who speaks three words, "Fetch some water." She is a peasant Jewess who has been raped the previous night by six of Makhno's Cossacks. She goes about her daily chores while a slow-witted boy, an aide-de-camp to the staff, reminisces upon what occurred the previous evening. The girl washes clothes. Her "legs, fat, brick red, swollen like globes, gave off a sickly sweet smell like fresh salted meat." (*Collected Stories of Isaac Babel,* World Publishing Co., 1955, p. 278. All page references are from this edition.) As he talks, the boy sticks "strips of gilt paper onto a German helmet" (278). This is not the "banality of evil," it is Babel's brutally understated prose assertion of an offense too awesome to become a story. A peasant girl ravished by diseased Cossacks, an idiot boy retelling her terror while posing before a mirror in a gilded helmet: Babel seems to carve these vignettes into the retina.

The short, lyrical sentences are a kind of anesthetic, numbing one's perceptions with literary conventions. It is, after all, a "story." It ends quickly, and with no mess, one progresses to the next short description of life with the Revolution's Cossacks.

West's syntax is neither as brief nor as brutal as Babel's. The self-conscious playfulness of *The Dream Life of Balso Snell* never entirely disappears. West cannot resist the one-liner, the "Chief Kiss My Towkus," even in *The Day of the Locust*. Yet this playfulness hovers over the novels like a bird of prey. While Babel catalogues horrors which are the fruits of war, West presents the lives of people who have the leisure to "come to California to die." Suffering in wartime Russia may be no more justifiable than in peace-time Hollywood, yet there is at least some rhetorical satisfaction that underlying Babel's violence is an ideological stance. This posture is of course the belief that the crimes of the Revolution are justified by its glorious end, the very attitude which destroyed Trotsky and ultimately Babel himself. Although West's novels are less bloody than Babel's stories, the overall effect of West's violence is at least as pervasive, since it is always gratuitous violence. There is no revolution, no political or moral ideology, not even a flawed one, to give pseudo-justification to the suffering.

By presenting the exploits of soldiers, Babel implicitly utilizes the most ancient literary motif of men at war. His Cossacks, like Agamemnon's legions, draw ironic force from the contrast between their mean lives and ugly deaths and the abstract ideas of glory in battle or revolutionary equality. West ironically creates his own "Homer," but utilizes no such classical literary heritage. His "armies" await only the opening of a theatre. Without any literary heritage, West relies on internal structural devices for a "historical" sense in *The Day of the Locust*. He recapitulates violence he has already described. Thus Homer kills Adore Loomis in the same way that Juju kills the red cock. Like Juju, Homer jumps in the air and jabs Adore from above. He uses his heels as Juju used his gaffs. The murder is the only act that Homer commits without his hands. His personality, his very humanity, is encompassed in the few rituals he performs with his hands and fingers. Without these outward signs of order, he is loosed from civilization to kill as a bird in a staged battle.

Tod's role in the final mob scene also recapitulates the iconography of earlier violence committed upon birds. Attempting to escape, Tod performs upon a man what Earle does upon a quail. When Earle poached, he trapped the quail in a small wire basket. The birds "ran wildly along the inner edge and threw themselves at the wire. One of them, a cock, had a dainty plume on his head that curled forward almost to his beak. Earle caught the birds one at a time and pulled their heads off." (*Complete Works of Nathanael West*, Farrar, Straus, and Cudahy, 1957, p. 330. All page references are to this edition.) Tod, trapped in the crowd, resembles the birds trapped in the cage. "He couldn't turn his body, but managed to get his head around. A very skinny boy, wearing a Western Union cap, had his back wedged against his shoulder" (416). The Western Union boy, like the cock with the "dainty plume," has his neck wrenched. Tod "finally got his left arm free and took the back of the boy's neck in his fingers. He twisted as hard as he could" (416).

Where Babel seemingly justifies the terror that precedes the dream of the Dictatorship of the Proletariat, West boldly mocks human affairs in the "dream capital." Hollywood is West's perfect symbol, for it offers not only "dreams" but sunshine and new hope. People slither into the California warmth for their last convulsive palpitations. They "writhe on the hard seats of their churches." At the "Tabernacle of the Third Coming," they listen to their messiahs shout "a crazy jumble of dietary rules, economics, and biblical threats." West's Hollywood is the dead end of the continent, the dream, and seemingly of sane personal relationships. It is on the edge not of revolution but of apocalypse. This is in sharp contrast to Babel's Russia of the 1920's where the "Messiah" has already arrived. Babel quotes Commissar Vinogradov as he tells the peasants of Berestechko, a recently plundered village, "You are in power. Everything is yours"

(121). Babel's narrator walks through the little town "awaiting a new era and instead of human beings there go about
mere faded schemata of frontier misfortunes." While the
Cossack commissar speaks in a voice "fired with enthusiasm
and the ringing of spurs," the peasants, Jews and tanners
listen beneath "walls where nymphs with gouged-out eyes
were leading a choral dance." Hollywood as much as
Berestechko is the place of "faded schemata" where the
visions of capitalism, Harry as salesman, Faye as actress, Abe
as entrepreneur, even Tod as artist are the tantalizing
manifestations of the American "new era," the revolution of
the daydreams.

It is in The Day of the Locust that West, who utilizes the
theme of dreams in each of his novels, confronts the rawest,
least institutionalized dream, the personal fantasy. In his
earlier novels, West chose the dreams of "art," "religion,"
and "success" as his satiric targets. In The Day of the Locust,
the target is dream itself, the bit of fantasy and hope in the
lives of the cheated and bored who have come to California
to die. They are the "nymphs with gouged-out eyes" whose
danse macabre is rhapsodic in Hollywood, stagnant in
Wayneville, everywhere sustained by boredom and violence,
and inevitably concluded in the chaos of its own empty
movements. These are the people who order their lives by the
everyday clichés "love" and "success" that are the heart of
their mediocre fantasies.

West strikes first and hardest at love. Faye, the desired
prize of virtually every man in the novel, is a classic bitch
goddess. Tod knows that Faye's love is "an invitation to
struggle hard and sharp . . . that if you threw yourself on her
it would be like throwing yourself from the parapet of a
skyscraper . . . Your teeth would be driven into your skull
like nails in a pine board . . . You wouldn't even have time to
sweat or close your eyes" (271). Faye is "hollow"; she is all
surface. "No matter how rough the sea got, she would go
dancing over the same waves that sank iron ships and tore
away piers of reinforced concrete" (406). Faye's youthful
surface, "taut and vibrant . . . shiny as a new spoon," (304) is

all there is. The dream of "love" is merely a combination of affectations.

After Faye, the love object, West's favorite target is "success." Only one character in *The Day of the Locust,* Claude Estee, is a Hollywood success. Stanley Edgar Hyman believes that Claude is "West's ideal vision of himself" (*Nathanael West,* University of Minnesota Press, Minneapolis, 1962, p. 44). If this is true, then West's image of himself is as grotesque as any of the characters he created. Claude is a member of another crowd, the bored rich, and this group is no less violent than the crowd of the poor and cheated. Claude lives in a house "that is an exact reproduction of the old Dupuy Mansion near Biloxi, Mississippi" (271). He is a dried up little man, but he dresses in flannels and tweeds. In his buttonhole is "a lemon flower" (272). "Here, you black rascal! A mint julep," he calls to a Chinese servant who comes running with a scotch and soda. Claude has the "success" that is the dream of the Greeners and the Mrs. Loomises, yet his act is as transparent as Faye's, without her "purity." He imagines a mythic past where the rich own the poor, and in his pool is a rubber model of a dead horse. Claude's crowd admires Mrs. Jenning, a madam "who runs her business as other women run lending librairies" (277). The only disappointing thing about Mrs. Jenning is her "refinement." The bored rich crave smut and obscenity as the bored poor crave the pretenses of taste and distinction. The causes of the two great scenes of violence in the novel are equally divided between rich and poor: Claude causes one, Homer and the "cheated" the other.

Babel's analogues to these American dreams of love and success are the Revolution's dreams of communal joy and glory in battle. The acts of Babel's soldiers are far less "decadent" than those of West's Californians. The Cossack cavalry is reduced by circumstance to testing itself through formal ritual. In one of Babel's most famous stories, "My First Goose," an intellectual gains his acceptance into the cavalry by killing a goose. "A severe-looking goose was waddling about the yard, inoffensively preening its feathers. I overtook it and pressed it to the ground. Its head cracked beneath my foot, cracked and emptied itself. The white neck lay stretched out in the dung, the wings twitched" (75). After demonstrating his brutality, the intellectual, a lawyer, is welcomed into the community. "Sit down and feed with us till your goose is done." After eating, he reads to his new comrades Lenin's speech to the Second Congress of the Comintern. He sleeps that night in the hay with his fellows. "We slept . . . warming one another, our legs intermingled. I dreamed and in my dreams saw women. But my heart stained with bloodshed grated and brimmed over" (77). Brutality has led to acceptance. Beneath a moon that hangs above the yard "like a cheap earring," the lawyer reads Lenin triumphantly aloud, only to be answered by a commander's cliché, "Truth tickles everyone's nostrils" (77). The men sleep, but this single goose casts a pall on the Revolution.

Babel's use of the bird to foreshadow and parallel the slaughter of men is similar to West's. Babel's intellectual kills when his best instincts become shrouded by the "new values" of the Cossacks. The cockfight in *The Day of the Locust* takes place under far more bourgeois circumstances. Claude "just wants to see a fight" (379). His fifteen dollars is impetus enough to bring about the action. It is here that Abe Kusich finds himself most at home. Abe too is sub-human: he suffers and writhes with the cock in perhaps the most genuine "love" West portrays in the novel. Abe and the bird are equals. "The dwarf eyed the bird and the bird eyed him" (380). Abe begs Claude, "Please mister let me handle him" (379). The dwarf speaks of himself and the bird as "we," ministering to the cock as if it were his child. "The little man moaned over the bird . . . he spit into its gaping beak and took the comb between his lips and sucked the blood back into it . . . he inserted his little finger and scratched the bird's testicles" (382). When the red cock dies, only Abe groans with anguish. "Take off that stinking cannibal" (383), he screams to the laughing Miguel. In Babel's story it is the intellectual who has become the "stinking cannibal." The intellectual's justification for his behavior is Lenin's pro-

nouncement that "there are shortages everywhere." Lenin
meant only the material shortages, but West and Babel turn
Lenin's truism into a brutal comment on the "new" men of
Hollywood and of Russia. For the "shortages" that are
apparent in *The Day of the Locust* and *Red Cavalry* are not
the bodily needs but those "noumenal" necessities that
define human behavior.

West and Babel, who resemble each other as highly
self-conscious literary stylists, are even more closely aligned
in their relationship to the past. Both writers are literally cut
off from the traditional roots of fiction in time and place.
Chaos is everywhere the Red Cavalry moves and in every
facet of Tod's life in Hollywood. In Russia, men speak to
each other in the sterile clichés of the Revolution; in
Hollywood the characters banter the disembodied jargon of
stale fantasies. No character has a "usable past": each is
"boxed in" by the random violence of a particular moment.
West speaks specifically of a "comic strip" technique in *Miss
Lonelyhearts*. "The chapters to be squares in which many
things happen through one action . . . I abandoned this idea
but retained some of the comic strip technique: Each chapter
instead of going forward in time, also goes backward,
forward, up and down in space like a picture ("Some Notes
on *Miss Lonelyhearts*," p. 2). Both West and Babel achieve
this "comic strip" technique in metaphysical as well as
stylistic terms. Babel's "picture" of Russia is done in short,
literally enclosed sentences. The continuity is in the narrative
voice and in the ride of the Cavalry. Yet the ride is a random
one and the narrator sees no particular order in the events he
records. Whether a village is plundered sooner or later, the
misery will always be there. This comic strip notion of
independent experiences, pictures with a few words, depends
upon easily recognizable figures who are not men.

The idea of the traditional novel and story has always
been to create the illusion of a "real life." An eighteenth or
nineteenth century novel is a "life and adventures"; even in a
modern short story, the "epiphany" depends entirely upon
the relation of the story's "illuminated moment" with the

cumulative experiences of the people involved. The boxed comic strip technique denies all but spatial and chronological relationships. But most significantly, it denies the past. What happened to Dagwood Bumstead yesterday has no necessary relationship with what happens today. Comic strips have no past, only the raw materials of character and situation. This is almost precisely Babel's condition as a writer in the midst of the Revolution. How does one create the past of the "new man" when the revolution obliterates yesterday the way the morning paper changes the old comic strip? Yet men live by their accumulated memories, a man is his past. Babel, caught in the "present" of the revolution, is too honest to buy the easy Utopian dream, yet too much a "Red" to lapse into a lament for the old Russia. Beneath his hard cool eye and dispassionate posture, he allows a very subtle nostalgia that permeates his work and serves as an implicit judgement upon the revolution.

The narrator is most readily nostalgic when he encounters anything Jewish. In the story "Gedali," the narrator admits that on Sabbath eves he is "oppressed by the dense melancholy of memory" (69). In such a mood he roams through the Jewish quarter of Zhitomir, where he finds amid the ruin of Jewish shops only one survivor, old Gedali, a man who has said "yes" to the revolution. As the Jewish cossack and the aged storekeeper await the Sabbath, Gedali asks the most telling questions about the revolution.

> The Poles, kind sir, shot because they were the Counter-Revolution. You shoot because you are the Revolution. But surely the Revolution means joy. And joy does not like orphans in the house. Good men do good deeds. The revolution is the good deed of good men. But good men do not kill. So it is bad people that are making the Revolution. But the Poles are bad people too. Then how is Gedali to tell which is Revolution? I used to study the Talmud, I love Rashi's Commentaries and the books of Maimonides. And there are yet other understanding folk in Zhitomir. And here we are, all of us learned people falling on our faces and crying out in a loud voice: "Woe unto us, where is the joy-giving revolution?" (71)

In Gedali's sentences lie all "shortages," the pressing ques-

tions: Who are the "good" and where is joy? What has the
Talmud to do with the Revolution? Why must learned people
fall on their faces? Gedali wants "an international of good
people where every soul is given first class rations" (72).
Gedali wants the utopia that coincides with his version of
history, the "good" based upon "joy." The Jewish Cossack
can only reply that the international "is eaten with gun-
powder . . . and spiced with the best quality blood" (72).
These two "new men" await the young Sabbath that comes
to them out of the "blue gloom." The narrator's melancholy
has led him to this confrontation with "the rotted Talmuds"
of his youth. He knows that Gedali, Rashi, and the Sabbath
are anachronisms, but if "joy" and "goodness" are also not
part of the Revolution, what is to become of Zhitomir, the
Cossacks, and the "faded schemata" who "own everything"
while they await the new day? Babel does not answer this
any more than he comments on other matters in *Red Cavalry*.
Faced with the problem of men whose pasts have become
immediately obsolete, Babel has created a spatial-temporal
Red Cavalry that reads like War and Peace stuffed into *Wines-
burg, Ohio*. The peasants and townspeople of Russia reek
with their "irrelevant" history in which there is no time to
explore in "dense melancholy."

West has a far less formal concern than Babel with
history. In Hollywood, "history" is as ill conceived and
transparent as everything else. West devotes most of one
chapter to "History" as Tod encounters it while searching for
Faye on the set of "Waterloo." Tod walks past "a forty foot
papier mache sphinx . . . the Last Chance Saloon . . . a Paris
street . . . Kamp Komfit . . . a Greek Temple dedicated to
Eros . . . the wooden horse of Troy . . . the bones of a
dinosaur . . . a corner of a Mayan temple" (353). Pausing to
catch his breath, Tod realizes that the studio lot is a "history
of civilization in the form of a dream dump. A Sargasso of
the imagination!" (353). Yet Tod, who has such metaphysical reflections, can continue after this brief revery to
search for Faye, his own hopeless two-dimensional dream.

Tod, like Babel's Jewish Cossack, brings with him the

paraphernalia of judgement based on the past. Babel's narrator still feels "dense melancholy" on Sabbath Eve, but he is unable to do anything to relieve the misery around him. He is in fact and in deed one of the Cossacks. And Tod too is one of the Hollywood "grotesques." It is Tod's failure that raises West's novel above a Hollywood burlesque, for Tod, who cannot be reduced to a language of "Vas you dere Sharley" or a stereotype plot outline, is no more effective in the world than anyone else.

Tod's failure is like the failure of Miss Lonelyhearts, and, West would surely add, of Christ himself. Tod is not a dwarf or an actor. He has legitimate values and artistic insights. By showing Tod to be as incomplete as the grotesques surrounding him, West has returned to the objective of *The Dream Life of Balso Snell*. The "artist" in West's first novel writes to facilitate his seduction of "fat girls," and Tod is another version of twelve-year-old John Gilson. Easily missed in West's tricky syntax is the suggestion that Tod is perhaps not a very talented artist. " 'The Burning of Los Angeles,' a picture he was soon to paint, definitely proved he had talent" (261).

In spite of his "historical" insights, Tod is as dream-infected as the other Hollywood grotesques. Although a bit more articulate than the rest, he is also a "case study" as West uses personal history rather than the compressed historical panoramas of Babel. West said that "the great body of case histories can be used the way ancient writers use their myths" ("Some Notes on Miss Lonelyhearts," p. 2). This is on the surface not a very striking comment, since the modern novel has obviously specialized in psychology. But West puts his own idiosyncratic twist to the modern novel. For he means not generally that case histories can be the basis of fiction, but that they can be used specifically the way ancient writers "use their myths." Thus West uses case studies by stringing a whole series of them together rather than by performing a Jamesian or Lawrentian case analysis of a single character or even a single family. West "packs" Hollywood with case histories the way Babel "packs" the Revolution into *Red Cavalry*. Like a modern Euripides, West strings out his "case studies"—Homer, Harry, Faye, Abe, Claude—often teasing the reader by giving an alternate version of the expected case study. West does not dwell on personal history any more than Babel does on the military past. He picks his case studies in the middle of their misery and mixes them into the random violence that is the texture of their lives. The "whys" of the past are as obsolete as Babel's "rotted Talmuds." The future lies ahead for West's case studies in the form of more premieres and plane crashes.

In both *Red Cavalry* and *The Day of the Locust*, the disenchanted crowd with its ubiquitous collection of misery and vice replaces the historical background. There is no sense of time nor place, no leisurely descriptions of men or nature, not even any relief in a "Big Two-Hearted River." Nature is as ominous as men in the literary landscapes of West and Babel. In *Miss Lonelyhearts* West quickly shatters the idea of pastoral retreat when Miss Lonelyhearts and Betty are told that "yids" have driven the deer away. When he looks about him, Miss Lonelyhearts sees that in the midst of spring "in the deep shade there was nothing but death—rotten leaves, gray and white fungi, and over everything a funereal hush" (114). Although he was the protege of Maxim Gorky, the great voice of "socialist realism," Babel resembles the Yiddish writers far more than the Russian in his treatment of nature. In the language of the ghetto there are not even words for the pastoral scenes that abound in all national literatures. Babel's Russian carries all the claustrophobic qualities of his life in the ghetto. Nature is only a series of images—words for literary effect. The only connection between men and the earth is that men are buried there.

In spite of the obvious terrors in both narratives, the effect of comparing *Red Cavalry* and *The Day of the Locust* is not as metaphysically debilitating as it would seem to be. In a society that has adopted "alienation," "violence," and "lack of communication" as intimate elements of a critical vocabulary it is not surprising that West and Babel have achieved such popular acclaim. Their fictions appeal to the sense of despair that the television news brings to our lives with regularity, often in color. Yet in our zeal for "brutal" and "apocalyptic" literature that seems to mirror our daily lives, West and Babel are no literary stand-ins for the one hour news special that tells us how bad the world is going to be because of air pollution, radiation, lack of birth control—whatever the topic and the sponsor of the day happen to be. West and Babel are not chroniclers of topical "issues" to be disregarded when the appropriate government agency takes charge. Whatever is wrong with Tod may be most clearly visible in Hollywood but is hardly confined to the dream capital. Similarly the milieu of Russian Civil War dramatically emphasizes the shadowy lives of the masses, but we knew they were shadows long before Lenin made them heirs of the earth. The pure and impenetrable Faye sitting in bed with her pack of cards, going through her daydreams with a formal and patterned dignity, is like a modern Helen taking a walk on the walls of a doomed city. We all know how the story ends, but the end is really the business of myth or science or religion. Even the knowledge of Troy's fall does not stem the momentary interest in Helen or the absolute judgement of her beauty. Because of their charged prose and their obvious appeal to the chaos of our times, West and Babel must not be mistaken for contemporary black humorists or chroniclers of the "absurd." They are literary formalists of impeccable stature who make out of human fragments and a surreal environment an ordered literary totality. Like Priam and the old men on the wall, they watch the movements of beauty which, at least in literature, can be isolated from the doom that echoes in her footsteps.

THE DAY OF THE LOCUST
AND THE PAINTER'S EYE
By Donald T. Torchiana

On rereading the novels of Nathanael West, one is struck by wide differences in narrative perspective and, at the same time, by an amazing agreement in characters and materials. Perhaps West's last novel best illustrates this impression. For in *The Day of the Locust* one meets, inescapably, an altogether hardened objectivity in point of view and a sustained uniformity of tone, accompanying materials already familiar from West's earlier work. There is no need to be exhaustive in showing these correspondences, though they certainly have a fascination of their own. For example, the inhuman laugh of an idiot no less than the ragbag of grotesques that people the alimentary canal of the Trojan horse in *Balso Snell* surely recall Harry Greener's laugh and his typical audience in Hollywood. Then too, there can be little choice between Earle Shoup's "two-dimensional face" and Shrike's "triangular face," or between the instruments of pain available in a saddlery store on Sunset Boulevard and those in a pawnshop window in New York. All such armories may only suggest the human and inhuman misery inflicted on such "holy fools"[1] as Miss Lonelyhearts and Homer Simpson in two different novels. And for every fearsome Mary Dove, Faye Greener, or Romola Martin in *The Day of the Locust* there is an equally ferocious flying predator in a Shrike or Faye Doyle in *Miss Lonelyhearts* or in a Squire Bird in *A Cool Million*. Moreover, the impervious sexiness of at least

249

two fays, Faye Greener and Faye Doyle, is clearly no solace for the torment they inflict: to sleep with either woman is to sleep "with a knife in one's groin" or, given Faye's "swordlike legs," to accept an invitation to murder. It follows, then, that frustration, crippling, or murder is the fate of the hero; the props of life are fake—whether they take the form of a giant hemorrhoid, a clock in the stomach of Venus, or the architecture of Hollywood; and good taste is rarely to be found outside the decor of a whore house.

For men en masse the gist is about the same: crowds can move with "dreamlike violence" in New York; or a Southern lynch mob can vie in joyous righteousness with its distant Midwestern cousins howling before a premiere showing in California. Then, needless to say, both New York and Hollywood become sites of the modern waste land, one seen in the dank parks where Miss Lonelyhearts broods and Lemuel Pitkin suffers the loss of an eye, the other viewed by Homer in his backyard vista of tin cans, incinerator, and ragged cactus plants. Such disporting chronicles could only conclude in the satisfactions of hysteria and violence. Homer and Miss Lonelyhearts approach catatonic states before they are killed; Balso winds up his dream with a mile-a-minute seduction; a fascist mob hails the martyred Pitkin as an All-American Boy; and even Tod discovers himself imitating a siren. But these examples may be enough, for they ought to make clear the means West employs in rendering his persistent themes—the betrayal of dreams, the inherent self-destructiveness of man in a world of animal violence, and the bankruptcy of the middle class, obvious in its yen for fascism, chaos come again.

Yet in *The Day of the Locust* these familiar materials are handled with a cool dispassion, even with a gaiety which shapes that novel into fiction altogether different from West's earlier self-conscious, frequently sentimental books. This difference arises, as I hope to show, from West's placing a painter, Tod Hackett, in the central role of the book and, again, from Tod's own persistent reference to his acknowledged masters, painters preoccupied, indeed obsessed, with the fantastic and the bizarre as they mysteriously define human life during its seemingly recurrent frenzies of the spirit.

In outline, the evidence is fairly clear. As recently as March 24, 1957, S. J. Perelman, West's literary executor and brother-in-law, hinted in the *New York Times* some of the novelist's affinity with the fine arts in the writing of *Balso Snell*: "it has a Goyaesque quality. West had that sort of talent...for the monstrous and the misshapen."[2] And so does Tod Hackett who, we may recall, had purposely fled the Yale School of Fine Arts to escape the dead end of "illustration or mere handsomeness"[3] to which his classmates seemed professionally doomed. But after sighting those who have come to California to die, Tod knows that he has discovered his metier, knows that "neither Winslow Homer nor Thomas [*sic*] Ryder could be his masters and he turned to Goya and Daumier" (261). Just as significantly, near the middle of the novel, Tod dreamily adds other masters: "He had lately begun to think not only of Goya and Daumier but also of certain Italian artists of the seventeenth and eighteenth centuries, of Salvator Rosa, Francesco Guardi and Monsu Desiderio, the painters of Decay and Mystery" (352). Then, a little later, while Tod sketches assorted lunatic worshippers in the temples of their Hollywood cults, we are told "he thought of how well Alessandro Magnasco would dramatize the contrast between their drained-out, feeble bodies and their wild disordered minds. He would not satirize them as Hogarth or Daumier might . . ." (365). These then are the painters who have a visible hand in Tod's future masterpiece *The Burning of Los Angeles*. Moreover, the perceptivity they teach him not only becomes the salvation of his art but also of his life. Hopelessly goaded by Faye's sexuality, Tod nonetheless contains himself by seeking figures and landscapes for his painting, indeed envisions its very progress while enduring mob violence and the added pain of a wrenched leg. The suffering he sees and withstands becomes the grist and impetus for his art. And just so Nathanael West. His final tone resembles Tod's point of view and that of

Tod's masters. It moves from satiric, cool amazement to a delighted, awed sobriety. The levity and the melancholy somehow enhance each other. As a result, different from his other novels, West's *The Day of the Locust* is something more than an extremely realistic, highly pictorial book. Its primary vehicle is, of course, the image or tableau;[4] but its central symbol is a painting, a panoramic burning, an urban last judgment. Hence, despite the too easy parallelism that critics often discover among the arts,[5] I think it can be shown that the final meaning of the book requires in part a knowledge of the grotesque tradition in painting. For, in allowing Tod to see through the eyes of Goya, Daumier, Magnasco, Rosa, Guardi, and Desiderio, West has permitted us to view the local chaos of Hollywood as a timeless image, a subject worthy of man's meditation, and a symptom crying for Biblical allusion and the utterance of prophetic art. In such manner, in the darting glance of the painter's eye, literature may fall heir to the added perspective and illumination of a sister art.

To speak of Goya's work, or that of any of these painters, as an aid in understanding *The Day of the Locust,* is not to insist necessarily on conscious influences or fortuitous parallels, although it must be apparent that West was familiar with the work of these artists. Nor need one always make sharp distinctions between the work of one painter or another, since frequently two or more may be said to amplify the meaning of the same scene or character. Nor, finally, need one deny that West's curious blend of fantastic and sordid images might also be derived from some of his favorite reading in Dostoyevsky, Flaubert, or Joyce. Yet the question remains, given the strategic reference to Goya at the start of the book, what illumination can a knowledge of Goya's art bring to an appreciation of *The Day of the Locust?*

One answer, I think, is that it can illuminate the depth of sexual folly, with its attendant viciousness and hypocrisy, a theme preoccupying Goya but seldom recognized in West's final novel. In viewing again the *Caprichos,* one marks this theme as predominant among the various abandonments of reason suggested by the central *Capricho* 43, "The Sleep of Reason Produces Monsters." Etching after etching discovers reason asleep while lust and violence roam abroad in the guise of flirtatious belles, lechers, prostitutes or crones, all later become flying cats, owls, witches, and demons. So a study of Goya can establish pictorially the underlying connection between West's murderous game cocks, impersonally lascivious women, and cheaters and masqueraders who would dispense as movie extras, promoters, or screen writers the celluloid lust of the dream factory. In the opening series of the *Caprichos,* such urgings take the form of prostitution of one sort or another. No differently, for an ambitious girl in *The Day of the Locust,* available in Hollywood is a range of opportunity stretching from a spot on Lysol Alley as a hustler (264), to a biological surprise awaiting the lovelies on call at Audrey Jenning's sex boutique, to the mythic assignations of a movie starlet.

To be specific, Faye Greener, only half way up this delectable mountain, is one of the performers or cheaters that Tod has included in a set of lithographs called "The Dancers." But in perspective, her giddy career also symbolizes the dim world of sensuality envisioned by these etchings of Goya and, before him, probably by the work of Hieronymous Bosch.[6] For in attempting to carry off her crude disguise as an aspiring movie star, Faye's hackneyed posturings are not unlike those of the full-bosomed *majas* of affected airs and flounces, attended by fawning or disreputable *majos* or crones in such typical *Caprichos* as Plates 5, 6, and 7. Even the elements of disguise and deception that surround girl and suitor in Plate 6, along with the glowering spectators in the background, can easily locate Faye among her pleasures in Hollywood, practicing her wiles, oblivious to the hard stares of those who have come to California to die. Understandably, Faye's "odd mannerisms and artificial voice" (304) puzzle Homer on his first meeting her. Serious actress and cool engima that she would affect to be, Faye is transparently a fraud as she gestures later before Claude Estees, the screen writer. Yet no one laughs at her, for her far more accomplished body commands respect, subtly gives the lie to her words, renders her audience "uncritical" (387). Exactly, one could add, as the false modesty and simpering expressions of·Goya's females are betrayed by the promise peeking from loosened fichus, exposed ankles, jutting hips, and swooping spinal columns. The obvious sequence of attempted rape, sexual excess, and violence attends the scenes that follow in Goya's etchings and West's novel. Yet in neither case is the condemnation a simple one: Goya compels us to see that his *majas* and prostitutes in *Caprichos* 23, 24, 32 and 34 are no worse than those who condemn them. West, too, discovers most men to be self-deceived masqueraders. For every Faye posing as an actress, there is a Kusich in a Tyrolean hat, an Estees impersonating a Civil War colonel, or an Indian extra asking, " 'Vas you dere, Sharley?' " (405), not to mention the daily crowd on Vine Street sporting yachting caps, Norfolk jackets, and tennis garb. In the gaudy plumage they assume, all men inherently deceive.

But the *Caprichos* offer an even sharper glance into the animality that lust exposes in prostitutes and their accusers alike. I think especially of the scrabbling birds and human beings plucking, eviscerating, and devouring each other, a motif most graphically etched in Plates 19-21. As pictorial witnesses to *The Day of the Locust,* Goya can probably offer no better illustrations than these to underline for us the peculiarly rapacious human folly in West's Hollywood, particularly since it is also extended by a fluttering world of feathery, flying things that suffer, kill, and gorge in a rich diapason of song and plaint.

First of all, how cunningly Goya and West derive and fuse this human mixture of pain and lust, flight and devouring. From the mindless, preening beauties in *Caprichos* 15, 17, and 31; from the simpering belle in consternation before one of her "dates" of the evening in Plate 27; and from the coy, teasing doxies, clad in brief, transparent shifts, chairs on their heads and admired by rogues, from all these stem the relentless flesh and desire that defeather and despoil birds with men's faces in *Caprichos* 19 and 20, or, transformed into seized, girlish hens, are torn and eaten by lawyers with cats' faces in Plate 21. Just as deftly, West also blends the fury of man and bird into a commonplace of animal existence. Pinyon Canyon, hinting clipped wings and violence, becomes a roost for Faye, Earle, and Miguel, from which they prey on Homer; in his daydreams of raping Faye, Tod listens to the accompanying bursting trills of a California night bird (407); atune to the book's strain of mutability, birds at twilight "sing as if sorry to acknowledge the end of another day" (314). The analogy becomes even closer when, in Miguel's camp, Tod is dazzled by the exotic plumage of the homicidal Jujutala, the gamecock that he will soon see in action, an action no less fierce than the fights between its owner and Earle for the possession of Faye. Outside the camp, other birds sound an equally human note: the melancholy call of trapped quail, a sound without "anxiety in it, only sadness, impersonal and without hope" (330). Goya was right. There is no distinguishing man from animal. After Earle finishes gutting the birds, the sight of feathers delicately tipped with blood and the insistent click of his metal scissors merely allow Faye a moment of affected skittishness before she too digs in and gorges like the rest. The orgy of gobbling, drinking, dancing, head-bashing, and attempted rape follows.

Goya and West also agree on the cause: desire—full, bursting, amoral, and mindless. Faye, like Goya's twittering vultures, is a seventeen-year-old lovely, intoxicated by sex, with "beauty . . . structural like a tree's, not a quality of her mind or heart" (346). She nevertheless unwittingly insists on her own Goyaesque identity with the scabby, garbage-eating hen that serves the fighting cocks, just as she, Faye, serves their owner. Thus she can easily defend the hen's filth and sexual activity as "only natural" (373). Truly, then, Faye is one of Goya's depredatory hens when, from the moment she sets foot in his house, she despoils Homer of his food, his money, his home, and finally his reason. Nor is she alone. Mrs. Schwartzen, the tennis champ who loves brothels, she of the "deep sunburn, ruby colored with a slight blue tint"

(272), resembles a huge iridescent blackbird. Then too, Mary Dove, laughing shrilly, can console Faye after Harry's death with the promise of a job in a brothel owned, of course, by Mrs. Jenning, the duenna who chirps Gertrude Stein and Juan Gris to her clients.

The depth of West's insight into the twists of human bestiality is best amplified in etchings of marmoreal frenzy among the more enigmatic *Caprichos* and in the starkly stressed or flying masses of humanity and animal flesh, winged or crouching, among the *Disparates*. Fay that she is, drunkenly chanting the refrain "If you're a viper . . .," Faye wails one line, "I'm the queen of everything" (390), that fits her neatly into the center of disorder—Goya would say the stupidities—of modern America. Like Goya's queens of night, companions to witches, devils, and phantoms, Faye leads the deluded in mad gyrations of folly, dances through the novel, bobs like a cork on the rough seas of human emotion, yet remains herself untouched. Hers are not the ancient accessories of witchcraft—the snakes, brooms, owls, and cats of *Caprichos* 60, 66, and 68. Instead, her studio picture reveals Faye in the more tritely modern witchery of harem costume complete with beer bottle and pewter stein (270). But she is no less ensorcelling. Half-naked and surrounded by the aficionados of the cock fight, she sings and dances just as enticingly as does the coy, exhibitionistic lady of *Capricho* 72 extending herself on one toe before leering, hovering males, an owl perched on their heads and shoulders, all counterbalancing the rhythm of her body, while a hooded, heavy-taloned bird of prey thrusts his face around the other side of her torso.

This mad scene, which Faye re-enacts in Homer's living room, recalls at least four of Goya's most stinging indictments of human animality in *Disparates*. For instance, caught in the heat of her own undulations, Faye is flushed with very much the same joyous intoxication that adorns the grinning, kicking woman pulled rudely over his back by a wild-eyed stallion in *Disparate* 10. Giant rats that devour other willing women in the background leave scant doubt as to the ends of female abandon. No less, the tipsy dance of three sagging males, drawn by three symmetrically swaying females in *Disparate* 12, retells the male foolishness that Faye's sexual witchery commands, at least before the inevitable brawl starts. Two erupt here, Kusich pitted against Earle and Miguel, and then the final Texas rassel between Miguel and Earle themselves. The third example from Goya, *Disparate* 6, shows just as irrevocably that violence is the climax of sexual folly: a maddened picador attacks a knife fighter, while a woman, the object of contention, turns her face. Significant is the arresting form of a misshapen, snarling, dwarfish figure beneath the legs of the picador. The same anguish racks West's imperiled dwarf as he attacks Earle in the groin. Otherwise, the picador's face duplicates Earle's "mean eyes" (400) and quick changes "from apathy to action without the usual transitions" (325). Clearly, then, the final vision of this unholy evening lies in the inevitable reduction of human relations to two battling males. Again Goya and West align: *Capricho* 62 depicts a fight to the death between what Goya terms "two accomplices." In like manner, Earle and Miguel tangle suddenly, explosively over Faye. In the etching, both naked fighters are seen as imminent victims of another of Goya's cat-like beasts, obviously the embodiment of the self-destruction inherent in their own combative energies. As usual, a baleful, fitful light plays upon their struggle, setting them off from the night around them. In the novel, beneath the same thin light of dawn, Earle and Miguel tear and claw at each other as Faye holds a sheet before her face. Then, just as mysteriously, the three disappear before Homer wakes again, just as, one suspects, Goya's embattled madmen and beast vanish in the surrounding dark.

These two fights over Faye come as thunder upon thunder to signal the final, the cumulative burst of random animal striving, humorous and deadly as always, in *The Day of the Locust*. This mounting extravagance reaches its crescendo in the grabbing, ripping, tearing premiere mob awaiting the appearance of its dream symbols. Gaping and wisecracking, milling men and women are thrust before our

eyes in much the same way that Goya thrusts forward the
aerie of contorted faces perched on the back of another
grimacing, middle-aged flying sprite in *Capricho* 64. Moreover, Goya's comment on this etching called "Bon Voyage"
is uncommonly apropos for West's middle-class mob.
"Where is this hellish company going to, filling the darkness
of night with their shrieks? If it were day it would be
different, the whole crew would be brought down by guns. It
is night. No one can see them." And in Hollywood under the
unreal light of Kahn's Persian Palace Theatre, men's faces are
just as preternatural, just as demonic as those of Goya's night
riders: one woman has "snaky gray hair . . . hanging over her
face and shoulders"; another one squeals; a youth near them
has "a kidney-shaped head." We hear them good-naturedly
joking about sex crimes and perverts. They are playful, too,
unaware, until goaded, of their tremendous collective
strength. In fact, West compares this mob to a "bull
elephant" (410) that allows itself to be cajoled and contained
only because it lacks direction. Goya seems to have been of
the same mind. For he too has symbolized massive, animal
power, wherever it might appear, in the symbol of an
elephant. In *Disparate* 21, "Animal Foolishness," four
seemingly wise men, registering looks of faith, hope, cunning,
and wonder, attempt to propitiate an elephant with written
rules and gaudy trappings. The elephant, apparently on the
edge of an abyss, stands silently, neither at bay nor relaxed,
eyeing something beyond them and, in terms of pictorial
composition, decidedly overbalancing them. Humor and attention, patience and bland defiance are in his face. Foolishness confronts foolishness.

One more comparison summarizes Goya's ability to
illuminate the theme of sexual folly, ultimately animal
energy and violence, in *The Day of the Locust*. I think of the
formal exhibition of sheer energy displayed in the cock fight,
a fight that comments directly on the lives of the novel's
main characters who watch so absorbedly. Arrayed like
human warriors, directing steel against flesh and bone, the
game cocks Jujutala and Hermano act out the stiff formalities

of a ritual that can only lead to murder, the most dramatic climax that any of the confused lives among the spectators can hope for. Little wonder, then, that sympathy is expressed for the dead game cock by the least sympathetic character in the book, Earle: "He handled the dead cock gently and with respect" (383). This sympathy enjoined with the murderous extravagance of a senseless yet necessary and absolutely ordered death comes as close as any act in *The Day of the Locust* to expressing the limits of human response that West permits in his art. And it is here that he is at his most objective. The relation of life to death is put with humor, dignity, and hopelessness. When Jujutala pecks at the dead Hermano's remaining eye, Kusich screams " 'Take off that stinking cannibal!' " (383). But in doing so he curses his own world too. He confuses his world and the animal world of a mutilated corpse, and yet, he had earlier, irresistibly, hoped to profit from the confusion: " 'I was going to make book' " (377). Some of this artful confusion and objective presentation of power stares equally impressively from Goya's *Disparate* 22, "Foolish Extravagance," an etching depicting four cavorting, tumbling bulls. One is upside down; the two facing us are wild-eyed and just as tough and lean as the fourth, whose sinewy hindlegs rigidly assume a stance to our left. The action is aimless, foolish; momentarily four bulls flash before us in space. Yet, though they might lack the ordered strife demanded by the cockpit, nevertheless, in their compositional depth and neat tangle of intersecting planes, they are as esthetically pleasing as a blend of the green, bronze, copper, lemon, and orange coloring of Jujutala is to Tod. Like West's fighting cocks in their human attitudes, these four plummeting, clustered bulls cast a glance of life altogether foolish, pronged, and colliding. Like the men and birds so tautly intimate and almost casually transposed outside the cockpit, these bulls whisper to us of our own stupid, powerful, magnificently aimless selves.

Yet Daumier provides the best graphic comment on West's development of the fraudulent performer-audience relationship in *The Day of the Locust*. James F. Light has probably put this relationship most concisely when he observes that West's world "can be divided into spectators (the cheated ...) and performers (the cheaters ...)."[7] Although West's total treatment of this middle-class world goes far beyond the manner of Daumier—the dirty movie which mocks a "very respectable" upper middle-class family (279) and the lower middle-class religious zealots who haunt the Hollywood streets are the obvious exceptions—the career of Harry Greener, Faye's "daddy," seems to be a natural for examination in the light of some of Daumier's work.

Like Faye and Abe, Harry is one of the dancers in Tod's set of lithographs. Naturally, Harry's years in vaudeville and burlesque endear him as a subject for Tod. What's more, Harry's constant clowning is his protective coloring. He realizes that he has been a failure on the stage, but "most people ... won't go out of their way to punish a clown" (282). More important, Tod feels, is the fact that Harry's "clownship was a clue to the people who stared (a painter's clue, that is—a clue in the form of a symbol), just as Faye's dreams were another" (282). In other words, like Faye's dreams, Harry's now inherent gesturing has become a means of duping his everyday audience, the prospective buyers of his silver polish made from "chalk, soap, and yellow axel grease" (284). He himself has become an image to excite the jaded sensibilities of those knots of staring Midwesterners who have come to California to die, those who had hoped to replenish the emotional life dried up in them during the dull round of their earlier lives. Harry is one of the *saltimbanques* who cheat them. But the point that West and Daumier also accent is that the Harrys of this world cheat themselves as well. As Jacques Lassaigne has shrewdly pointed out, in Daumier's work ". . . the supreme betrayal which affected him more than any other was that human beings should descend of their own accord to the status of bogeys and puppets."[8]

Harry's willingness to exploit his stock-in-trade of crude emotions is clearly visible in his first meeting with Homer. He snarls, becomes folksy, unleashes his hideous laugh, and even successfully mimicks his own true condition, that of a man suffering from a heart attack and soon to die. In focusing on the stances of two carnival men advertising a side show, Daumier's drawing *La Parade* shows at least two extremes of Harry's perpetual act. The first performer, a relaxed, middle-aged drummer, beams at us a seemingly frank and ingenuous appeal while his muted drumbeats proclaim just as forthrightly the delights of the fat lady inside; the other, a clown on a chair to his left, is frozen in a military brace, hands out at his sides, knees together, eyes up, and shoulders rigid, with an altogether contrasting, know-nothing grimace on his face. Harry's propitiations are no less violently in contrast. Moreover, in releasing them he is also something of the puppet or mechanical. In his outlandish banker's outfit, he inevitably appears too small for his clothes. Once he starts a performance, he resembles a toy that must be allowed to run down. Essentially, then, he is no different from three of Daumier's seedy drummers in a water color called *Les Saltimbanques*. They too mechanically yet energetically urge us to come inside and view what might well pass for one of Faye's daydreams, an alligator chasing a vague running figure. Behind the two screaming, gesticulating men and beckoning hoyden, two spare, impassive musicians await their cues to play. The contrast and yet the sameness in the attitudes displayed by drummers and musicians alike must be obvious.

However, in repose—and here one thinks of Daumier's oil painting *Les Saltimbanques au Repos*— Harry betrays a gravid haggardness that foreshadows his imminent death. Ironically enough, his first heart attack in Homer's cottage strikes at the moment that he usually switches his vaudeville routine from exaggerated high jinks to pathetic fatigue. But now his life and art converge. He stands hesitantly, head back with his hands at his throat, then collapses but refuses to accept his sickness. This has been his greatest act; he should net at least five dollars from his captive audience, Homer. Thus Harry, like those who stare at him and are duped by him, cannot, given the unreality of his and their lives, accept or understand the fact of death. Even shortly before his own death, Harry inflicts another of his unsolicited routines on Tod, and again manages to exploit his real sickness. At last, however, real sleep seems to overcome the actor's pose. Yet not altogether: Tod sees "how skillfully he got the maximum effect out of his agonized profile by using the pillow to set it off" (336). Now it is that Tod can describe Harry's head as "almost all face, like a mask, with deep furrows between the eyes, across the forehead and on either side of the nose and mouth, plowed there by years of broad grinning and heavy frowning" (336). Here, then, and in the death sleep, Tod can compare Harry's "worn, dry skin" to "eroded ground" (338), a striking resemblance to the texture of permanent distortion that one catches beneath the wreath of provoking bravado in Daumier's performer's head in the drawing *Chanteur au Tambourin.*

As befits his cheating act, Harry's greatest performance is his own funeral. Abetted by the stage manager's efficiency of Mrs. Johnson, whose hobby is funerals, it could be nothing else. Harry is tucked snugly in his casket, registering all the silent aplomb of an "interlocutor in a minstrel show" (344). Faye, now on the turf at Mrs. Jenning's, has never been more stunning; Tod is drunk; the Lee sisters, the Gingos, Abe Kusich, Mary Dove, and the roomers at the San Bardoo help make a full house. Ironically, a Bach chorale is played. To the extent that we have before us one of Daumier's rapt and uncomprehending audiences, West, like his French master, has drolly summarized the folly of performer and spectator by underlining the grotesqueness of their ceremonial selves gaping at mysterious death or acting it out, in either case collaborating in another misunderstood, thrilling, overacted show.

At the same funeral, it is the "scattering of men and women who looked very much out of place" (347) that really absorbs Tod. They are those for whom Harry living had been a clue in the form of a symbol; these are the people who stare. Incongruous even in Hollywood, they become Tod's real subject and West's means for ultimately joining the malaise of Hollywood to all of America. The extremists among them, had they appeared in the work of Daumier, would probably have been satirized, or so Tod feels (365). But neither Tod nor West satirizes them; nor, as Tod recognizes, would have Alessandro Magnasco, whose creatures these fanatics are (365).

In the early pages of *The Day of the Locust,* Tod spotted these starers skulking along the byways of the average Hollywood citizens. They were

> ... people of a different type. Their clothing was somber and badly cut, bought from mail-order houses. While the others moved rapidly, darting into stores and cocktail bars, they loitered on the corners or stood with their backs to the shop windows and stared at everyone who passed. When their stare was returned, their eyes filled with hatred. At this time Tod knew very little about them except that they had come to California to die.
>
> He was determined to learn much more. They were the people he felt he must paint (261).

Invariably they are Midwesterners, usually of the Iowa picnic variety. We have already viewed some of them in the background of Goya's etchings of folly and violence. Dangerously bored, lacking the brains, money, and juice with which to enjoy themselves, they become "cultists of all sorts . . . the wave, airplane, funeral and preview watchers" (420), the scavengers of accidental violence and death. Clearly, then, they comprise Goya's bull elephant, the ordinary hopped-up members of the lower middle-class premiere mob. If not always the torch-bearers in Tod's picture-to-be, "they would run behind the fire and do a great deal of shouting" (347). But among them are an elite, the fanatics, the torch-bearers themselves who must be taken even more seriously. Of more consequence than the apathy which Tod seeks to depict in men, their rage and infectious anger sober him. For these are the extremists, comparable in their bedraggled, misdirected enthusiasms to the strained and baffled figures of Magnasco.

Like West in the 1930's, Magnasco joins his monks, eremites, and distracted holy men with brigands, entertainers and outcasts, all one in the twilight world of the grotesque as conceived by the elaborate treatment of baroque art. In

staring from their churches, cells, and desert caves, Magnasco's fanatics reflect the plight come to the holy men of the
seventeenth and eighteenth centuries in their slow recognition of a world quite indifferent to the fury of religious
conviction. Perhaps recording the scepticism arising from the
conflicting claims of the Reformation and the Counter-
Reformation, Magnasco was sometimes "content," as one
critic has put it, "to view the world with the detachment of a
satirist, and enjoyed the paradoxical contrast between men's
good intentions and their ruthless behavior."[9] Under an
almost identical blue and white California sky, West assumes
the same detachment. Yet both West and Magnasco see much
more than the simple disparates that lie between men's
motives and actions. Instead, the resulting power, the
misplaced energy and the possible consequences of both
sober the artist. Before such a spectacle, an artist need not be
committed to satire or pity but, as West concedes, he may
register an even deeper "respect" (366). In fact, we are
vouchsafed this very "respect" from Tod's own eyes after he
has sought out some of the gatherings of the Hollywood
cults:

> One Friday night in the "Tabernacle of the Third
> Coming," a man near Tod stood up to speak. Although his
> name most likely was Thompson or Johnson and his home
> town Sioux City, he had the same countersunk eyes, like the
> heads of burnished spikes, that a monk by Magnasco might
> have. He was probably just in from one of the colonies in the
> desert near Soboba Hot Springs where he had been conning
> over his soul on a diet of raw fruit and nuts. He was very
> angry. The message he had brought to the city was one that an
> illiterate anchorite might have given decadent Rome. It was a
> crazy jumble of dietary rules, economics and Biblical threats.
> He claimed to have seen the Tiger of Wrath stalking the walls
> of the citadel and the Jackal of Lust skulking in the shrubbery,
> and he connected these omens with "thirty dollars every
> Thursday" and meat eating.
>
> Tod didn't laugh at the man's rhetoric. He knew it was
> unimportant. What mattered were his messianic rage and the
> emotional response of his hearers. They sprang to their feet,
> shaking their fists and shouting. On the altar someone began
> beating a bass drum and soon the entire congregation was
> singing "Onward Christian Soldiers" (366).

The sobering fact for Tod is that these madmen of the thirties have "it in them to destroy civilization" (366); "the Angelenos would be first, but their comrades all over the country would follow. There would be civil war" (335). This last thought leaves Tod strangely happy with a vaticinal pleasure parallel to the depth of his artistic respect.

As Tod's cultists "writhe on the hard seats of their churches" (365), he is reminded of "how well Alessandro Magnasco would dramatize the contrast between their drained-out, feeble bodies and their wild, disordered minds" (365). The truth of this thought may be seen in paintings by Magnasco like *Christ on the Sea of Galilee* in which the strained attitude of the intent Hollywood believer is duplicated in the figure of St. Peter sinking while he attempts to emulate his master. Or, typically, the distraught Angeleno may again be seen in the two friars engulfed in a tidal wave, quite the opposite of any "sea of faith," from which both psychopathically pray for deliverance in Magnasco's *Seascape with Friars*. Both pictures illustrate restless, stretching, elongated bodies nevertheless become one with a sea of matter surrounding them, while their frantic appeal to some power beyond goes unregarded. Whether disciple or friar, Magnasco's fanatic seems just as much a victim of his own turbulent desires, rebounding from an indifferent world, as does Thompson or Johnson from Sioux City venting his wrath in the bromides of modern chiliasm. Then, too, Magnasco's use of holy men and women as subjects during a period marking the decay of the religious orders nicely parallels West's preoccupation with a decayed middle class. The original intent of the orders had been to strengthen the spiritual arm of the church by enlisting the most devout souls in a close and daring imitation of the life of Christ, by Magnasco's day a highly suspect imitation. Similarly, since the time of the Puritan revolution in England, the middle class has tended to adapt the religious fervor of Prostestantism to the workaday realm of material progress, industry, and sober good sense. Thus, in both instances, West and Magnasco were confronted with the disturbed remnant of

originally successful movements. In West's case, religious
fervor had further dwindled from good sense to nonsense:
holiness was now made available to the believer in Hollywood
temples by a cockeyed reliance on weight lifting, fortune
telling, eliminating salt from the diet, and learning " 'Brain-
Breathing, the Secret of the Aztecs' " (365), a reliance no less
precarious than that suggested in Magnasco's ascetics with
their rickety, makeshift crosses.

As befits the modern American leadership of the middle
class, two women highlight this inverted religiosity. They
are Mrs. Johnson, the janitress at the San Berdoo whose
hobby is funerals, and Maybelle Loomis, a typical American
housewife in appearance, mother to the child actor Adore,
who "thinks he's the Frankenstein monster" (363) and is.

Mrs. Johnson is absorbed in the formalities of funeral
ceremonies. There is nothing perverse about her; she is
merely elaborately indifferent to the mystery of death. At
Harry's leave-taking, she scolds Holsepp the funeral director
over the quality of the casket handles, curtly directs
mourners to their seats, makes sure the casket is properly
placed, stops the Bach Chorale suddenly, and is insulted
when the congregation hesitates to inspect the open casket.
The simple affirmation of faith in the Bach chorale is just as
wasted on her world of decorous funeral arrangement, as
Magnasco's shining figure of Christ is wasted on the natural
world in the painting *The Baptism of Christ*, where the holy
rite lies obscurely centered in a raging mass of water, trees,
and hurling wind.

Maybelle Loomis, is no less a variation on the same theme
of the deflection of middle-class energies into the decadent or
monstrous. And again, the desperate twist of her religious
observances is just as apparently sane as Mrs. Johnson's
abandonment of the rites of the dead. Mrs. Loomis is a
devotee of the "raw-foodest" leader, Dr. Pierce; she has also
found a paradise in California; and her explanation of death
is just as irrelevant as Mrs. Johnson's passion for funerals:
"Death comes from eating dead things" (362). Her smolder-
ing unholy determination that Adore shall succeed as a child

star is no less characteristic of her middle-class orientation. Behind her friendly exterior there is the everpresent savagery, the hushed imperative in her voice, with its threat of the strap should Adore refuse any audience his talents. For that matter, her own baffled, misdirected psyche lies embedded in the features of her child. Lost, sick, and wandering in mind, he is half-boy, half-adult, all monster with his pale, staring, troubled face. At one moment he can be contorted with all the affected tortures of sex as he croons a well-rehearsed song; at the next moment he can pull a sail-boat around a yard, tooting in imitation of a tugboat. In West's Hollywood, then, it comes to this: all the trivialities of life, love and death—raw food, torch songs, and casket handles—become the major channels, the distractions, for man's religious drive. Thus are Magnasco's overwhelmed believers transposed to a modern, middle-class setting.

A final observation may well fix this likeness. I have already suggested that the leaders of the premiere mob clearly resemble the zealots of Magnasco in the easily induced hysteria by which they command and drive their followers. In this regard, Magnasco's paintings *The Synagogue* and *The Ecstatic Congregation* may serve as adroit summaries of this mass reverence of excitement. Here at the Hollywood premiere, the modern evangelist is appropriately a radio announcer, determined to whip up the drained minds and bodies before him into public bedlam, and then insinuate the excitement to a similarly apathetic audience throughout America. One is peculiarly recalled to Magnasco's flickering lines and colors as he reveals the nervous restlessness in the figures of the Jews surrounding the guttering flares in the cupola of a synagogue. Similarly, amid equally nervous violet shafts of light that illumine the modern temple, Kahn's Persian Palace Theatre, the announcer's excited rant urges on his own ecstatic congregation, or in West's words: "His rapid, hysterical voice was like that of a revivalist preacher whipping his congregation toward the ecstasy of fits" (409). In turn, it is the potential destructiveness of this ecstasy that excites the announcer and his listeners. In a stutter of superlatives he revels in the fact that the police cannot control the crowd. Yet among these " 'ten thousand excited, screaming fans,' " as the young revivalist of the airways puts the horrible fact, Tod sees no working men, few really rough individuals. Instead, "the crowd was made up of the lower middle classes, every other person one of his torchbearers" (410). They, like Magnasco's frenzied monks, friars, worshippers, and anchorites with their makeshift crosses, obscure and unflagging meditations, and eccentric stances, they are the elite of a nation's madmen ready to kill, rip, tear, and burn for reasons no longer understandable to them. Or as an anonymous critic of Magnasco's work said in the year of West's death, it is not the hostile universe that man is no longer able to cope with that excites the modern Magnasco; rather, "the Magnascos of today . . . feel man's inhumanity to his fellow man to be the force with which they are unable to cope."[10] How easily, one muses, he might have illustrated his thesis by reference to West's inhuman destroyers in *The Day of the Locust*; for these destroyers command Tod's and West's profoundest attentions.

The obvious example in the novel of man's inhumanity to man is the career of Homer Simpson, Hollywood's victim and martyr, and yet also partially his own. On first sight Tod marks him down as "an exact model for the kind of person who comes to Hollywood to die, perfect to every detail down to fever eyes and unruly hands" (285). But Tod quickly sees his mistake: "Homer Simpson was only physically the type. The men he meant were not shy" (285). Otherwise, to be sure, Homer does fit the description of the cultists whom Tod assumes Magnasco would have taken seriously. Homer is a Midwesterner; pictorially speaking he resembles "one of Picasso's great sterile athletes" (290); and for all his bulk, he appears "neither strong nor fertile" (290). In the enormity of his hands, the rigidity of his stance, and the smallness of his head he bodies forth one of Magnasco's anguished and penitent monks. Yet Tod is right. Different from the torchbearers and their followers, Homer is a self-effacing, thankful, unpretentious, friendly man, incapable of hate or mockery. But Romola Martin, the hotel floozie, is also right: for, despite his anguish, Homer does indeed have something temptingly bovine, something ripe for the slaughterhouse in him. He is saintly at his own peril, to paraphrase William James's caution on holy men in *The Varieties of Religious Experience,* a book familiar enough to West.[11] As James states, there is a general "dislike of the saintly nature," so that even a kindly nature like Tod's can find Homer's humble, retiring decency irritating. There is even a covert snobbishness about his goodness and willingness to suffer. Hence, masochistic, clumsy, and unadaptable to the world— "no one was ever less a Negro than Homer" (367)—the modern saint is fittingly the self-propelled victim of crazed secular millenarians and cultists whom he appears to resemble, and, at the same time, of unsaintly pagans to whom he is attracted against his will. And here it is that painting and literature again combine to give us the historical perspective by which to gauge Homer's abbreviated hagiography.

In other words, as we watch Homer brooding over his incinerator, cactus garden, and fly-stalking lizard, we can probably compare him to one of the most conspicuous saints in painting and literature, Saint Anthony, particularly as he is depicted in Flaubert's *The Temptation of Saint Anthony,* a book which seems to have made a deep impression on West.[12] The further relevance of this source to the theme of the painter's eye in *The Day of the Locust* is not only based on the exaggerated pictorial element employed by Flaubert but also stems from the influence of the paintings of Saint Anthony by Callot and Breughel the Younger, Flaubert's acknowledged guides in planning his own rendering of the temptation theme.[13] In addition, not only Magnasco but Desiderio, Guardi, and Rosa together also handled the same subject, a fact that might suggest the closeness of Flaubert's image to the tradition of grotesque art that West summons to his aid. In any event, the parallels between the vicissitudes of Flaubert's and West's saints seem close, and their divergences seems equally telling, since Homer not only succumbs to temptation but is also martyred.

Peculiarly appropriate to the modern martyrdom of Homer Simpson is the scenery and skyline of Hollywood which West relates, in their architectural and imaginative lunacy, to the imaginary landscapes of Rosa, Guardi, and Desiderio.

Resting in the shade after he has hurried through the tangled acres of Hollywood movie sets—an astounding melange of Egypt, Paris, Troy, frontier towns, Greek and Mayan temples, and a scattering of windmills, elevated stations, palaces, forts, dinosaur bones, stockades, "half of the Merrimac" and "the skeleton of a Zeppelin" (352)—Tod sits down to catch his breath while his mind turns to the art of Rosa, Guardi, and Desiderio:

> Looking downhill now, he could see compositions that might have actually been arranged from the Calabrian work of Rosa. There were partially demolished buildings and broken monuments, half-hidden by great, tortured trees, whose exposed roots writhed dramatically in the arid ground, and by shrubs that carried, no flowers or berries, but armories of spikes, hooks and swords.
>
> For Guardi and Desiderio there were bridges which bridged nothing, sculpture in trees, palaces that seemed of marble until a whole stone portico began to flap in the light breeze. And there were figures as well. A hundred yards from where Tod was sitting a man in a derby hat leaned drowsily against the gilded poop of a Venetian barque and peeled an apple. Still farther on, a charwoman on a stepladder was scrubbing with soap and water the face of a Buddha thirty feet high (352-53).

These thoughts apply immediately to the panorama of movie sets stretched out before Tod. He has come to know intimately these quickly decaying and dilapidating structures while learning set and stage designing. But in a much more exciting way these thoughts also apply to the daft architecture, the grotesque landscape and figures, and ultimately the chaotic trappings and decor of the Hollywood mind as it symbolizes America. And to revisit the Calabrian works of Rosa is to encounter a romantically sinister decay in landscape and persons, a decay not far removed from the one that hangs like a pall over the uprooted, lower-middle class in its imitation Spanish, Irish, or Arabian houses, in its dreams of romance, violence, and adventure, or in its chronic movie going, a class lurking in the shadows of such fantastic edifices as a saddlery store that resembles an armory of torture instruments or a one-story building with a sign on the roof reading "Malted Milks Too Thick For a Straw" (322). Lady Morgan, more than a hundred years earlier, had already described the models for such beings, men who had attracted Rosa in Italy's Calabrian district and who were fomenting revolt against the Austro-Spanish control. The lower-middle class world of movie extras, game bird enthusiasts, broken-down actors, bookies, and religious nuts in *The Day of the Locust* could blend almost imperceptibly into Rosa's circle of disaffected conspirators, brigands, and monks: "The chief conspirators were the celebrated Tomaso Campanella, the author of several philosophical works, and a number of monks under the protection of some Calabrian bishops. One thousand five hundred banditti were subsidized as allies, and with three hundred monks, were already under arms when the conspiracy was detected. . . ."[14]

Aside from the relevance of the many brigand figures that Rosa completed at this time, there is one picture that is especially representative of his Calabrian work and equally useful in extending Tod's thoughts to the milieu of Holly-wood. I think specifically of the famous *Passage over the Bridge,* where unwary travellers, though warned, approach a ruined bridge that leads into a mountain path disappearing into a maze of heavy foliage, twisted branches, and jutting rocks. In the recesses of this formidable topography lie waiting what appear to be the fierce inhabitants of Calabria. They are comparable in the imaginative vigor that invests their tiny ambuscade to the knot of admirers that surround Faye with their ever constant threat of violence sprung from desire and indolence. We, too, become unwary travellers as we accompany Tod to the camp belonging to Earle and Miguel in the hills surrounding Los Angeles, discovered in a "valley thick with trees, mostly eucalyptus, with here and there a poplar and one enormous black live-oak" (328). There Tod encounters "a ramshackle hut patched with tin signs that had been stolen from the highway" (329); there he

watches Earle poaching game; and, as we have seen, there he
is witness to the drinking, dancing, and violence of the
modern brigand's life in and around Hollywood.

From Guardi, according to this drift of Tod's thoughts,
comes the *veduta ideata,* the imaginary view, often an
architectural *capriccio,* a pastoral scene containing incongruous pieces of architecture and equally incongruous figures.
Tod's vision of derby hat, Venetian barque, charwoman and
towering Buddha among the movie sets answers very well to
this formula, not, after all, an extraordinary sight when
among the sanely capricious Angelenos "a dead horse, or,
rather, a life-size, realistic reproduction of one" (274) is to be
found submerged in an illuminated swimming pool. Then
too, for all those creatures who visit Glendale airport on the
chance of seeing a plane crash, there is an equal number in
the holiday throng in Guardi's *The Ascent of a Balloon from
the Giudecca Canal* to remind us that the daily foolishness in
eighteenth-century Venice also included the mass appeal of
sudden, aerial disaster.

But the most illuminating of these three painters whom
Tod has taken as guides is Francisco Desiderio, in West's day
still known by the first name Monsu. Aside from his mixing
renaissance and medieval architectural forms, as A. Everett
Austin has said in commenting on the first great showing of
Desiderio in this country, this painter is always "reiterating
his constant theme of saintly martyrdom, central to the
Baroque psyche."[15] The martyrdom usually occurs against
the background of a fantastic city, just as often on the brink
of destruction or in the throes of disaster. It is essentially the
dreamy unreality of this background that enhances so
strangely Desiderio's concomitant martyrdom, or that makes
the scene of saintly Homer's martyrdom, in all its rich
architectural non sequiturs, so oddly appropriate for his
death. Again and again and again, the gross but nevertheless
satisfying merger of oriental spires, Corinthian columns,
Gothic motifs, and bits of Roman architecture stands
moodily in gleaming white, ghostlike and immemorial, often
quietly revealing destructive figures hunched around a bat-

teringram in a corner of the canvas; or, symptomatically, a broken column, toppled unexpectedly behind the center of injustice at the moment of execution; or suddenly in another canvas the fissured, toppled remnant of the same city, now abandoned, crumbled partially into dust, subsumed in a tangle of encroaching vegetation or simply left standing, the shards of a civilization destroyed and judged by some higher, mysterious power. Usually the initial hint of such disaster accompanies the frozen gesticulations of an urban mob beholding, say, the muscular swing of an executioner's arms as he decapitates an abstracted, mild-mannered saint in *The Martyrdom of a Bishop Saint.*

In this light, how ominous become the juxtaposed and fake architectures in a skyline that waits the descent of locust fury, according to Tod's prophetic painting. The San Berdoo, despite its plain and unadorned back and sides, has a fantastic facade of "diluted mustard and its windows, all double, were framed by pink Moorish columns which supported turnip-shaped lintels" (263). No less monstrous is Homer's Irish cottage, with its Spanish living room and two trumped up New England bedrooms, its grotesqueness termed "cute" by the agent (287). At the end of the first chapter, halting after his climb from Vine Street to Pinyon Canyon, Tod decided that "only dynamite would be of any use against the Mexican ranch house, Samoan huts, Mediterranean villas, Egyptian and Japanese temples, Swiss chalets, Tudor cottages, and every possible combination of these styles that lined the slopes of the canyon" (262). Such an explosion might compare with the boiling glare and fragments of flying architecture in Desiderio's *Explosion in a Temple,* its amazed figures rocked by the mysterious and unaccountable detonation. And, could we recall after such destruction Homer confronted by Adore before the milling crowd in Hollywood, we might also share the melancholy of one of Desiderio's many paintings of ruined cities. This one, *Ruins by the Seashore...,* depicts Saint Augustine before a small boy attempting to bail the sea with a shell, virtually in the shadows of the hulking remains of a city. Instead of fantastic architecture that nearly hides the hints or beginnings of the destruction about to be loosed, we see only ruins behind a few boats and occasional loungers, fisher folk sustaining life along the shore where once a great city stood. In any case we don't laugh. Nor, for that matter, does Tod after his long climb to Pinyon Canyon. For the architectural nightmare before him seems as symptomatic of anguish in the human soul as one suspects it was for Desiderio:

> On the corner of La Huerta Road was a miniature Rhine castle with tarpaper turrets pierced for archers. Next to it was a little highly colored shack with domes and minarets out of the *Arabian Nights*. Again he was charitable. Both houses were comic, but he didn't laugh. Their desire to startle was so eager and guileless.
>
> It is hard to laugh at the need for beauty and romance, no matter how tasteless, even horrible, the results of that need are. But it is easy to sigh. Few things are sadder than the truly monstrous (262).

If one cannot be sure of the motives that prompted Desiderio in his work, it is fairly plain that the analogues to it that we have seen in movie sets and Hollywood architecture inspired Tod to pity, awe, and finally to the dire prophecy of *The Burning of Los Angeles* for the lives that sustain and create such architecture. Thus Tod makes an imaginative leap from the crude disorder of the sets, to the mind of those for whom movies are made. This leap parallels the transition we have just seen Tod make from the mad architecture of Pinyon Canyon to the emotional needs that lay behind it. Hence, after reminiscing over Rosa, Guardi, and Desiderio, Tod, we are told, considers

> ... a ten-acre field of cockleburs spotted with clumps of sunflowers and wild gum. In the center of the field was a gigantic pile of sets, flats and props. While he watched, a ten-ton truck added another load to it. This was the final dumping ground. He thought of Janvier's "Sargasso Sea." Just as that imaginary body of water was a history of civilization in the form of a marine junkyard, the studio lot was one in the form of a dream dump. A Sargasso of the imagination! And the dump grew continually, for there wasn't a dream afloat somewhere which wouldn't sooner or later turn up on it, having first been made photographic by plaster, canvas, lath

and paint. Many boats sink and never reach the Sargasso, but no dream ever entirely disappears. Somewhere it troubles some unfortunate person and someday, when that person has been sufficiently troubled, it will be reproduced on the lot (353).

So the imaginary landscape of the studio, with its distortion of life, love and history—the god Eros lies "face downward in a pile of old newspapers and bottles" (352)— becomes a dumping ground of the modern mind and finds another illuminating image, this time in the novel by Thomas Allibone Janvier, *In the Sargasso Sea* (New York, 1898). There one follows the hero, Mr. Roger Stetworth, in his rather incredible triumph over the imaginary marine waste said to lie in the Atlantic somewhere northeast of the West Indies. A central passage, if only for its pictorial description, shows the implications of Tod's comparison:

And, indeed, it has a good deal the look of being a real island ... But in spite of the golden light which hung over it, and which ought to have given it a cheerful look, it was the most desolate and sorrowful place I ever saw; for it seemed to belong—and in a way really did belong, since every hulk in all that fleet was the slowly wasting dead body of a ship slain by storm or disaster—to that outcast region of mortality in which death has achieved its ugliness but to which the cleansing of a complete dissolution has not yet been brought by time (97-98).

In such manner, too, the Hollywood death-in-life—landscape and figures—is projected from the substantial insubstantial of the movie set, and derives its original, fetid, golden being from the minds of the cheated and the cheaters in America, apparently in constant, inevitable collaboration. The point is clear: the landscape of Hollywood becomes only an exaggeration of the troubled landscape of the middle-class American mind.

The final connection, then, between the architectural fantasies that mar Pinyon Canyon and the destructive day that Tod will paint can be seen in the increasingly explicit demonic motifs in the progression of Desiderio's work: from urban fantasy, to occasional dilapidation, to martyrdom accompanied by destruction, to desolation, to dust. And thus

The Day of the Locust. Tod comments on the grotesque edifices and on the minds that created them and will destroy them. West insists that the day is close at hand. But perhaps I go too far. For, in the end, it is the dream-like serenity that surrounds the destructive fire or cataclysm in a painting by Desiderio, the same serenity that attends the mile upon mile of rotting vessels in Janvier's Sargasso Sea that is so disturbing in West's Hollywood novel, yet no less disturbing than the news in our day of the strange flashes and fires on the desert and city horizon clearly visible to Angelenos everywhere in the sixties as they take their serene psychopathic ways along the same fantastic pathways of the mind that West observed in their parents during the Thirties.

To focus attention on the central symbol of *The Day of the Locust,* Tod's prospective canvas, *The Burning of Los Angeles,* is to pull together the many pictorial analogues that give the book its added dimension of historical terror. This is possible since Tod is both artist and prophet, yet a man who refuses to concede the confusion of the two roles and one who is at the same time "a very complicated young man with a whole set of personalities, one inside the other like a nest of Chinese boxes" (260). Hence, despite his dominant skill, Tod can also be "amused by the strong feeling of satisfaction this dire conclusion" (335) in his painting offers him. It is as artist, prophet, and complex personality that Tod can provide us with a clue to the composition and meaning of his yet unpainted work. Here, then, is Tod's own resume of the painting he has so far blocked out in charcoal. The vision crisscrosses his mind as he awaits rescue from the mob at the end of the book:

> Across the top, parallel with the frame, he had drawn the burning city, a great bonfire of architectural styles, ranging from Egyptian to Cape Cod colonial. Through the center, winding from left to right, was a long hill street and down it, spilling into the middle foreground, came the mob carrying baseball bats and torches. For the faces of its members, he was using the innumerable sketches he had made of the people who come to California to die; the cultists of all sorts, economic as well as religious, the wave, airplane, funeral and

preview watchers—all those poor devils who can only be stirred
by the promise of miracles and then only to violence. A super
"Dr. Know-All Pierce-All" had made the necessary promise
and they were marching behind his banner in a great united
front of screwballs and screwboxes to purify the land. No
longer bored, they sang and danced joyously in the red light of
the flames.

In the lower foreground, men and women fled wildly
before the vanguard of the crusading mob. Among them were
Faye, Harry, Homer, Claude and himself. Faye ran proudly,
throwing her knees high. Harry stumbled along behind her,
holding on to his beloved derby hat with both hands. Homer
seemed to be falling out of the canvas, his face half-asleep, his
big hands clawing the air in anguished pantomime. Claude
turned his head as he ran to thumb his nose at his pursuers.
Tod himself picked up a small stone to throw before
continuing his flight.

He had almost forgotten both his leg and his predicament,
and to make his escape still more complete he stood on a chair
and worked at the flames in an upper corner of the canvas,
modeling the tongues of fire so that they licked even more
avidly at a corinthian column that held up the palmleaf roof of
a nutburger stand (419-420).

Individual elements of this disaster, although they are
characteristically Tod's, are perhaps not surprisingly related
to the work of the painters so far discussed. For instance, the
great conflagration is a subject that seemed to preoccupy
many of them. Guardi's *The Fire at St. Marcuola,* with its
accompanying holiday spirit, accented diminution of the
throng watching it, and blending of noonday sunlight and
licking flames seems especially apropos; earlier we had been
told that Tod's flaming city would burn "at high noon, so
that the flames would have to compete with the desert sun.
. . . He wanted the city to have a gala air as it burned, to
appear almost gay. And the people who set it on fire would
be a holiday crowd" (334). Then, too, the great combustion
of conflicting and fantastic architecture resembles nothing so
much as three spectacular burnings set forth on canvas by
Desiderio in the pictures of three symbolic cities succumbing
to the self-generated flames of their own wickedness: *The
Burning of Sodom and Gomorrha, The Burning of Troy,* and

The Burning of Rome. Of course the hodge-podge of styles, especially the merge of palmleaf roof, Corinthian column, and nutburger stand, reflects as unholy a combination of tastes as any found in Desiderio. And, as we have seen, the millenarian promise of a Dr. Pierce is quite enough to spur the illusory joys and deadly enthusiasms of those who stare, those who have come to California to die, the febril, unadjusted descendants of Magnasco's restless crew. On the other hand, the pursuing Angelenos could also recall a horde of Rosa's Calabrian banditti, come trumpeting down from their mountain strongholds. But this time they take out after the cheaters, more particularly after the titillating form of one of Goya's foolish females, Faye, running as Tod once before imagined her for his picture, "enjoying the release that wild flight gives in much the same way that a game bird must when . . . it bursts from cover in complete, unthinking panic" (321). The unfettered, dreamy animal energy she expends in flight is, of course, no different from her equally errant, amoral bursts of animality in ordinary life. Nor is it very far removed from the exuberant elan of the *majas* and proud, heavy-limbed prostitutes of Goya's etchings. Harry, too, remains his true self. His prop, a derby, is his first concern. He is no less the entertainer, this time on the lam after the bad performance of a lifetime, stumbling and self-deceived in the value of his costume which he confuses with the importance of his life, just as Daumier might have pictured him. Finally, only the artist and thinker make any token resistance. Claude, in the armor of his "involved comic rhetoric" (276), and Tod, in the puny imperviousness of his art, can make some show of resistance, while Homer, striking the pose of the modern saint, who has nowhere to turn, can only claw the air, attempting to leap from a canvas that allows no leap to heaven.

Given its surrealistic surface, Tod's painting would tend to suggest a curve of sensibility stretching from Bosch and Breughel to the present, a curve that marks Tod's masters and himself as students and exploiters of the fragmentary but eternal ugliness and perversity that flash in the actions of

men at any time, especially when an age or nation is under
extreme stress. Here one would like to know more about
whatever social impetus, if any, helped create the typical
schizophrenic city of Desiderio. But the ravages of the
Counter-Reformation, "the humors of Venice," and the
possibility of ethnic revolt with all its promise for romantic
art, these stand in fairly clear evidence in the work of
Magnasco, Guardi, and Rosa respectively. One need hardly
mention the time of troubles that surrounded the man Goya
in his personal life and in his position as a Spanish citizen at
the end of the eighteenth century and the turn of the
nineteenth. No less obvious is the derivation of Daumier's
realism from the political broil and dissent of the middle of
that century.

A recent study by Norman Cohn, *The Pursuit of the
Millennium,* offers a powerful statement of the "long-term
preconditions" that usually precede religious and totalitarian
outbreaks of collective madness; one of them, the breakdown
of "emotional means of satisfaction," seems most apropos to
the great onslaught in Tod's painting.[16] But superimposed on
such a precondition are what Cohn terms more immediate
psychological fantasies, chiefly paranoiac, which include "the
megalomaniac view of oneself as the Elect . . . the refusal to
accept the ineluctable limitations and imperfections of
human existence . . . [and] the obsession with inerrable
prophecies" (Cohn, p. 309), cankers which turn men into
grotesques, and, like the destructive fire, ignite other less
flammable minds:

> This does not of course mean that hitherto sane individuals
> suddenly turn into downright paranoiacs. But there are always
> very large numbers of people who are prone to see life in black
> and white, who feel a deep need for perfect saviours to adore
> and wicked enemies to hate; people, in other words, who
> without being paranoiac yet have a strong tendency towards
> paranoid states of mind . . . the appearance of a messianic
> leader . . . can produce remarkable reactions . . . Those who
> are first attracted will mostly be people who seek a sanction
> for the emotional needs generated by their own unconscious
> conflicts. It is as though units of paranoia hitherto diffused
> through the population suddenly coalesce to form a new

entity: a collective paranoiac fanaticism. But these first followers, precisely because they are true believers, can endow their new movement with such confidence, energy and ruthlessness that it will attract into its wake vast multitudes of people who are themselves not at all paranoid but simply harassed, hungry or frightened (Cohn, 311-12).

Beyond the common subject matter of Tod's masters, and beyond the peculiar psychological state of pursuers or pursued that they suggest, remains the third matter of esthetic effect that seems to relate their work to Tod's own graphic art and the literary art of Nathanael West. For each has taken a repulsive subject and has dwelt most longingly on just those aspects—prostitution, murder, self-delusion, martyrdom, hysteria, brigandage, and urban cataclysm—which we ordinarily crowd to the far reaches of our minds. Moreover, West, Tod, and his mentors yoke them with all the glee, the joy, the clear blue skies, or the sunny, gala hilarity and exhilaration of an otherwise dark, indifferent world. This joy and repulsion, though they may seem to indicate the splintered state of the artist's mind, remain joined and true, and thus beautiful on his canvas, plate, or page. Hence to liken West's art to the art of the surrealists is to make at best an incomplete comparison. For here in *The Day of the Locust,* West has not only discovered a powerful modern symbol, *The Burning of Los Angeles,* but has also made systematic reference to an established line of painters, not of the first rank yet highly relevant as mockers of our overblown, mediocre values, who lend him an established perspective. That perspective does not celebrate man's self-conferred glory nor, on the other hand, does it limit itself to satirizing him. It merely holds up to us the enervating excitement, the frail demonic, and the sublime perversity of that which we are pleased to call genuine or normal. In evoking the painter's eye, in placing Tod Hackett's vision of traditional art in the midst of mob disorder, Nathanael West has looked both ways: at the present and at history, at a symbol and at its traditional vestiges, at an idea and at its eternal, recurring images. In doing so he has given his novel a solid depth of realism that most American fiction cannot command, indeed would probably be shabbier for recognizing, a realism of glittering presences, powerful voices of silence, beyond the call of reform or idealism, seemingly delighted merely to relume the sameness of man's day and the locust hovering over his short span.[17]

FOOTNOTES

1. Arthur Cohen, "Nathanael West's Holy Fool," *Commonweal*, LXIV (June 15, 1956), 276-78.

2. "Book Review Section," *New York Times*, March 24, 1957, p. 5.

3. Nathanael West, *The Complete Works of Nathanael West* (New York: Farrar, Straus and Cudahy, Inc., 1957), p. 261. Unless otherwise indicated, all references to West's work are to this edition.

4. West has made interesting remarks on the pictorial and lyrical quality of his work in "Some Notes on Miss L.," *Contempo*, III (May 15, 1933), 1-2.

5. For example, see the caveat in G. Giovannini's "Method in the Study of Literature in its Relation to the Other Fine Arts," *JAAC*, VIII (March, 1950), 185-95.

6. Among recent commentators who make this connection, see especially F. D. Klingender, *Goya in the Democratic Tradition* (London, 1948), pp. 102-05, 168-69, 179 and André Malraux, *Saturn: An Essay on Goya*, translated by C. W. Chilton (London, 1957), p. 46.

7. James F. Light, *Nathanael West* (Evanston, 1961), p. 158.

8. Jacques Lassaigne, *Daumier*, translated by Eveline Byam Shaw (Paris, 1938), p. 16.

9. Grose Evans, "The Subtle Satire of Magnasco," *Gazette des Beaux-Arts*, ser. 6, XXXII (July, 1947), 40.

10. "Magnasco's Precarious, Picaresque World," *Art Digest*, XIV (January 15, 1940), 13.

11. "Some Notes on Miss L.," *Contempo*, III, 2.

12. A letter from Professor I. J. Kapstein of Brown University, a college friend of West's, states "West had a strong feeling for the grotesque and the eccentric and ... something of the technique in

rendering these came from Flaubert's *The Temptation of Saint Anthony"* (May 7, 1957).

13. Jean Seznec, *Nouvelles Etudes sur la Tentation de Saint Antoine* (London, 1949), p. 61. The same author's essay, "The Temptation of Saint Anthony in Art," *Magazine of Art*, XL (March, 1947), 87-93, is a pertinent account of the continued attraction of this subject to painters since the middle ages.

14. Lady Morgan, *The Life and Times of Salvator Rosa*, I (London, 1824), 106-107n.

15. *The Fantastic Visions of Monsù Desiderio*, with a "Foreword" by A. Everett Austin (Sarasota, Florida, n.d.), p. 4.

16. Norman Cohn, *The Pursuit of the Millennium* (London, 1957), p. 313.

17. This essay was begun in 1958. I discussed the matter with Mr. Light at the time, but he did not choose to develop my theme at any length in his subsequent book, *Nathanael West*, pp. 169-74.

NO REDACTOR, NO REWARD
By James H. Bowden

Inquirers there are and many of them who have asked after the place of Nathanael West in American literature: will he be cannonized, ought he be? If he is, where will he go: with the Prophets or the Writers, and will he be among the minor prophets or writers, if so? Should one who seems initially, enduringly, and finally so negative really be considered at all? Negative, negative—even Nietzsche said Yea by saying Nay. West seems all Nay. Is he only a surrealist, distorting figures before fun-house mirrors—except that there is no way out of the fun-house? Therein lie if not most of the objections, at least the final cavil: people who introduce editions of his works, even those who write full length books on him (books longer than any he wrote), all seem to end with a *yes, but . . . .*

Perhaps if he'd lived longer. No. West shares some attitudes with Scott Fitzgerald, who died at 44 the same month West did, and no one doubts the bulk of *his* work would have been behind him in any case. The same for West, dead at 37, who began work almost as young but who was always more careful and precise, spelled a little better too. Since his four novels, though of uneven quality, agree in outlook, there is no reason to suppose he would have done more than produce another one or two or three of the same. More refined, perhaps, and it would be nice to have them, but that's all. He said his say, he was negative, he distorts.

Except we know all artists distort in order to bring into focus what they want seen, excluding one way or another the rest. Saying West is a "painter of the grotesque" is therefore worthless as such; anyway, his people aren't all that odd—few people are, outside of asylums. Then all this says is that he didn't manage it so well, did he? For we see as grotesque what we should accept as usual. He makes us uncomfortable, makes us feel *we're* all grotesques, that all the world is an Unfunny Farm. But if he's right in that, then we are left with no place whereon to stand—even to evaluate his own work. We are trapped like the man in Chekhov's "Ward Eight," mistakenly caught in an institution for the insane, except we know in his case it was an error and in ours (if West is right) all the world's insane. This situation really is intolerable.

Partly this is a problem of point-of-view, a tough problem with writing that is surreal or satirical or naturalistic: at a party of drunkards the latecomer is thus disproportionately sober and is obviously not normal. You can't have a healthy or good or sober man in such a situation, he messes up the continuity. *Deus ex machina*, he seems, and all that. (Hence Graham Greene puts garlic on the breath of the confessional priest who appears at the end of *Brighton Rock*: he's got to have *something* wrong with him, and even so he's an intruder from another world.) West is careful never to have any such hero emerge or enter. Thus it is better art, but it challenges our sanity. In order to handle such a threat the easiest retort is the one Betty makes when Miss L pinches her tit and otherwise bullies her: with her we say the man, though brilliant, is sick.[1] If it's him or us, usually we say it's him.

This is an unfair though general response. In order to classify him more aptly, return to the initial metaphor of whether he fits into the canon and judge him against the book against which all books might well be judged: the Bible, the Book. Is he a prophet, perhaps a Nathan coming out of the West to reprimand David for stealing Bathsheba? A Jeremiah, more likely, except one expects a prophet to speak for a God and there doesn't seem to be any in West's work. True, he could be only affecting the mein of a prophet of old while really speaking in behalf of a modern urgency; but that too implies at least a deification if not a deity and there simply is no god of any sort, secular or sacred, found overtly in his novels.

Clearly, then, he cannot be Job either, for if there is one thing—or person—Job believes in, it's the deity, for otherwise he would have no problem: the world would be only a random and ceaseless flux of errata, phenomena, meaning nothing at all. Rather like Ecclesiastes, in fact. Ah, yes: Ecclesiastes; may it not be that this is our man's niche? Vanity of vanity, says the Preacher: forget your palaces, gold, whores and all—it all comes to nothing; forget about the life of wisdom (though you ought to be a *little* wise) for it won't get you much either, indeed "neither make thyself over wise" (Eccles. 7:16b).[2] But that nice little book of soap bubbles, intending to show wandering young Jews that Hebraicism also had Wisdom, that the Greeks didn't have it all, that book is awfully *detached.* West isn't. Or, more precisely, *West* is detached, Miss Lonelyhearts and Tod Hackett are not detached; thus he qualifies. Still one asks, how did Ecclesiastes make it? It differs from the bulk of the Book: is it leaven? A little will leaven the whole lump.

Most critics agree that the book of Ecclesiastes got into the canon of Scripture for two reasons, and just barely got in at that: it was first of all attributed to Solomon—which also helped the Song of Songs get in, but he didn't do either of them (how *could* the same man do both, even if you were willing to believe he did one?)—and second there is a tagged-on ending to this rather existential work, an ending supposedly to "correct" what had gone before. Correct or—in the printer's sense of the word—justify it, to make it come out even, tight, acceptable. This ending is thought to be the work of a redactor, a copyist-editor who forgot for the moment he was supposed to be only the former and did the latter too and then got taken seriously by later copyists. A descendent, perhaps, of the fellow who gave Job everything back twice over, after the whole import of the book before then had been that God is obscure, but has His reasons (Job 42:7ff).

This answer is similar to the Ecclesiastes answer to the Problem of Theodicy (How to reconcile a good God with a suffering creation) but it is not very satisfactory to questioners whose religion emphasizes the God of History, with justice in this world. It is all very well to say that the real answer to the doleful situation in Job is found in the person of Jesus of Nazareth, and Christians have long found supportive proof-texts (Job 9:32-33, 19:25-27) for this claim: here is the Perfect Man, by whom men said No to God on Friday and through whom God will make things right, by and by, or there is the somewhat rarefied Jewish view that the God who acts decisely in history at certain points for His people as a whole nevertheless cannot be expected to pay everyone accurately on a one-to-one basis personally.[3]

That is, one can accept the implied but hidden and certainly longed-for Christ, or one can, with Job, repent in sackcloth and ashes for having challenged even in one's private thoughts the Most High. Is that good enough? "Sure, Manny," says the hairy-chested director, irate behind his sun glasses, gesticulating to his associate, both of them watching the filming of a gross bedroom copulatory scene, "Sure, Manny," he says, "*I* get it and *you* get it—*but will the man in the street get it?!*" Possibly not: he might read *sport* where he's supposed to see *love* or is even supposed to decide *hate*. You can't tell, so what you do is add those last eleven verses to Job and the extra two to Ecclesiastes. Then they get it. The cognoscenti will understand, even as they sigh, and the multitude will be *so* pleased.

This situation it seems, is what explains both West's success and failure, says why he makes it beautifully with some but misses utterly with most; in short, it explains his place in the canon of American Literature. His *Miss Lonelyhearts* is a sort of Ecclesiastes without the last two lines. The case with his other good book, *The Day of the Locust,* is similar, though it is not an abbreviated Ecclesiastes but rather it is an adumbrated Revelation instead: the last book in the Christian Scripture, written for reasons of caution to sound futurist, really was aimed at the Rome of the Neronian persecutions; but the Intentional Fallacy seems to have worked then, too, and it speaks of the Heavenly Jerusalem to follow the Divine Judgment. The analogous parallel here is that while in the case of *Lonelyhearts* West leaves off the Summing Up of the Duty of Man, in *Locust* he leaves off the heavenly reward for the faithful. He even leaves off the faithful. Some are simply more *aware*.

Rather than questioning West for not adding an explicit antidote to the bulk of *Lonelyhearts,* an artistically impossible feat, perhaps we should chide the redactor for messing the ending of Ecclesiastes. Does he commit artistic error? What if that book could have ended with the sentence preceding the addenda, a thoroughly Westian line: after giving terminal prudent advice, the advisor urges the reader not to take even him too seriously: "And further, by these, my son, be admonished: of making many books there is no end; and much study is a weariness of the flesh" (12:12). This statement is as goodly self-condemnatory as Miss McGreeney's biography of Samuel Perkins, biographer of Fitzgerald, biographer of Hobson, biographer to Boswell, biographer to Johnson: four tin cans tied to the Doctor's tail with a fifth coming up. And it is as satisfactory a closing as that of *Miss Lonelyhearts,* where—after finding the Rock and after Accepting—Miss L goes to his sudden and ridiculous death.

Appended endings aside, the Preacher and West speak similarly on main points: consider the job Shrike does on destroying all the panaceas (Tangible Goals, the psychologists call them) that are immediately available. Dictating to Miss L, Shrike begins with Art:

"Art Is a Way Out.

"Do not let life overwhelm you. When the old paths are choked with the debris of failure, look for newer and fresher paths. Art is just such a path. Art is distilled from suffering. As Mr. Polnikoff exclaimed through his fine Russian beard, when, at the age of eighty-six, he gave up his business to learn Chinese, 'We are, as yet, only at the beginning. . . .'

"Art Is One of Life's Richest Offerings.

"For those who have not the talent to create, there is appreciation. For those. . .

Then Shrike says, "Go on from there" (69).

And he does go on: eventually Shrike asks *How About Back to the Soil*, or perhaps the *South Seas, Life to the Hilt, Art* (again), *suicide, drugs* (107-110). No, only the Church will do. Except, well, the Church *is* rather strange these days, ranging from Adding Machine Cult to thomistic synthesis. Shrike mentions "the First Church of Christ Dentist," and the "Trinity new style: Father, Son and Wirehaired Fox Terrier" (110). In *The Day of the Locust,* Tod, gathering material for his "Burning of Los Angeles" painting, is given to sketching worshippers in such as the weight-lifting "Church of Christ, Physical" and the "Church Invisible," where spiritualism is practiced (365). The examples are strange, but no one denies the edge has been dull for some time on the sword of the Church. Or, as Koheleth would say, approximately, God is far off and you are here (5:2b).

Well, is it not holiness to deny that these escapes are anything other than what they are? If denying is what the Preacher is doing, even if with more calm than West, then what's wrong with West saying the same? Nothing, if it can be shown that he speaks in the name of Someone Else. The same cannot be said for *Balso Snell*, but *Balso Snell* doesn't count, it being a trying-out, a getting-it-out-of-your-gut *tour de force*; it never goes beyond the level of wit, and is mercifully short.

Nor is there such a concern in *A Cool Million*, reminiscent of *Candide* while satirizing the Horatio Alger stories; at times it even mimicks Alger's style. The difficulty is that satire is always parasitic, dies if that which it lives on dies. (*Candide* lives because while technically aimed at Leibniz it will do to curb any facile optimism that occurs.) Also, Alger's works make laughable that which he claims to endorse; his is thus already a satire, and it is simply not possible to satirize a satire, which is why *Candy* fails: proclaimed as a satire on pornography, it became porn itself instead, since pornography is already a satire on sexuality. In its overt form the particular myth Alger tried to vivify was well dead. So reading it becomes for the already convinced merely an exercise in self congratulation.

It is different in *Miss Lonelyhearts,* where from the first
we are inundated with Christ-talk, being told just Who is the
ultimate Miss Lonelyhearts; Miss L the newspaperman knows
well that "Christ was the answer, but, if he did not want to
get sick, he had to stay away from the Christ business" (68).
What West means, of course, is that we'll get sick—sick of
hearing it: art always serves a god, but it had better be
Pascal's *deus absconditus* unless you're prepared to listen to
an allegorical lecture.

Especially would this idea be out of place in a journal-like
(rather than journalistic) novel: *Miss Lonelyhearts* partakes
of the flavor of journalism, even as *Balso Snell* sounds as if
batted off the clever walls of academe ("the books smelt like
a closet full of old shoes through which a steam pipe passes"
[17]) and *A Cool Million,* as noted, like Alger (". . . dear
reader. . . . Alas, to such a sorry pass had he come. . . . for our
hero. . . ."[192-193]); *The Day of the Locust* sounds apocalyptic whenever Southern California is mentioned, but what
doesn't? All West's writing is sentence-centered, the mark of
all journalism, good or bad; it is spare and so epigrammatic it
is hard to collapse sections together for ellipsized quotation—it's already compacted as much as it will stand. All this
is not to say his writing is small-beer or that he skates on ice
twenty feet thick, with no chance of hollowing scholarly ice
palaces or of discovering what strange finny shapes swim
below; rather does he conform style to mood. Most journal-
ists have a novel in them (a good place for it, too), but on
emitting it they tend to believe their work worth upwards of
300 pages of one's time. West eschews prolixity in that too;
but since the milieu of the journal-novel does not admit of
metaphysics, he keeps the Christ-talk on the surface. Still we
know what's under the ice: either there is meaning or there is
not.

The alternative offered this frustrated Christ-riddenness is
being a one-dimensional person and (more or less) liking it, as
does Shrike, named for the bird that appears to kill without
purpose. Perhaps Shrike is ultimately unhappy, but, eventually, if one has sought at all, one either *finds* or else one

prudently decides to *call off the search*. He has called it off. Looking is good, the unexamined life is not worth living, and all that. But inquiry either leads your car somewhere or else you get out and walk home. No good just spinning your wheels. Miss L is an annoyance to those around him because he is serious enough and young enough at 26 still to be looking.

Mary Shrike's response to inquiry that, designed to or not, brings her a little too close to admitting the unsavory quality of the salt of her life, is a response similar to Betty's: don't ask. In the El Gaucho night club "her movements [become] languorous and full of abandon" (93), while Miss L compares this mentally to the dreams of those who think life will be full if only they become civil engineers, learn cartooning, develop a bust on which to pillow Raoul's head. Mary is perceptive enough to sense his criticism of her sudden adoption of what she imagines to be Spanish ways and she defends herself, saying "It's a little fakey, I know, but it's gay and I so want to be gay." Asked why, she claims "Everyone wants to be gay—unless they're sick" (94). Had she admitted first off the limitations under which man labors and the *ultimate* vanity of earthly works, then she might be right in claiming a season for gaity and a desire always to wear shining garments and to anoint her hair (3:1-9, 9:7-9). She'd have to do that with Shrike, of course, but anyway she doesn't admit it, though she is considerably more aware than Betty.

Betty is the sort protected by Powerful Limited Vision, protected thereby and enabled to overcome obstacles by a total inability to see that they are there. Her limitation is surely congenital and one wonders why Miss L has picked her: longing perhaps for what he might read as an innate innocency, a spiritual virginity inviolable even by intellectual dynamite? Then why Mrs. Doyle, whom he rightly loathes but still beds? She didn't rape him, after all, and he *pursues* Mary Shrike, an unlikely target even if she weren't another man's wife. Does he envy Shrike, and also want to sleep with a knife in his groin? And then of course there is Faye, desired by Tod Hackett, store-dummy Faye, an ignoramous, panted after by a Yalie art grad. It makes no sense on a superficial level, sounds as if West might have been harboring some sort of homosexual resentment. "One man among a thousand have I found, but a woman among all those have I not found" (7:28b).

These women do make sense if the alternative is considered. Suppose a simpatico female did crop up, what then? It would be an *Answer,* no? Live your life with a person you can talk to: "Again, if two lie together, then they have heat; but how can one be warm alone?" (4:11). Good advice, a nice hedge against the night, and it might be the one palliative West would have permitted in a later book since his own marriage was reportedly happy. This good advice cannot be admitted here, though, before he has made his point: if the salt has lost its savor. . . .

Thus it is for sake of his art that he limits the sort of women allowed, though giving us just one engaging one for female readers to identify with would have secured him much greater popularity. Damn all else but leave us Eros and the rest is forgiven—even applauded—for such works do elevate the god that much higher. Also he varies in not submitting to the American myth of the Purity of Nature. Instead his are strictly city novels, and cities are unlikely places to receive revelations of burning wheels within wheels—not in a luncheonette, says Shrike—nor where the earth of the park is packed down from many feet, and no grass grows, where the sky is as if rubbed by a dirty eraser and a stone obelisk begins to swell and ejaculate, and dirty newspapers (appropriately enough) play around your ankles. Betty, incisive for once, sees this situation and says all his troubles are city troubles.

So Nature is another escape that needs destruction, and we learn that it really is a place of clean boredom, of ignorance: the man at the Aw-Kum-On Garage explains that the reason there are still deer around is the yids haven't ruined it. Not hunters, yids. Dumb. West is most Biblical when he says go to the city to see what it's like: both Old and New Testaments begin in Gardens and both end in

Jerusalem, albeit a Heavenly Jerusalem in the case of the latter. He and Betty return and enter the Bronx slums and "He saw a man who appeared to be on the verge of death stagger into a movie theatre that was showing a picture called *Blonde Beauty*. He saw a ragged woman with an enormous goiter pick a love story magazine out of a garbage can and seem very excited by her find" (115).

The ultimate American city, everyone knows, is Los Angeles. Here is where every dream attacked in *Miss Lonelyhearts* is realized, damnably realized. In olden days, people in the game had to make predictions that could soon be confirmed or else seen through quickly, and it was customary to stone false prophets; West's prophecy is realized. Not only do the people living there now seem to enshrine the billboard life in their own habitat, one of their leading industries is the fabrication of more of the same for viewing around the rest of the land, and in other unfortunate countries not yet converted.

Were West writing today the locale could be the same—though the exporting of L.A. seems sufficiently successful that the suburbs of almost any large city would do—except a few details would change: the car, his killer, would be more influential, serving even more to isolate while uniting in standardization, and instead of writing of architecturally variegated bungalows he would note the repetitious ranch houses. It comes to the same thing, the same Disneyland vision that puts Tombstone round the bend from instant New Orleans (with happy coons plinking banjos and no Storeyville), only a few minutes by Mississippi sternwheeler to the hourly shoot-out at the OK Corral with a few hippopotomi on the way, mowed down by a Jungle Jim on the bow. West had to use conglomerate movie sets to get this effect, but now the Surreal has gone legit. Oh, West was no false prophet.

Disneyland, by denying validity to History, denies that meaning is found in history: "On the corner of La Huerta Road was a miniature Rhine castle with tarpaper turrets pierced for archers. Next to it was a little highly colored

shack with domes and minarets out of the *Arabian Nights*"
(262). The plastic reflects the non-plastic—our buildings show
what we believe. Obviously, then, Time and Place mean
nothing to us. There is no History so there is no God of
History and hence no in-breaking of the God is expected.
Nothing is expected. That even Death is not real can be seen
by the cemeteries, which are called anything other than what
they are: Parks, Gardens, Lawns. Disneyland-for-the-Dead,
which, denying suffering and death, denies as well joy and
life.

Harry Greener, old vaudevillian and manqué actor, dies
and is buried in customary California pattern, being painted,
plucked, rouged—packaged. Wisely West doesn't over-do it,
by trying to make an entire work out of these funeral habits,
which are yet another self-parody, one that causes *The Loved
One* to appear banal (though popular) next to *Locust*. So
there are no tombstones at Forest Lawn, there presumably
being no dead—but, ah, for one granite phallic marker
trusting in eventual resurrection.

Into this situation comes Tod, under contract to do art
for the flicks. His love is Faye Greener, long-leggedly healthy
and destined for prostitution. Unlike most of her sort who
are glorified in films, *e.g., Butterfield Eight, Irma la Douce,
Never on Sunday,* she operates from a profound sense of the
economics of the profession and not from tender-hearted
love. Tod, his soul aching, is terribly out of it by Hollywood
standards when he tries to persuade her not to become a
whore: he doesn't comprehend that by ordinary American
literary algebra (obviously unacceptable to West) it is
reasoned that that which Society calls Bad must be Good
since Society is itself Bad—two negatives make a positive;
accordingly, that which Society (Bad) calls Good is concomi-
tantly Bad—a negative and a positive make a negative.

This is a commonly supposed Truism in Hollywood, as if
when Jesus observed that the formerly sinning woman had
been forgiven because she loved much, He had meant "her
loving justified her sinning" instead of the better exegesis
that "you can see her sins are forgiven because she is *able* to

love." She couldn't love if her sins were not shriven (Luke 7:36-50). Faye, if she can be said to think, thinks of herself as a Thing; words such as "sin" and "love" and "meaning" are thus not relevant to her. Nor are they for Tod, who though infinitely more aware, is of her same pagan outlook; he realizes this and at the end of *Locust* loses his grip since though he hates the L.A. style he has no grounds for an alternative. Similarly, all he can say against her turning herself into a thing is that it will be bad for her health:

> ... She wouldn't understand the aesthetic argument and with what values could he back up the moral one? The economic didn't make much sense either. Whoring certainly paid. Half of the customer's thirty dollars. Say ten men a week.
>
> She kicked at his shins, but he held on to her. Suddenly he began to talk. He had found an argument. Disease would destroy her beauty. He shouted at her like a Y.M.C.A. lecturer on sex hygiene (346).

If *Miss Lonelyhearts* tells people that half realize it that their gods are false, *The Day of the Locust* says this is the result of calling off the search. That is, *Lonelyhearts* follows the same tack used by the Preacher in Ecclesiastes: here are all the baals, he says, now do you not realize they are no more than gold-painted bulls? Don't you see that in your agnosticism you have been led to idolatry? What you must do, says Koheleth, is become agnostic about agnositicism. Once you consider the possibility that Meaninglessness might itself lost meaning—and it is toward achieving this insight that the book of Ecclesiastes works—then space will be cleared for the Hidden to be made manifest. And you may "hear the conclusion of the whole matter: Fear God, and keep his commandments: for this is the whole duty of man. For God shall bring every work into judgment, with every secret thing, whether it be good, or whether it be evil" (12:13-14). See, there are no gods; therefore, remember God.

West doesn't include this proviso, which really isn't so foreign to what has gone before it as it might seem: the job in both cases has been to destroy the half-gods. Emerson says in "Give All to Love" that "when half-gods go / the Gods arrive." C. S. Lewis has rightly called that a very doubtful opinion; more likely, then will the quarter-gods come. Then will Los Angeles succéed New York. Then there will be dryness and madness. Persons not knowing this, slave at uninteresting jobs in order to retire to Ultima America.

> Once there, they discover that sunshine isn't enough. They get tired of oranges, even of avocado pears and passion fruit. Nothing happens. They don't know what to do with their time. They haven't the mental equipment for leisure, the money nor the physical equipment for pleasure. . . .
> Their boredom becomes more and more terrible. They realize that they've been tricked and burn with resentment. Every day of their lives they read the newspapers and went to the movies. Both fed them on lynchings, murder, sex crimes, explosions, wrecks, love nests, fires, miracles, revolutions, war. This daily diet made sophisticates of them. The sun is a joke. Oranges can't titillate their jaded palates. Nothing can be violent enough to make taut their slack minds and bodies. They have been cheated and betrayed. They have slaved and saved for nothing (411-412).

Thus comes the so richly deserved Apocalypse, the Day of the Locust:

> And there came out of the smoke locusts upon the earth: and unto them was given power, as the scorpions of the earth have power. And it was commanded them that they should not hurt the grass of the earth, neither any green thing, neither any tree; but only those men which have not the seal of God in their foreheads (Rev. 9:3-4).

This is only the first woe, and two more are to follow. After hearing the eight-year-old Adore Loomis, son of the raw-only vegetarian, sing "Mama Doan Wan' No Peas," after seeing Claude Estee's copy of the Dupuy Biloxi mansion, after enduring MR. KAHN A PLEASURE DOME DECREED, it is almost a pleasure. No, it *is* a pleasure, if only to have done with it. (Especially since no one has the seal of God in his forehead.) It is a pleasure to have done with it, which means really we're a bit glad to have done with Mr. West: Ecclesiastes is at the least a good little bit of *Nachtmusik*, though it hardly sums up the Old Testament; similarly, Revelation concludes but does not encapsule the New.

It *was* clever of him to have a newspaper/written-record

metaphor for the Old Testament novel, and film for the comparatively (Once-in-History) flashy consummation of the New. In this ·case both media were liars, however (Cf. the previous quotation from *Locust*, above). A contemporary sequel would use TV and its world—as the New Israel? And it too might keep on asking *Why?*, though no one likes a person to go about forever asking Why? Why? What Does It Mean? One either finds an answer and tells it, or one doesn't find an answer and shuts up, or if one doesn't shut up, one suffers having a bowl of soup dumped on his head.

In accepting the challenge of asking the Most High questions West has tacitly accepted this rider: yet he sits there grunting and grunting without produce, but declines to get off the pot. Now this will not do.

As Romano Guardini, S. J., has said, "I want none of your pallid humanisms: if Christ be not God, I will hack my way through existence alone." In the Western World, especially in America, Most High Questions always involve Christ. Our West, however, says no to both of these alternatives: he can't hack Christ (*Balso Snell, Miss Lonely-hearts*) and he can't hack without Him (*A Cool Million, The Day of the Locust*). And thus his appeal is to that narrow band of fellows who similarly cannot leave off asking and who cannot the while find satisfactory answers, people who believe there is no God hidden anywhere but who can't call off the search.

There is no Hidden God in West, no more than there is in the fabric of the everyday culture of the West. In these novels the Christ is banal (not vulgar—Jesus was himself deliberately vulgar) and so is the Absence-of-Christ banal. This is so because the questions have to be asked on or nearly at the level on which they are raised, and they happen most often to be asked with banality. This is one of the features of democracy most galling to the intelligent aesthete and it is as much as an aesthete as it is as an intellectual that West works, using the first to illustrate the second: hence the force of his double-barreled shot. The reason, then, that there is no corrective additive to his Ecclesiastes, to *Miss Lonelyhearts*, is that he doesn't think God will assuredly bring every act eventually into Judgment; the reason there is no Heavenly City offered as an alternative after the Abomination is burnt down is that he isn't at all sure that we can expect one. He does not offer a negative by which the discerning gnostic few can print off a clear picture. His Preacher asks and goes on asking until he's shot; his Just (or Concerned, or Aware) sees everything destroyed, himself included.

FOOTNOTES

1. Nathanael West, *The Complete Works of Nathanael West* (New York: Farrar, Straus and Company, 1963). Henceforth, parenthetical pagination will refer to that edition.

2. Since this is an essay aimed at literature and not at theology, the King James Version is used throughout for Biblical quotation. Unless otherwise noted, Scriptural excerpts are from Ecclesiastes.

3. The Christian view tacitly assumes—as with, say, Abp. Anselm, in *Cur Deus Homo*—that everyone owes a crashing debt he can't possibly pay so we all deserve whatever evil befalls. In this regard Ecclesiastes complements Job when it says *Vanity* to those who protest, "But what of those whose windfall in this life is great houses, vineyards, pools, men singers and women singers?" Do not all go to the same place?

NATHANAEL WEST AND THE CONFIDENCE GAME
By Warwick Wadlington

"There's a game we want to play and we need you to play it.—'Everyman his own Miss Lonelyhearts.' "

Americans have always been, in one sense or another, confidence men. This is why, now that an existential failure of confidence cuts at the very quick of our experience, we have discovered the Melville of *The Confidence-Man*, the Twain of *The Mysterious Stranger*, and the novels of Nathanael West. In the case of West, one influential critical portrait that has grown over the last several years is an intriguing Daumier creation: West as an exotic plant on our shores whose genus is really the Continental Decadent-Existentialist family of literature (represented, say, by the major Dostoevsky-Rimbaud-Céline branch). Obviously there is a great deal that is accurate and suggestive in this classification. But it seems to me that such a categorization is primarily significant because it is a response to something underlying the Continental label. It essentially identifies in West's fiction a crisis of confidence that is not exotic but indigenous. While West's kinship with an American tradition including Melville has been pointed out (by James Light, R. W. B. Lewis, and others), it has been insufficiently explored. If confidence is the American Way, West saw that the modern failure of confidence is a national as well as an individual catastrophe. He saw that the attempted American Way Out (as Shrike would say) of a schizophrenic loss of selfhood is a game of confidence that easily becomes a confidence game. Like Melville, West found in the linked possibilities *confidence man* and *man-of-confidence* the prototype of both the traditional American and the creative artist. But West's modern American exists primarily as a diminished variation of the prototype: he is the conned-man, the conned-artist, the unconfident confidence man.[1] Thus at the outset it will be helpful to recall the American iconography that serves as the basic vocabulary of West's fiction.

I

In the national iconography Americans are peddlers of assurance. The iconography was shaped early by the historical uniqueness of the experience open to the nation, by the new Romantic faith in the self, and by the competitive energies of capitalism. The mood that is central to the nineteenth century love of tall talk and of patriotic oratory in a particular "spread-eagle style" is also fundamental to the advocacy of confidence by Franklin as well as Emerson, the self-reliance that in its various forms was *The Way to Wealth*, to wholeness of spirit, and to the Oversoul. The vibrant national mood vivified, if it did not alone create, the loftiest metaphor of Protestant America's Dream—the identification of America as the land of promise, the New Jerusalem trustfully awaiting its secular and transcendent Redeemer. At a more immediate level, the matrix of robust confidence produced a figure who was the most popular national type from the Revolution to the Civil War—the Yankee. Yankee became a synonym for both American, a man of confidence, and New Englander, a confidence man. In the first versions of the comic type, the "Jonathan," the bumptious certitude that was often scornfully attributed to Americans by foreigners was picked up by the fledgling culture as a nose-thumbing badge of identification. As the Yankee appeared on the stage, in the literature, and sub-literature of the century, he increasingly reflected the deprecation of everything sophisticated and the exaltation of a shrewd, peasant commonsense that was thought to be a native gift. The primary manifestation of the Yankee was the Peddler, whose lonely, wandering life-style, true to the promptings of democratic patriotism, Romanticism, and free enterprise, was the icon of self-confidence above all.

In the familiar mythology, America, disembarrassed of the weight of European institutions and traditions, placed all its trust in the untrammeled self. The song of the open road was the native Song of Myself, and the only weight to be reckoned with was the Peddler's bag of "Yankee notions," borne willingly because it was his own, because what he was marketing was chiefly himself.

Insofar as the Yankee Peddler was seen as upholding the American virtues, he was a benign figure, like Sam Slick, whose slyness in trading was the harmlessly comic consequence of the national game of merchant self-reliance vs. customer self-reliance. The benign Peddler was our cracker barrel mentor, a Romantic rustic given to apothegms on trust in oneself, in one's fellow-man, and in the benevolence of "Natur." And the wise cunning of a Sam Slick was an amusing lesson in the necessary game of confidence that is involved not only in a money economy but especially in an expanding capitalist system. In 1849 the *Merchants' Ledger*, as might be expected, found comfort in the exploits of a swindler who achieved a great notoriety in the newspapers of the time as "The Original Confidence Man": "That one poor swindler, like the one under arrest, should have been able to drive so considerable a trade on an appeal to so simple a quality as the confidence of man in man, shows that all virtue and humanity of nature is not entirely extinct in the nineteenth century. It is a good thing . . . that . . . men *can be swindled.*" The *Merchants' Ledger* article was quoted approvingly in the *Literary World* (West and Melville would have smiled knowingly at the literary angle), which added, "It is not the worst thing that may be said of a country that it gives birth to a confidence man."[2] The con man's game, as in Melville's novel, was to ask ingenuously that the intended dupe display his trust in the trickster by a loan or a purchase.

The formula was the quintessentially American mode of Romantic capitalism: an ingenuous pose concealing a private, secret self, confident of its powers, confident particularly of its power to elicit trust in the pose. The stronger one's feeling of secure selfhood, the more successful the persona; and the more successful the mask, the surer one's private sense of self, confidence breeding confidence.

The Peddler, "The Original Confidence Man," and another famous bunko-artist, P. T. Barnum, excited the American imagination as iconic marginal figures, on the periphery of "ordinary life," whose values were inherent in the dominant culture. Like all marginal figures, however, the Yankee trickster could also represent the dangerous side of cultural values. When the focus shifted to the exploitation of trust, as in accounts like Timothy Dwight's *Travels* (1821), the Peddler was regarded with moral distaste. Especially in the Old Southwest humor (for example, the Sut Lovingood and Davy Crockett stories), the Peddler with his wares was a detested image of Northern mercantilist attitudes. Still another widely popular figure, the frontier picaro of the Old Southwest, further exemplified the deceitful abuse of confidence. While there is a comic relish in the frontier trickster's duplicity, there is also a recognition of the more grotesque impulses of the confidence game, often combined (as in the Simon Suggs tales) with a satire of Jacksonian faith in the common man and rugged individualism.

The major examination of the American gospel of confidence, Melville's *The Confidence-Man* (1857), climaxes the author's long preoccupation with life's pasteboard deceptions. At one level, Melville seems to confront the national confidence in the self with the revelation that there is only persona. The protean being who voices assurance in himself and the wares he peddles and asks that his customers put their faith in *him* above all is a kaleidoscope of identities, a Cosmopolitan whose conglomeration of discordant colors and anomalous items of clothing make up a non-identity. In his instant readiness to respond to the expectations and desires of others with pose after pose, the Confidence-Man seems precisely like the colorless, all-color white in *Moby-Dick*: capable of being everything and therefore essentially nothing in itself. Yet the total thrust of the novel is not this clear-cut; the book also sets up counter-currents to the extractable "meaning" I have just outlined. In a well-known passage, Melville says that the genuinely original character in literature is a revolving Drummond light, raying away from itself all round it—everything is lit by it, everything starts up to it . . ." (Chapter XLIV). The description points directly to the miraculous effect of the book's hero. The Confidence-Man is a Drummond light in that he literally causes people to betray selves—to betray, seemingly, the self that is the autonomous source of the light as well as that which responds. Our experiential sense in reading the book is that we have somehow become aware of the profoundest being of the characters. Paradoxically, we come to believe most of all in the selfhood—the single, essential identity—of the Confidence-Man, and for the same reason that we believe in all the characters. If the protagonist relentlessly reveals that all men are actors, the flexibility and success of his roles suggests a strong and definite selfhood, though it may be a highly fluid, quicksilver entity that can be experienced only through roles and never directly known. As Melville also demonstrates in *Moby-Dick*, illusion and self are inextricable, and the Confidence-Man seems the most *real* because he is the best actor. But the sense of a real self is also produced by the strength and adequacy of the roles played by other characters—most notably, the invulnerable Emersonian figure, Mark Winsome ("a kind of cross between a Yankee peddler and a Tartar priest"), whose doctrine of absolute self-confidence in practice denies placing trust in others.

The double pull of the book's implications, one seeming to deny the reality of selfhood and the other to affirm it, is the basis for Melville's thorough-going game with the reader. The novel's prose plays powerfully on the surfaces of things, convincingly directing our attention to costumes, gestures, roles. Yet often the very garishness of appearances—the Missourian's coonskin trappings, the Cosmopolitan's incredible dress—urges us to be suspicious of surfaces; and the ironic, involuted style suggests that truth is only hinted at in the surfaces of things, or perhaps is nowhere at all. The confidence game, both the author's and his protagonist's, is a wry tribute to reality and, conjointly, to what Melville called the Art of Telling the Truth. The double implications of the book are the dual implications of life's pasteboard masks, immediately experienced as concretely real and trustworthy, but upon reflection suspected of being a Chinese box sequence, layer upon layer, all surfaces and no core. Whether the immediate experience or the later suspicion is true, *The Confidence-Man* does not finally say—that would be a form of certitude in itself. The point of the book is to capture the felt duplicity of reality, private or public, as a kind of concrete uncertainty. Beneath the metaphysical, psychological, and aesthetic meanings, the first premise of the novel's irony is that the American gospel is, finally, no more than a confidence in confidence. For Melville the ground of American being, selfhood, is a question wrapped in an enigma, and from that source there rays out a gigantic, indeed a cosmic, fraud.

II

"Life is a pic-nic en costume; one must take a part, assume a character, stand ready in a sensible way to play the fool." The Confidence-Man

The Cheated was the original title of West's last book, *The Day of the Locust*. All of West's characters have been cheated of self, whether they belong to the frenetic group of performers West calls masqueraders, or to the faceless, uneasy mob whose appetite for a vital identity is served by the masquerade. As Tod Hackett reflects, the anarchic audiences who throng Hollywood's cinema openings are the cream of America's madmen because they realize that they have been betrayed by the promise of life for the free individual. Con men like Dr. Know-All Pierce-All have beckoned them to the "Road to Life," the national Dream culminating at the frontier's end in movie-set façades and the millennial expectations of the Church of the Third Coming ("O Come Redeemer" beseeches the music at Harry Greener's funeral). As in Melville, the relationship between cheater and dupe is profoundly symbiotic. But in West, distinctive emphasis is on the state of being cheated—the *a priori* existential condition—on a civilization of cheaters and façades both symptom and result, created on demand: "the group of uneasy people . . . stood staring at the performers in just the same way they stared at the masqueraders on Vine Street. It was their stare that drove Abe and the others to spin crazily and leap into the air with twisted backs like hooked trout."[3] West's characters are all poorly made, like Homer Simpson, because all that remains of real identity is a vestigial self felt as a restless desire for completion. The audience's demand that they be furnished with a full, authentic existence is insatiable, so that they are always ready to provoke and then to follow "the necessary promise" of a new con man into the violence that makes them feel alive. The growing recognition runs throughout West's work: the dissolution of self makes the existence of individual, artist, and nation three dependent coordinates of a con-game.

West described his first novel, *The Dream Life of Balso Snell*, as "a protest against writing books," and the reasons for the protest are perfectly clear in the artist's hatred of the audience who requires him to be a confidence man:

> Some day I shall obtain my revenge by writing a play for one of their art theatres. A theatre patronized by the discriminating few . . . .
> In this play I shall take my beloved patrons into my confidence and flatter their difference from other theatre-goers . . . . Then, suddenly, in the midst of some very witty dialogue, the entire cast will walk to the footlights and shout Chekov's advice:
> "It would be more profitable for the farmer to raise rats for the granary than for the bourgeois to nourish the artist . . . ."
> In case the audience should misunderstand and align itself on the side of the artist, the ceiling of the theatre will be made to open and cover the occupants with tons of loose excrement.

> After the deluge, if they so desire, the patrons of my art can
> gather in the customary charming groups and discuss the play
> (30-31).

As another character explains, "Art is a sublime excrement"
(8). The book's studiedly clever, self-ironic protective color-
ation should induce, not block, our awareness that West is
dealing with his own precocious crisis of confidence as a
writer.

Art is an excrement in that it seems to be a waste, a
by-product, of the fundamentally selfish, yet symbiotic,
relationship of artist and audience: the audience needing the
stimulating illusions of the artist in order to feel that it exists
and the artist needing someone to see his illusions for the
same reason. More specifically, as the anecdote about
dumping excrement suggests, art is a sadomasochistic shell
game in which the artist's covert desires to demean are
released to the delight of the victims, who have in effect
"asked for it" by stimulating his desires. The epitome of this
alliance is the anonymous artist's relations with his mistress
Saniette ("exactly those of performer and audience"). The
casualness of her responses "excited me so that I became
more and more desperate in my performances." But because
of the extravagance of his complaint to her, "Saniette was
able to turn my revenge into a joke. She weathered a second
beating with a slow, kind smile" (25-30). The secondary,
by-product nature of art is further indicated by the book's
repeated explanation that creativity is a vehicle for sexual
conquest and by the frequent suggestion that the content of
art is inconsequential as long as it seems excitingly porten-
tous; standing before his "cringing audience," another performer climaxes his act "by keeping in the air an Ivory
Tower, a Still White Bird, the Holy Grail, the Nails, the
Scourge, the Thorns, and a piece of the True Cross" (56).
The thesis that art is a deceitful act of aggression fulfilling the
ulterior needs of performer and viewer is chiefly borne out in
the long literary leg-pull of the book. We begin by entering
the anus of the deceitful Trojan horse, and after complicated
stories-within-stories-and-dreams which explode in our faces

after asking to be taken seriously, we finally come to a conclusion that defines the whole work as an excremental act, a wet-dream. There is little doubt that the excrement of West the con-artist is aimed at the "discriminating few" who read *Balso Snell.*

West's career after *Balso Snell* is very much like Melville's later phase—a kind of high-wire act carried out in large part as a dramatization and defiance of the recognition that *Pierre* puts in these words: "Like knavish cards, the leaves of all great books were covertly packed. He was but packing one set the more . . ." (Book XXV, chapter III). The "modern" art which, at base, attacks art has few more distinguished examples than West's second novel, *Miss Lonelyhearts.* The third work, *A Cool Million,* is almost ruined by another outbreak of West's scorn, though it is less shrill than that of *Balso Snell.* In *Miss Lonelyhearts,* however, Shrike serves as a lightning-rod who draws off from the novel itself West's coruscating desire for parody and delivers it as stunning irony directed at Miss Lonelyhearts' realization that he can no longer play a joke with the needs and sufferings of his readers.

In both *Miss Lonelyhearts* and *The Day of the Locust* West extends his inquisition of the art-game to an exhibition of the art by which everyone lives. Human life is exposed as a set of tricks and rituals by means of which one person asks another for assurance, with the implied promise that confidence will be returned if the other cooperates in the game. People exist by inducing others to trust roles. Miss Lonelyhearts and Tod Hackett both make repeated, knowing attempts to stimulate themselves by concentrating on the artifices of existence: "[Miss Lonelyhearts] tried to excite himself into eagerness by thinking of the play Mary [Shrike] made with her breasts . . . . One of her tricks was to wear a medal low down on her chest" (90); "She thanked him by offering herself in a series of formal, impersonal gestures . . . and there was something clearly mechanical in her pantomime" (94). Tod's paintings are completely inspired by trickery—Faye Greener's "elaborate gesture[s] . . . so completely meaningless, almost formal, that she seemed a dancer rather than an affected actress" (304); Harry's mask-like face and intentionally burlesque devices; and the countless charades of Hollywood, where even the landlady's interest in Harry's funeral "wasn't morbid; it was formal. She was interested in the arrangement of the flowers, the order of the procession, the clothing and deportment of the mourners" (341). But whereas Melville's characters can still present persuasive performances, the roles West's people put on display are inordinately unconvincing. The players lack sufficient selfhood to act confidently; the poses are transparent, obviously second-hand, loose-fitting, as if originally intended for someone else. In West's extravagant comedy, the very lizards of *The Day* are inept, "self-conscious and irritable" (297).

The supreme form of confidence, religious faith, is the dramatic center of *Miss Lonelyhearts* as it is of *The Confidence-Man*. Christ, the ultimate Miss Lonelyhearts, is the sovereign conferrer of belief; and West's protagonist, once he finds it impossible to betray his readers' trust anymore, is forced to search for a self that will give validity not only to his role but to Christ's. The design is basic West. A tormented, cheated mob forces a man to attempt to fashion an authentic self that will make his role effective in giving the mob authenticity in turn. Miss Lonelyhearts must play the part that the shadowy Dr. Pierce-All does in *The Day*. He must indicate the road to life. Such is the interdependence of all of West's huddled artifacts—people, animals, and things in a continuum of gaudy sterility—that one has the awesome sense that if anyone in this world came to genuine life, Miss Lonelyhearts' whole "world of doorknobs" would indeed follow suit miraculously. Christ is the answer, Miss Lonelyhearts knows, but he is also aware that for him Christ is another trick, a "hysteria" in whose "mirrors . . . the dead world takes on a semblance of life" (75). However, tricks and mirrors are all that is available, so in a grimly comic parody of the existentialist hero's quest to create himself, West's hero willfully attempts to indulge the deception to the hilt.

As Shrike says, " 'the Miss Lonelyhearts are the priests of twentieth-century America' " (69).

The hero's dreams begin to reflect the shamanistic magician-priest's role that is part of the trickster's basic repertoire: "he found himself on the stage of a crowded theater. He was a magician who did tricks with doorknobs. At his command, they bled, flowered, spoke." But when he tries to continue by leading the audience in prayer, he fails: "no matter how hard he struggled, his prayer was one Shrike had taught him and his voice was that of a conductor calling stations. 'Oh, Lord, we are not of those who wash in wine, water, urine, vinegar . . . . Oh, Lord, we are of those who wash solely in the Blood of the Lamb' " (76). For most of the novel Miss Lonelyhearts is the unconfident confidence man whose rituals are impotent and whose world remains stubbornly dead. The Drummond light does not give even the illusion of working—nothing starts up to it.

Skeptical of his own roles and the illusions on which they are built, the West hero is vulnerable because of his inability to cloak himself completely with a façade. Wanting to find a believable role, yet despising the lies of which roles are made, he maintains an envious love-hate relationship with those who have apparently achieved invulnerability through manipulation of illusions—Shrike and Betty in *Miss Lonelyhearts* and Faye Greener in *The Day*. Betty and Faye share the "power to limit experience arbitrarily" (79), Betty to the order bounded by gingham apron and party dress, and Faye to the mental screen where she projects a bright confetti of fragmented film-strips.

Just as Miss Lonelyhearts is an eviscerated con-artist, Shrike is a joke at trickery. The avatars of Melville's Confidence-Man are designed to convince immediately, although their chilling hints of duplicity may cause the dupe later to reconsider the ideas of faith and trust. Shrike's diabolic mockery is open. He is a papier-mâché Satan for our times, his dead-pan trick and patter about a goat and adding machine religion pointedly derived from the cinema and newspapers. He is the master-player in the novel, admired, emulated, and feared because his game is to destroy games. Other people are poor, unpersuasive players; Shrike's exaggerated pretense at pretense establishes him as an expert at being unconvincing, and his superlative shoddiness doubly mocks their ineptitude. His dead-pan fleers at their deadness. His complementary simpleton act ironically reflects the shams by which everyone asks for confidence: "While talking, he kept his face alive with little nods and winks that were evidently supposed to inspire confidence and to prove him a very simple fellow." Yet even Shrike is not wholly invulnerable. As he tells about his sterile relationship with his wife, "the dead pan broke and pain actually crept into his voice . . . . It was Miss Lonelyhearts' turn to laugh. Shrike tried to ignore him by finishing as though the whole thing were a joke" (92). There is apparently a limit of tolerance for everyone in a world of tricks when the joke is no longer funny and one can no longer fool oneself sufficiently. At the moment this limit is reached in West, we tetter precariously between apocalyptic outrage and terrible laughter. The moment of laughter is particularly horrifying, for the sound is an automatic hedge against a crushing self-knowledge, and it resonates mechanically with the emptiness it seeks to shield. In traditional comedy the grace of laughter descends to dissolve difficulties in the end. West's comedy is black because it says that laughter is not enough, not nearly enough. Shrike's anti-game says the same thing of the specious assurance that has no foundation except mutual complicity.

Shrike's transparent simpleton's pose is a parodic version of the fool-character that fascinates West, who exhibits his diverse clowns, from Peter Doyle to Harry Greener, with the connoisseurship of a collector. Miss Lonelyhearts too tries at times to play the fool in a desultory way, but the paramount role he eventually tries to perfect is that of the Holy Fool, the Pauline fool in Christ. The traditional energy and dominion available to the fool-role is evident in the literary convention and religious paradox that identifies ultra-simplicity with divinely inspired wisdom. In the trickster's search for power, the fool-pose is ideal because it disarmingly tends to elicit a responsive simplicity from others. As Melville's hero advises, one must learn to play the fool in the human masquerade, and he follows his own counsel in the first two of his avatars—the Christ-like deaf-mute and Black Guinea—as well as in the extreme ingenuousness he later relies on heavily. In West's fiction the fool-role is crucial above all because it represents a way of dealing with a diminished self; in this sense, we may say, all of West's characters are fools.

Miss Lonelyhearts is thus more successful as the Holy Fool than as the magician-priest. In fact, in the transformation that takes place in the last pages of the novel he seems to achieve his desire to become a man of confidence. The inner sureness and stability that he suddenly comes to possess are unshakeable when Shrike fetches him for a sport intended as the paradigm of Miss Lonelyhearts' hapless cheating: " 'There's a game we want to play and we need you to play it.—"Everyman his own Miss Lonelyhearts." I invented it, and we can't play without you' " (132). The sturdy rock that Miss Lonelyhearts has within him has made him invulnerable to Shrike, whose party mock-game he ignores in order to play a "real" game with Betty. "The party dress had given his simplified mind its cue," and he finally becomes like the instinctive con man, responding accurately and effectively to the needs of his audience, manifested in its poses: "He was not deliberately lying. He was only trying to say what she wanted to hear . . . . He begged the party dress to marry him, saying all the things it expected to hear . . . . He was just what the party dress wanted him to be: simple and sweet, whimsical and poetic, a trifle collegiate yet very masculine" (137). Miss Lonelyhearts' religious experience and his murder follow with inevitable logic from this successful artistry. The rock upon which all these phenomena are founded is West's ironic summation of modern selfhood—a compromise between schizophrenia and a catatonic state. In simpler words, it is little more than Betty's ability to limit experience arbitrarily. "He did not feel. The rock was a solidification of his feeling, his conscience, his sense of reality, his self-knowledge" (138). Earlier, he had felt that his confusion was more significant than Betty's order, although when he tries to pretend that his confusion is "honest feeling . . . the trick failed" (79). But he also reflects that "Man has a tropism for order" (104). The tropism at length dominates his confusion, which is a function of his painful awareness and sensitivity. When these precipitate out into his private rock, he becomes another stone object, congruent with the "enormous grind-stones" (101) that are Fay Doyle's buttocks and the obelisk in the park "about to spout a load of granite seed" (89). In short, he has not revitalized the world but has become more solidly a part of what Balso Snell called the mundane millstone.

Miss Lonelyhearts' final return to his bed is a continua-tion of the illness that had prostrated him earlier: "he realized that his . . . sickness was unimportant. It was merely a trick by his body to relieve one more profound" (111). The pronoun *one* hangs provocatively between the antecedents *sickness* and *trick*. With the arrival of fever, which "promised . . . mentally unmotivated violence," the ironic revelation and martyrdom of Miss Lonelyhearts commences. The vision is of everything the protagonist lacks, a light-source which rays out life to the world: the transcendent Miss Lonelyhearts, Christ, "is life and light"; he is "a bright fly, spinning with quick grace" to which "the black world of things" rises like a fish. The same simplified, limited ordering of experience causes Miss Lonelyhearts to mistake Peter Doyle's cry of warning for a cry of help. The hero rushes to perform for his last audience—Desperate, Sick-of-it-all, and all the rest—with fatal, and false, confidence. As he had told Betty earlier, he is really the victim of a joke, not its perpetrator.

One major attribute of West's self-doubt as an artist, his haste to laugh at himself before we do, gets the best of him in his next novel, *A Cool Million*. It is a bit like listening to the run-away laughter of Harry Greener. In the parody of Alger that turns into a self-travesty, West yields again to the con-artist's aggressive temptation to flaunt his props and mechanisms. In *The Day* Tod is charmed by Faye's amateurish artificiality: "because he saw the perspiring stagehands and the wires that held up the tawdry summerhouse . . . he accepted everything and was anxious for it to succeed" (316). The triumph of urgent need over acting skill that captivates West as it does Tod has an obvious ironic counterpart in Shrike's simulations. Yet West is unable to bring off a satiric work which gets stuck in a grey monotone somewhere between the amateurish charm of Faye's artifice and the expert counterfeiting of Shrike's. West can neither make us share a "camp" interest in Horatio Alger's sweating stagehands nor a savage bitterness in response to the Algeresque chicanery of the American Dream. Nevertheless, *A Cool Million* is not merely regressive; seen in the context of West's career, it represents his progressive generalization from the self-doubt of the artist to an understanding that this provides a key insight into a national as well as a personal malaise. Whenever West has a new or deepened perception his first instinct is to parody it. Thus *A Cool Million* bears much the same relationship to West's last novel that *Balso Snell* does to *Miss Lonelyhearts*.

Although con men, frauds, shysters, and masquerades abound in comic plenty on every page of *A Cool Million*, the novel is built on a simple sequence of proportions with three major terms: the patriotic con man Shagpoke Whipple is to the nation as the literary con man Sylvanus Snodgrasse is to the Chamber of American Horrors as Nathanael West is to the novel.

The confession of faithlessness by Snodgrasse is a set-speech bit of hyperbole that asks to be discounted: "Like many another 'poet,' he blamed his literary failure on the American public . . . and his desire for revolution was really a desire for revenge. Furthermore, having lost faith in himself, he thought it his duty to undermine the nation's faith in itself" (238). West is clowning at himself and the truth. The book's ridiculous over-stylization itself is revenge enough on the reader, and the nation's confidence is not undermined but exposed and found to be rotten. Although the massive national fraud, the "surfeit of shoddy," is burlesqued to the point that the indictment loses force, in places the power of West's own doubt isolates the native virus sharply. " 'We accepted [the white man's] civilization,' " orates an Indian chief, " 'because he himself believed in it. But now that he has begun to doubt, why should we continue to accept? His final gift to us is doubt, a soul-corroding doubt' " (232).

Over against this secret modern doubt is set the absurd confidence of traditional American iconic figures like the "ring-tail roarer" Missourian, which are made into flat, stereotyped pop-up targets for satire along Lemuel Pitkin's picaresque road. The chief target is Shagpoke Whipple, ex-President, cracker barrel expounder of faith in America, enemy of "sophistication," Fascist dictator, and confidence man from first to last. Lemuel Pitkin, the stock-fool, is conned, beaten, or otherwise exploited by everyone in the book. His adventures touch on every kind of fraudulent victimization in the whole American Chamber of Horrors. Finally, after his dismantling and martyrdom, he is apotheosized as the American Boy and held up as an icon and mirror to Whipple's followers in order to fleece them further. The moral is shouted at us so loudly it is a sneer: the *schlemiel* Huck Finn's trust in the American dream of success means betrayal for himself and triumph for the native confidence game.

A Cool Million allows us to see still more clearly that in dealing with the duplicity that he perceived at the center of existence, West could not create a potent master-manipulator of confidence as Melville could. Melville makes the existence of the self an enigma, but the figure he places before us has a full, probing power even if the source of the power be a mystery. In West, the dissatisfied boredom and sense of vague betrayal indicate that the self does in fact exist, but only as a minimal presence. It is significant that West can only present the confidence tricksters who objectify this inner state as burlesque puppets (Shagpoke Whipple), disembodied symbols (Dr. Know-All Pierce-All), and failed or inverted con men (Miss Lonelyhearts and Shrike). "Lies only never vary," Melville writes in *Pierre* (Book XXV, chapter III). West's rigid automata never vary, and that is the point.

The suspicion that somehow, some unnameable agent has cheated them of something valuable sifts like the smell of smoke through the empty souls of *The Day of the Locust*. West's ability to capture this mood is perhaps the most remarkable quality of the novel, but the book also has a certain diffuseness everyone has noted. In *Miss Lonelyhearts* plot was coterminous with meaning; the flesh and bone of *The Day* never quite connect, in part because West makes his most ambitious attempt to deal with the individual, artistic, and national crises of confidence that he feels are inter-related. The three threads of plot weave in and out of each other in the sort of disquieted ballet performed by the masqueraders and the mob that watches.

Melville's and Twain's innocents repeatedly discover that their glamorous dreams are false and cast them aside. West's heroes have already lost their innocence but still attempt an open-eyed, desperate, fool's indulgence in resplendent fakery—Miss Lonelyhearts in the hysteria of the Christ-dream, and Tod in the sex-fantasy centered on Faye Greener. If Beagle Darwin in *Balso Snell* talks like "a man in a book" (47), Faye is a girl out of a movie, personifying and acting out Hollywood's virgin-bitch-goddess role. The destructive force of this sexuality is plain ("it would be like throwing yourself from the parapet of a skyscraper"), but Tod needs the artificial stimulation as badly as anyone in the novel: "he would be glad to throw himself, no matter what the cost" (271). Towards the end of the novel he begins to suspect that he too suffers "from the ingrained, morbid apathy he liked to draw in others. Maybe he could only be galvanized into sensibility and that was why he was chasing Faye." Tod's paintings of Faye at first had been the sublimation of his desire for sexual stimulus; once he sees the truth, he turns again to art as a saving game. He uses "one of the oldest tricks in the very full bag of the intellectual," which is to tell himself that he had drawn Faye enough times and to seek new models in Hollywood's insane religions. "It was a childish trick, hardly worthy of a primitive witch doctor, yet

it worked" (365). Tod escapes temporarily into art from
Faye's attraction; but for all his intellectual awareness of
affectation, perhaps he is never capable of the deeply buried
horror Homer Simpson instinctively feels at the small "dirty
black hen" hidden within the statuesque blond sham. For
Homer there is no escape at all.

Tod's (and West's) reaction to Hollywood is also his
reaction to Abe Kusich's "grotesque depravity": indignation
coupled with an excitement that "made him feel certain of
his need to paint" (264). Neither Abe the bookie nor
Hollywood come off as really depraved, however, nor are
they meant to. There is no Evil in West's fiction, there are
only voids and needs. The suffering that is everywhere seems
the result of the same vast scheme of raking violence that
produces the physical and spiritual cripples of *The Confidence-Man*. But despite the omnipresence of suffering in both
books it seems sourceless—no locatable evil has produced it.
Depravity is a pose inseparable from an original warp of the
soul, the same trick of creation itself that made Homer a
defective automaton and Melville's Goneril an icy piece of
clay. And yet where is the Trickster? Melville's "metaphysical
scamp" bears the obvious yet ambiguous trappings of
sacrality, both divine and diabolic. But, lacking such a figure,
West's fiction has no cosmic targets for resentment. When
Miss Lonelyhearts searches the sky for a target, it "looked as
if it had been rubbed with a soiled eraser. It held no angels,
flaming crosses, olive-bearing doves, wheels within wheels"
(71). Later when he again examines the sky "for a clue to his
own exhaustion," it is merely "canvas-colored and ill-
stretched" (100). The gods have departed, addresses
unknown, after untidily erasing a few mistakes and putting
up a covering that fools no one.

However, Miss Lonelyhearts does find a clue to his
personal exhaustion in the skyscrapers that rear up around
him: "Americans have dissipated their radical energy in an
orgy of stone breaking" and in building a civilization of
"forced rock and tortured steel" (100). *The Day of the
Locust* elaborates the idea of radical exhaustion in image

doubtless many ways of achieving the pure vision to which I refer. Nor is it a matter of Jamesian point of view and technical authorial absence form the work that is at issue. The question I am addressing concerns an extreme remoteness of tone, a positive chill, that readers have often misunderstood or criticized not only in West but in the later Melville and the modern black humorists. The suspicion arises that these writers are really *ill*-humored. The truth is of course that West and the others are capable of being, and sometimes are, as peevish and as aloof from their creations as Milton's God. This is the West of *Balso Snell* and *A Cool Million*. But in his best writing West sustains a detachment from the infernal regions he depicts that is remote in the way Dante's sphere of Light is remote. Then in West's chill tonal brilliance the shears close on the quail and a bright drop of blood hangs on a feather-tip; Homer Simpson watches lizards eating flies and is himself dragged down by the mouth to be torn apart; the letters come in relentlessly about an idiot girl's rape, about aching kidneys, and a demonic husband staring out from under the bed. The judgments, the cruelty, are *pure* and, it seems, self-actuating; and so, therefore, is our compassion.

But it is a strange feeling. There is no catharsis. Laughter is not enough, we know, and tears, real or metaphorical, seem excessive. Instead of being self-transcending, the compassion is finally reflexive. The conclusions of West's superior works produce an effect as if a dead-pan audience or a large camera were suddenly turned close by to face us. Our consequent uneasiness is a groping toward that secret interior place where we keep our selves hidden from view, to see whether the secret is still safe, or whether it is even there any more. The search is unsettling, yet it is also oddly detached; for if the artist has communicated, over a great distance, his self-doubt to us, he has also lent us an impersonal compassion toward what we find.

The camera faces us now, the audience stares its old dead stare and waits. And so we go into our acts . . . .

Or do we?

FOOTNOTES

1. The last term is borrowed from James Hall, *The Tragic Comedians* (Bloomington, Indiana, 1963).

2. In Paul Smith, "*The Confidence Man* and the Literary World of New York," *N C F*, XVI (March 1962), p. 334. See also Johannes Dietrich Bergmann, "The Original Confidence Man," *A Q*, XXI (Fall 1969), 560-577.

3. *The Complete Works of Nathanael West* (New York, 1957), p. 264. Hereafter cited in my text.

4. H. D. F. Kitto, *Greek Tragedy* (New York, 1954).

AN ANNOTATED BIBLIOGRAPHY
Selected by Helen Rushton Taylor

Not until 1957, with the publication of *The Complete Works,* was Nathanael West rescued from—in William Peden's words—"this unmerited sojourn in limbo." Until then, he had attracted little critical interest. His neglect in the 1930's, when his novels first appeared, has been explained on the grounds of his radical departure from the "gravymash-potato" school of social consciousness in fiction, and his unproletarian dismissal of dogma, idealism, and socialism. This lack of interest lasted for the next couple of decades, with Edmund Wilson virtually a lone voice in hailing West as an important, original writer who was making a thoroughly new departure in modern fiction.

However, with publication of *The Complete Works* in 1957, suddenly the critical world began to notice West, and to speak of the "West revival" in excited tones; indeed, critics quickly adopted him as a new cause, which he has remained ever since. The cult of Westiana has grown steadily since the late 1950's to its present scope, and, with the plethora of new material constantly appearing, has become a bibliographer's nightmare.

Much criticism of West is unfortunately very repetitive—if I have read once that *A Cool Million* is a present-day *Candide,* I must have read it a hundred times. I suspect that a thorough reading of Robert Edenbaum's essays in *Arts in Society* on Dada and Surrealism will save many a weary scholar from wading through the multitude of articles about these influences on West's novels.

Most critics comment only on the favorite books, *Miss Lonelyhearts* and *The Day of the Locust,* but much of this criticism reeks of a drearily conventional approach to a unique writing style, which surely deserves a vitally fresh approach. I was disappointed to find very little critical work on the film versions of the novels, or on West's screenplays and the extraordinary dichotomy between their style and that of the four novels.

William White remains West's most faithful, rigorous bibliographer; I refer you, in all humility, to his work for its thorough, exhaustive citations. My own bibliography is fairly selective, and excludes details of the films, screenplays, translations and the like, all of which are to be found in White's bibliographies.

The method of direct quotation from articles and books which I have used through much of this bibliography is, I hope, a fresh approach to annotation which attempts to give the reader a feeling for the content and approach of each work cited, rather than a paraphrase of the central thesis.

Finally, there is much here to delight any reader who has a taste for the morbid (something which all writers about West apparently share to some degree), but much to frustrate the researcher, who will find, as I did when I went West, that the book remains to be written which will fully explain the fascination and the profound originality of Nathanael West's style and techniques.

WORKS BY NATHANAEL WEST

West, Nathanael. *The Complete Works,* with introduction by Alan Ross. New York: Farrar, Straus and Cudahy, 1957.

———. "L'Affaire Beano." An unpublished short story quoted in Richard Gehman's Introduction to Nathanael West, *The Day of the Locust.* New York: New Directions, 1950.

——. "Bird and Bottle," *Pacific Weekly* 5 (November 10, 1936): 329-31, reprinted in Martin, *Nathanael West: A Collection of Critical Essays.*

——. "Business Deal." *Americana*, October 1933, p. 14.

——. "Christmass Poem." *Contempo*, 21 February 1933, p. 4.

——. (Nathan von Wallenstein-Weinstein). "Death." *Casements*, June 1924, p. 15.
An interesting sample of West's undergraduate writing.

—— (Nathan von Wallenstein-Weinstein). "Euripides—A Playwright." *Casements*, July 1923. Unpaginated.
Another undergraduate essay.

——. "Miss Lonelyhearts and the Dead Pan," reprinted in *Years of Protest: A Collection of American Writings of the 1930's,* ed. Jack Salzman. New York: Pegasus, 1967. pp. 406-12.
A shorter, early version of the first chapter in the novel.

——. "Soft Soap for the Barber." *New Republic,* November 1934, p. 23.

——. "Some Notes on *Miss Lonelyhearts.*" *Contempo*, 15 May 1933.

——. "Some Notes on Violence." *Contact*, October 1932, p. 132.

BOOKS ABOUT NATHANAEL WEST

Comerchero, Victor. *Nathanael West: The Ironic Prophet.* Syracuse: Syracuse University Press, 1964.

The second full-length study of West published. Comer-chero considers West's protagonists as "the dramatized victims of a declining Western culture," and examines perceptively the tensions and archetypal figures in West's work, by close verbal analysis.

Hyman, Stanley E. *Nathanael West.* Minneapolis: University of Minnesota Press, 1962. (University of Minnesota Pamphlets on American Writers, No. 21)

Hyman believes West found "objective correlatives for our sickness and fears" and sees him as a "true pioneer and culture hero, making it possible for the younger symbolists and fantasists who came after him . . . to do with relative ease what he did in defiance of the temper of his time, for so little reward, in isolation and in pain."

Jackson, Thomas H., ed. *Twentieth Century Interpretations of "Miss Lonelyhearts."* New York: Prentice-Hall, 1971. Selected essays on this novel reprinted.

Light, James F. *Nathanael West: An Interpretative Study.* Evanston: Northwestern University Press, 1961.

At the time, this was the most extensive treatment of West's life and work to appear in print. Predicting a growing interest in and serious appreciation of West, Light notes: "West's universe . . . is a limited one, but . . . to introduce the normal into it would be to destroy its very fabric."

Malin, Irving. *Nathanael West's Novels.* Carbondale: Southern Illinois University Press, 1972. Close reading of texts.

Martin, Jay. *Nathanael West: The Art of His Life.* New York: Farrar, Straus and Giroux, 1970.

The first full-length biography of West, including detailed analysis of West's involvement with the Dadaist and Surrealist Movements, the Depression, radical politics, the movie industry, etc.; interviews with his friends and admirers, Malcolm Cowley, Erskine Caldwell, Edmund Wilson, Alfred Kazin, and an appendix on his film writing. Also 20 pages of photos, most previously unpublished.

———, ed. *Nathanael West: A Collection of Critical Essays.* New York: Prentice-Hall, 1971.

Perry, Robert M. *Nathanael West's "Miss Lonelyhearts": Introduction and Commentary.* New York: Seabury Press, 1969.

This book, one in a series entitled "Religious Dimensions in Literature," seems to me a fine example of the ways in which West has been badly misinterpreted: "Will anyone save Sick-of-it-all in time? We do not know, because there is no revelation. We only know what we have faith to believe. That the anguish must not be and must not have been in vain."

Reid, Randall. *The Fiction of Nathanael West: No Redeemer, No Promised Land.* Chicago: University of Chicago Press, 1967.

"In the deflationary world of his books, simple mockery collapses as completely as simple self-pity. So do all the customary poses; ironic detachment, passionate involvement, heartfelt compassion. A reader who wants a simple attitude to take toward his world will therefore get no help from West."

White, William. *A Bibliography of the Writings By and About Nathanael West* [The Serif Series: Bibliographies and Checklists]. Kent State University Press [in preparation].

This will be the most complete bibliography published so far, and will include the entries in White's earlier bibliographies in *The Serif, Studies in Bibliography, The American Book Collector,* etc. It will include bibliographical descriptions of West's novels, material he wrote for magazines, newspapers, and movies, all the translations (with collations), printings, impressions, etc. Also, books about West, articles, Ph.D. and M.A. theses, and reviews of his books. This work will be of utmost importance to all scholars, critics, collectors, librarians, and bibliographers.

DISCUSSIONS OF WEST IN BOOKS

Abrahams, Roger D. "Androgynes Bound: Nathanael West's *Miss Lonelyhearts*," in *Seven Contemporary Authors,* ed. Thomas Whitbread. Austin: University of Texas Press, 1966. pp. 49-72.

Allen, Walter. "The Thirties: America," in *The Modern Novel in Britain and the United States*. New York: E. P. Dutton, 1964. pp. 167-72.

"The human condition, for West, is outrageous and intolerable; it can be borne, one feels, only when translated into the comic, when the comic absurdity is as it were clowned into further absurdity."

———. *Tradition and Dream: The English and American Novel from the Twenties to Our Time*. London: Phoenix House, 1964. pp. 166-72.

Calls West "probably the most economical novelist who ever wrote . . . an extreme and desperate concentration."

Auden, W. H. "Interlude: West's Disease," in *The Dyer's Hand, and Other Essays*. New York: Random House, 1962. pp. 238-45.

"His books should, I think, be classified as Cautionary Tales, parables about a Kingdom of Hell whose ruler is not so much the Father of Lies as the Father of Wishes."

Coates, Robert M. Introduction to *Miss Lonelyhearts*. New York: New Directions, 1946, 1950.

Cowley, Malcolm. *Exile's Return: A Narrative of Ideas.* New York: Norton, 1934. pp. 230-33. (Viking paperback, 1951).

Interesting that, as early as 1934, Cowley could hail *The Day of the Locust* as "still the best of the Hollywood novels" and *Miss Lonelyhearts* as "a brilliant novel that had few readers."

Fiedler, Leslie A. *Love and Death in the American Novel.* New York: Criterion, 1960. pp. 316-18, 461-67.

Sees in West "a willingness to reinterpret the formulae of Gothicism in the light of Freudian psychology."

——. *Waiting for the End.* New York: Stein and Day, 1964. Consult index for references.

Gehman, Richard B. Introduction to *The Day of the Locust.* New York: New Directions, 1950.

Gehman quotes a letter from West to Jack Conroy: "I believe there is a place for the fellow who yells fire and indicates where some of the smoke is coming from without actually dragging the hose to the spot."

Kernan, Alvin B. "The Mob Tendency: *The Day of the Locust,*" in *The Plot of Satire.* New Haven: Yale University Press, 1965.

"The progress in *The Day of the Locust* of the painter-satirist from realist, to painter of grotesques, to the loud wail of disaster is but one instance of the classic pattern which most satirists picture themselves as following."

Madden, David, editor. *Proletarian Writers of the Thirties.* Carbondale: Southern Illinois University Press, 1968. Consult index for references.

McKenny, Ruth. *Love Story.* New York: Harcourt, Brace, 1950. pp. 175-76, 195-97.

Story of West's wife, Eileen, written by her sister.

O'Connor, William Van. *The Grotesque: An American Genre, and Other Essays*. Carbondale: Southern Illinois University Press, 1962.

Olson, Bruce. "Nathanael West: The Use of Cynicism," in *Minor American Novelists*, Charles Alva Hoyt, ed. Carbondale: Southern Illinois University Press, 1970, pp. 81-94.

Parry, Idris. "Kafka, Gogol, and Nathanael West," in *Kafka: A Collection of Critical Essays*, ed. Ronald Gray. Englewood Cliffs, N. J.: Prentice-Hall, 1962. pp. 85-90.

The three writers cited "choose the irrational because they must, and because they know they will find there, as in a dream, the roots of their own human dilemma. And if we can follow them, we too may find that the nonsensory world is really anything but nonsensical."

Podhoretz, Norman. "Nathanael West: A Particular Kind of Joking," in *Doings and Undoings: The Fifties and After in American Writing*. New York: Farrar, Straus, 1964. pp. 66-75.

"His 'particular kind of joking' has profoundly unpolitical implications; it is a way of saying that the universe is always rigged against us and that our efforts to contend with it inevitably lead to absurdity."

Ross, Alan. "The Dead Center: An Introduction to Nathanael West," in *The Complete Works of Nathanael West*. New York: Farrar, Straus and Cudahy, 1957.

Of West's slight reputation at the time, Ross suggests: "Perhaps the ruthlessness of West's portrait, his making of the whole political and economic racket so undisguisedly repulsive and meaningless, was too near the bone for an American audience with a mass neurosis, and a guilty conscience."

Soupault, Philippe. "Introduction" to *Mademoiselle Coeur-Brisé (Miss Lonelyhearts)*. Paris: Editions du Sagittaire, 1946. Reprinted in Martin, *Nathanael West: A Collection of Critical Essays*.

Widmer, Kingsley. "The Sweet Savage Prophecies of Nathanael West," in *The Thirties*, ed. Warren French. Deland: Everett/Edwards, 1967.

Talks of West's idea of a "master-joker—the sweetly savage nihilist whom we contemplate in his artful mirrors of hysteria."

Wilson, Edmund. "The Boys in the Back Room," in *Classics and Commercials*. New York: Vintage Books, 1962.

"Mr. West has caught the emptiness of Hollywood; and he is, as far as I know, the first writer to make this emptiness horrible."

ARTICLES ABOUT WEST IN PERIODICALS

Aaron, Daniel. "The Truly Monstrous: A Note on Nathanael West." *Partisan Review*, 14 (February 1947). 98-106.

Of Miss Lonelyhearts, he notes "the ineffectualness of this neurotic Charlie Chaplin, this two-bit Dostoevsky."

——. "Late Thoughts on Nathanael West." *Massachusetts Review*, 6, No. 2 (Winter-Spring 1965), 307-17.

"His vision of man was religious rather than ideological . . . [his humor stems from] his wry awareness of the disparity between secular facts and his suppressed religious ideals."

——. "Writing For Apocalypse." *Hudson Review,* 3 (Winter 1951), 634-36.

In *The Day of the Locust* "Hollywood . . . is not an isolated piece of dreamland or a national joke; it is

America carried to its logical conclusion."

Andreach, Robert J. "Nathanael West's *Miss Lonelyhearts*: Between the Dead Pan and the Unborn Christ." *Modern Fiction Studies*, 13, No. 1 (Spring 1966), 251-60.

"Because Pan can be resurrected only through the violation of one's conscience and Christ can be born only through the violation of one's nature, modern man lives in a wasteland."

Bittner, William. "A la Recherche d'un Ecrivain Perdu." *Langues Modernes*, 54 (July-August 1960), 274-82.

Article written in English discussing the rediscovery of American writers in Paris, referring to West as "the classic discovery in American letters in our time."

Breit, Harvey. "Go West." *New York Times Book Review*, 24 March 1957, p. 8.

Quotes S. J. Perelman on *Balso Snell*: "It has a Goyaesque quality. West had that sort of talent, a feeling for the monstrous and the misshapen."

Bush, C. W. "This Stupendous Fabric: The Metaphysics of Order in Melville's *Pierre* and Nathanael West's *Miss Lonelyhearts*." *Journal of American Studies*, 1, No. 2 (October 1967), 269-74.

"Both Pierre and Miss Lonelyhearts experience the dark night of the soul. Both aspire to some form of Christian order and are frustrated in the attempt, achieving their dreams of order only in death."

Coates, Robert M. "The Four Novels of Nathanael West, That Fierce, Humane Moralist." *New York Herald Tribune Book Review*, 9 May 1957.

"West, first and last, was a moralist, and an Old Testament one at that."

Cohen, Arthur. "Nathanael West's Holy Fool." *Commonweal*, 15 June 1956, pp. 276-78.

"West may be remembered by us for having attempted to make a saint and a fool a convincing hero of modern fiction."

Collins, Carvel. "Nathanael West's *The Day of the Locust* and *Sanctuary*" *Faulkner Studies*, 2, No. 2 (Summer 1953), 23-4.

Cites West's borrowings from Faulkner (e.g. Earle and Tod Hackett bear resemblances to Faulkner's Popeye and Horace Benbow), and observes that West satisfies E. E. Cummings' maxim that "a good artist does not borrow from another, he steals."

Contempo, 3, No. 3 (July 25, 1933). A critical symposium: Bob Brown, "Go West, Young Writer," pp. 4-5; William Carlos Williams, "Sordid? Good God!," pp. 5, 8; Josephine Herbst, "*Miss Lonelyhearts*: An Allegory," p. 4; Angel Flores, "Miss Lonelyhearts in the Haunted Castle," p. 1; S. J. Perelman, "Nathanael West: A Portrait," p. 2.

Cramer, Carter M. "The World of Nathanael West: A Critical Interpretation," *Emporia State Research Studies,* IX, June, 1971, p. 4. Uses Northrop Frye's classifications of fiction: novel, romance, confession, and anatomy, or satire. *Dream Life of Balso Snell* and *A Cool Million* are satires; *Lonelyhearts* is a romance and *Day of the Locust* is an anatomy. Critics who fail to use these concepts succeed only in distorting the novels.

Daniel, Carter A. "West's Revisions of *Miss Lonelyhearts*." *Studies in Bibliography*, 16 (1963), 232-43.

Comparisons of the periodical appearance of 5 chapters in 1932 with their final revised appearance in book form in April 1933, showing how the revisions were almost always an improvement and that West was "a mature and conscious craftsman."

Edenbaum, Robert I. "Dada and Surrealism in the United States: A Literary Instance." *Arts in Society,* 5 (1968), 114-25.

Like the dadaists, West "was capable of using every weapon that offended, everything that exasperated society, including obscenity, scatology, and sacrilege."

———. "A Surfeit of Shoddy: Nathanael West's *A Cool Million.*" *Southern Humanities Review*, 2, No. 4 (Fall 1968), 427-39.

Fiedler, Leslie A. "The Breakthrough: The American Jewish Novelist and the Fictional Image of the Jew." *Mainstream,* 4 (Winter 1958), 15-35.

———. "Master of Dreams." *Partisan Review*, 34, No. 3 (Summer 1967), 339-56.

Notes on the archetypal myth of the Jewish emissary to the non-Jews, and the roles of Freud and Kafka in shaping Jewish-American writing of the twentieth century.

Flavin, Robert J. "Animal Imagery in the Works of Nathanael West." *Thoth* 5 (1964): 25-30. Animal violence in West's world.

Galloway, David D. "Nathanael West's Dream Dump." *Critique* 6, No. 3 (Winter 1963-4), 46-64.

For West, Hollywood contained "both an instant symbolism and a microcosm of his favorite subjects: the ignoble lie, the world of illusion, the surrealistic incongruities of the American experience."

———. "A Picaresque Apprenticeship: Nathanael West's *The Dream Life of Balso Snell* and *A Cool Million.*" *Wisconsin Studies in Contemporary Literature*, 5, No. 2 (Summer 1964), 110-26.

"Balso Snell is a catalogue of the delusions which were to

be the subjects of his later work—Christianity, the success dream, artistic detachment, the innocence of childhood, the return to nature, and political idealism."

Gilmore, Thomas B., Jr. "The Dark Night of the Cave: A Rejoinder to Kernan on *The Day of the Locust.*" *Satire Newsletter*, 2 (Spring 1965), 95-100.

Lists reasons why the book cannot be considered as satire.

Hand, Nancy W. "A Novel in the Form of a Comic Strip: Nathanael West's *Miss Lonelyhearts.*" *Serif*, 5, No. 2 (1968), 14-21.

Hassan, Ihab H. "Love in the Modern American Novel: Expense of Spirit and Waste of Shame." *Western Humanities Review*, 14, No. 2 (Spring 1961), 149-61.

Hawkes, John, D. J. Hughes, and Ihab Hassan. "Notes on the Wild Goose Chase; Symposium: Fiction Today." *Massachusetts Review*, 3, No. 4 (Summer 1962), 784-97.

"For Nathanael West, love is a quail's feather dragged to earth by a heartshaped drop of blood on its tip, or the sight of a young girl's buttocks looking like an inverted valentine."

Herbst, Josephine. "Hunter of Doves." *Botteghe Oscure*, 13 (1954), 310-44.

———. "Nathanael West." *Kenyon Review*, 23, No. 4 (Autumn 1961), 611-30.

Sees the novels as "dark parables" in which "there are no big shots; no tycoons; no one can be said to be in the money. The only valid currency is suffering. If there is a vision of love it is etched in the acid of what love is not."

Hollis, C. Carroll. "Nathanael West and Surrealist Violence."

Fresco, 8, No. 3 (Spring-Summer 1957), 5-13.

Discussion of West's treatment of Christianity, including an interesting comparison with Graham Greene (the only one I have seen).

————. "Nathanael West and the 'Lonely Crowd'." *Thought*, 33, No. 130 (Autumn 1958), 398-416.

"An apostate artist finds in himself the endemic symptoms of the spiritual plague that threatens us all."

Hough, Graham. "New Novels." *Encounter*, 10 (February 1958), 86.

Reviewing *The Complete Works*, he notes "a strange contrast with the general tone of reassurance breathed by current American letters."

Jacobs, Robert G. "Nathanael West: The Christology of Unbelief." *Iowa English Yearbook*, 9 (1964), 68-74.

"Lonelyhearts is a recognizable American type, the American Puritan whose sensitive nostrils can detect even the faintest aroma of sin."

Liebling, A. J. "Shed a Tear for Mr. West." *New York World Telegram*, 24 June 1933, p. 14.

Light, James F. "Miss Lonelyhearts: The Imagery of Nightmare." *American Quarterly*, 8 (1956), 316-27.

"In this world of decay and violence the only way that man is able to exist is through dreams," the "commercializing and stereotyping" of which has reduced their efficacy.

————. "Violence, Dreams, and Dostoevsky: The Art of Nathanael West." *College English*, 14, No. 5 (February 1958), 208-13.

Lokke, V. L. "A Side Glance of Medusa: Hollywood, the

Literature Boys, and Nathanael West." *Southwest Review*, 46, No. 1 (Winter 1961), 35-45.

He sees West's thesis in all the novels to be: "We have succeeded in tying the very human needs in our lives for poetry, romance, a sense of mystery, and religion itself to a mechanical production process whose output must be ever expanding."

Lorch, Thomas M. "The Inverted Structure of *Balso Snell*." *Studies in Short Fiction*, 4, pp. 33-41.

Rather than a dismissal of literature per se, *Balso Snell* is "a scathing critique of its misuses, abuses and perversions."

———. "Religion and Art in *Miss Lonelyhearts*." *Renascence*, 20 (Autumn 1967), 11-17.

Lorch suggests that West as it were "found religious belief of itself not so important as the ability to express it; thus art emerges as more immediately relevant to modern man's problems."

———. "West's *Miss Lonelyhearts*: Skepticism Mitigated?" *Renascence*, 18, No. 2 (Winter 1966), 99-109.

Influence of William James' *Varieties of Religious Experience* on *Miss Lonelyhearts*.

Mann, Nora J. "The Novels of Nathanael West." *Dissertation Abstracts*, 29 (1969), 2716A (Mo., Columbia).

McLaughlin, Richard. "West of Hollywood." *Theatre Arts*, 35 (August 1951), p. 46.

Nichols, James W. "Nathanael West, Sinclair Lewis, Alexander Pope, and Satiric Contrast." *Satire Newsletter*, 5, No. 2 (Spring 1968), 119-22.

Peden, William. "Nathanael West." *Virginia Quarterly Review*, 33 (Summer 1957), 468-72.

Perelman, S. J. "Nathanael West: A Portrait." *Contempo*, 25 July, 1933, pp. 1, 4.

Interesting, if only because Perelman was a close friend, and later brother-in-law of West.

Phillips, Robert S. "Fitzgerald and *The Day of the Locust*." *Fitzgerald Newsletter*, No. 15 (Fall 1961), 2-3.

Cites parallels between *Locust* and *Tender is the Night*— use of a movie set to mirror the world, masquerade imagery, death of culture in a world of brutality, etc.

Pinsker, Sanford. "Charles Dickens and Nathanael West: Great Expectations Unfulfilled." *Topic* 18, 40-52.

Both saw worlds in which "great expectations went unfulfilled and the dark insights of the satirist hid just beneath their respective surfaces."

Popkin, Henry. "The Taming of Nathanael West." *New Republic*, 137, No. 18 (October 21, 1957), 19-20.

Review of Howard Teichmann's play, an inaccurate adaptation of *Miss Lonelyhearts*. Popkin exclaims, "If the purpose was to put the commonplace on the stage, why on earth did Teichmann begin with the wild world of Nathanael West? I give up."

Ratner, Marc L. " 'Anywhere Out of This World': Baudelaire and Nathanael West." *American Literature*, 31, No. 4 (January 1960), 456-63.

Influence of the French symbolists, especially Baudelaire, discernible in West's "terse epigrammatic style, poetic imagery, and satiric content."

Reynolds, Stanley. "Life Sans Everything." *New Statesman*, 24 May 1968, p. 469.

"The message of West is life sans everything, and one is left with only the hope implied in the act of making."

Rosenfeld, Isaac. "Faulkner and Contemporaries." *Partisan Review*, 18 (January-February 1951), pp. 106-14.

Brief consideration of West, with the following acute observation: "He saw, as everybody has seen, the starvation latent in the popular media, but he stayed clear of the platitudes and condolences over the death of culture."

Sanford, John. "Nathanael West." *The Screen Writer*, 2 (December 1946), 10-13.

Memorial essay on the sixth anniversary of West's death by a personal friend.

Schneider, Cyril M. "The Individuality of Nathanael West." *Western Review*, 20 (Autumn 1955), 7-28.

Discusses West's "loyalty to the concrete and particular and human, and a reluctance to enter the realm of the abstract and the general and the mechanical." This essay suffered grave plagiarism charges in the Spring *W.R.* by Herman H. Levart, who calls the article "a patch work quilt (and a badly made one) of great uncredited portions from my own Columbia University Master's thesis on West."

Schwartz, Edward Greenfield. "The Novels of Nathanael West." *Accent*, 17 (Autumn 1957), 251-62.

Shepard, Douglas H. "Nathanael West Rewrites Horatio Alger, Jr." *Satire Newsletter*, 3, No. 1 (Fall 1965), 13-28.

Smith, Marcus. "Religious Experience in *Miss Lonelyhearts*." *Wisconsin Studies in Contemporary Literature*, 9, No. 2 (Spring 1968), 172-88.

"The main critical issue concerning *Miss Lonelyhearts* is whether the title character and protagonist is a tragic saint or a psychotic fool."

Solberg, S. E. "The Novels of Nathaniel [sic] West—A Sargasso of the Imagination." *The English Language and Literature* (Eng. Lit. Society of Korea), No. 14 (1963), 125-46.

Tibbetts, A. M. "The Strange Half-World of Nathanael West." *Prairie Schooner*, 34, No. 1 (Spring 1960), 8-14.

"The public will swallow a satirist's work if his world is complete and recognizable; West's was not. His world was cut in two—and half of it was missing . . . [this half was] real people doing real things." (Bibliographer's note: extraordinary grounds for adverse criticism—this charge could be levelled at most of the greatest literature.)

——. "Nathanael West's *The Dream Life of Balso Snell.*" *Studies in Short Fiction*, 2, No. 2 (Winter 1965), 105-12.

Troy, William. "Four Newer Novelists." *Nation*, 14 June 1933, pp. 672-73.

Miss Lonelyhearts is "without that proletarian self-consciousness which has become the keynote of recent American fiction."

Volpe, Edmond L. "The Waste Land of Nathanael West." *Renascence*, 13, No. 1 (Autumn 1960), 69-77, 112.

West's novel, *Miss Lonelyhearts*, is an answer to "the optimism implicit in Eliot's version of man and society. . . . Eliot's victims can repent sin; West's only innocence."

Wadlington, Warwick P. "The Theme of the Confidence Game in Certain American Writers." *Dissertation Abstracts*, 28 (1968), 3691A (Tulane).

White, William. " 'Go West!' Notes from a Bibliographer." *American Book Collector*, 19, No. 5 (January 1969), 7-10.

Both a summary of recent scholarship on West, and a bringing up to date of his earlier bibliographies. (See the White entry under "Books on West.")

——. "A Novelist Ahead of His Time: Nathanael West." *Today's Japan: Orient/West*, 6 (January 1961), 55-64.

Widmer, Kingsley. "The Hollywood Image." *Coastlines*, 5, No. 1 (Autumn 1961), 17-27.

Referring to Schulberg, Mailer, and Fitzgerald as Hollywood novelists, like West: "For the American, even when an intelligent novelist, the image of Hollywood, like the image of Babbitt, remains sentimental, no matter how harshly used."

Williams, William Carlos. Review of *The Day of the Locust*. *Tomorrow*, 10 (November 1950), 58-9.

"Had he gone on there would have unfolded, I think, the finest prose talent of our age."

——. "A New American Writer," reprinted in Martin, *Nathanael West: A Collection of Critical Essays.*

ABOUT THE CONTRIBUTORS

Max Apple is assistant professor at Reed College, and has taught at Stanford and Michigan. He is writing a historical novel about the Russo-Japanese War. His essay on West won a Hopwood prize at the University of Michigan.

James H. Bowden teaches English at Indiana University Southeast, and has taught at Kentucky, Montana, and Colgate. His first job was as a printer's devil, and for a brief time he was editor of a weekly newspaper in Wisconsin. Although his Ph.D. was in American Studies, he has studied at the Seabury-Western and Louisville Presbyterian Theological Seminaries. His poetry has appeared in *Prairie Schooner, Chelsea Review, Trace, Motive, St. Andrews Review, Christian Star,* and *Kansas Quarterly,* and in an anthology of poems about Emily Dickinson.

John M. Brand teaches literature at the University of Northern Colorado. For seven years, until 1966, he was a Presbyterian minister in West Texas. His essay received honorable mention in a Nathanael West essay competition conducted by Everett/Edwards and *The Southern Review.* He has two articles on Mark Twain that have been accepted for publication.

Lawrence W. DiStasi lives in Berkeley, California, working on his doctoral dissertation, writing articles, and preparing a book "probing the common bases in form-anxiety-myth-literature." He states that he was "formalized at Dartmouth, sanforized at New York University, and re-cycled by Vietnam, Tullio and Zaslow."

Robert I. Edenbaum has taught literature at Temple University since 1961; he has also taught at the University of Minnesota and the University of California at Berkeley. His articles on West, John Hawkes, Dashiell Hammett, F. Scott Fitzgerald, Henry Adams, Lucian, Delacroix, and the military draft have appeared in various journals and in collections of essays. His work with the draft problem and related activities are a major avocation. A study of West's "collateral descendants" is underway.

James W. Hickey teaches writing and film at SUNY Purchase, Mount Vernon campus. In college, he received awards for his poetry, fiction, play directing, and oil painting. He has completed a novel entitled *The Codpiece Memoirs*.

Gerald Locklin has taught literature at California State College in Long Beach since 1966; he has taught at California State in Los Angeles. He has published nearly a hundred poems in *Minnesota Review, New Orleans Review, Florida Quarterly, Beloit Poetry Journal, Southern Poetry Journal, Wormwood Review, Trace, Western Humanities Review, Kansas Quarterly,* and other magazines. He has also published numerous book reviews and a few stories and essays.

Lavonne Mueller is an instructor in English at Northern Illinois University. Three of her plays were produced at the University of Iowa when she was a student in the writers workshop. She has published a poem in *Quinto Lingo* and essays in *English Journal, Forum, Rocky Mountain Review,* and *Finnegans Wake Newsletter.*

Marcus Smith is associate professor of English at Loyola University in New Orleans; from 1964 until 1970, he taught at the American University of Beirut. He wrote his doctoral dissertation on West. His articles and poems have appeared in *Contemporary Literature, Modern Fiction Studies, American N & Q, Southern Humanities Review, Middle East Newsletter, Southern Writing in the Sixties: Poetry,* and other magazines.

T. R. Steiner is Assistant Professor of English at the University of California, Santa Barbara; he has taught at Hunter and at Brooklyn College. A student of English Literature from 1660 to 1800, he has published essays on Neoclassical translation in *Comparative Literature Studies* and *Arion*. He is working on a book about the city and its images in Neoclassical literature. His essay on West won the Nathanael West essay contest conducted by Everett/Edwards and *The Southern Review.*

Helen Rushton Taylor is a 23-year-old British subject, born in Bolton, Lancashire, and raised and schooled in Birmingham. She completed her bachelor's degree at London University. She completed work on her master's degree at Louisiana State University. Her interest in American literature led her to the United States, and a visit to California during the summer of 1970 led to her involvement with Nathanael West's work. Her major field of interest is feminism in Britain and America; she has become actively involved in the women's rights movement. She is currently lecturer in literature and liberal studies at Bristol Polytechnic.

Donald T. Torchiana is professor of English at Northwestern University, where he has taught since 1953. He served as a Fulbright lecturer in American literature at University College, Galway, Ireland, in 1960-62 and 1969-70. A member of the Dublin United Arts Club and the Irish Georgian Society, he is also a consultant to the Royal Irish Academy. He is the author of *W. B. Yeats and Georgian Ireland.*

Kingsley Widmer is Professor of Comparative Literature at San Diego State College; he has taught "in a variety of institutions, here and abroad." Among his more than one hundred publications are four books of literary criticism: *The Art of Perversity: D. H. Lawrence; Henry Miller; The Ways of Nihilism: Melville's Short Novels;* and *The Literary Rebel.* He also writes satiric verse and social essays and is currently a regular contributor of social-cultural criticism to *The Nation, Anarchy, The Village Voice,* and other magazines.

Warwick Wadlington teaches literature at the University of Texas, Austin. His essay "Pathos and Dreiser" appeared in *The Southern Review.* He is working now on a book about the confidence game theme in the works of Melville, Twain, West, and several contemporary writers. His essay on West received honorable mention in a Nathanael West essay competition conducted by Everett/Edwards and *The Southern Review.*